Near Death Experience (NDE):

A Holographic Explanation

Oswald G. Harding Ph.D.

LMH Publishing Limited

© 2006 Oswald G. Harding
First Edition
10 9 8 7 6 5 4 3 2 1

All rights reserved. No part of this book may be reproduced, stored in a retrieval system, or transmitted, in any form or by any means, electronic, mechanical, photocopying, recording, or otherwise, without the prior written permission of the publishers or author.

The publishers have made every effort to trace the copyright holders but if they have inadvertently overlooked any, they will be pleased to make the necessary arrangements at the first opportunity.

If you have bought this book without a cover you should be aware that it is "stolen" property. The publishers and author have not received any payment for the "stripped" book, if it is printed without their authorization.

All LMH titles, imprints and distributed lines are available at special quantity discounts for bulk purchases for sales promotion, premiums, fund-raising, educational or institutional use.

Cover Design: LeeQuee Design
Executive Editor: Charles-Anthony Moore
Book Design, Layout & Typesetting by: Michelle M. Mitchell, PAGE Services

Published by: LMH Publishing Limited
7 Norman Road,
LOJ Industrial Complex
Building 10
Kingston C.S.O., Jamaica
Tel: 876-938-0005; 938-0712
Fax: 876-759-8752
Email: lmhbookpublishing@cwjamaica.com
Website: www.lmhpublishingjamaica.com

Printed in the U.S.A.

ISBN 976-8202-09-2

To my dear departed father,
Sylvester Alexander Harding,
Who did everything in his life
To make mine a success

PREFACE

An original experience is always enduring. The writing of this book is no exception.

When I began this odyssey, I had only a sense of general direction; I truly did not know where the road would lead, where it would turn, or much less where it would end. It has been a fascinating journey for me, passing through many fields of knowledge and a rich landscape of concepts, exciting my imagination and testing my beliefs.

My intellectual explorations opened into an ever-widening estuary of understanding and an enlarging vista of ideas. All this became for me an imperative to reconnect with speculative philosophy, allowing an escape from the narrow canyons of logical positivism or empiricism, to investigate the richness of metaphysics in the search for the meaning of a specific human experience. This approach was not an invitation to abandon scientific knowledge, but a call to resuscitate other fields of reflective human endeavours and not to confine our mental activities solely to the problem of analysis. On account of the dominance of our intellectual life by science, we may be in danger of forgetting the fundamental speculative nature of philosophy.

This publication has incorporated current research in near-death-experience, evaluating the competing arguments for and against. It has provided a plausible explanation of the phenomenon of near-death-experience by the application of some of the scientific postulates of holographic theory as a working model for transpersonal experiences. It is contended that, consistent with our changing world-view, the holographic model offers the best understandings of the phenomenon of NDE.

ACKNOWLEDGEMENT

I owe a debt of gratitude to many persons, who, by their assistance, enabled me to complete this work. I wrote the first version of this work in part fulfillment for the Degree of Doctor of Philosophy. I record my appreciation to my sponsors, Professors Edward Baugh and Errol Miller, who thought I had the capacity to complete this project. I must mention, for special thanks, Mrs. Delva Cameron and Miss Kayla Young, both of New York, who helped to locate many books that were not locally available. To Miss Edris Hill of the University of the West Indies Registry at Mona, and Mrs. Michelle Ennis of the Department of Language, Linguistics and Philosophy, who both walked me through the maze of campus regulations and Mrs. Paulette Kerr, Librarian, who was always willing to assist in the search for materials. Throughout my attachment to the faculty, I have had much valuable assistance and support from Mr. Joseph R. Pereira, Dean of the faculty and Professor Hubert Devonish, Head of Department, and from Dr. Earl McKenzie in the early days of the research.

My debts are many but my greatest debts are to Dr. J. A. I. Bewaji of the University of the West Indies, Mona and Professor George Graham of the University of Alabama without whose guidance and encouragement this work could never have been completed. I must also thank: Professor Kenneth Ring for his interest shown and his many courtesies; Professor Robert Almeder of Georgia State University for his many suggestions; Dr. Hugh Vaughn for his comments on Chapter 7; Mrs. Norma Rodney Harrack, my personal assistant, typist and factotum, who struggled through many pages of my often indecipherable manuscripts and without whose dedication and demonstrable interest this undertaking would have been many times more difficult; Dr. O. Harry for his many useful suggestions on format and Kevin Chang whose skills on the computer were invaluable.

Finally, to Dr. Phillipe Garrique, formerly of McGill University, who during my undergraduate days, first whetted my appetite for knowledge and research which has lasted me a lifetime. To my family, especially my wife Marigold, for their patience and tolerance during the period of execution of this work and to my many friends who withstood the constant bombardment of my ever-changing philosophical speculations.

FOREWORD

The question of the intrinsic nature, composition and end of human person is one of the philosophical matters that the human intellect has reflected on perennially. Different disciplinary areas have advanced different theories relating to human person, nature and manifestation – these have ranged from the natural scientists such as biologists, chemists and physicists to social scientists such as economists, sociologists, psychologists and anthropologists, and from historians to philosophers. But no one theory has proven universally acceptable or genuinely satisfactory.

That is why it is even more peculiar that a Queen's Counsel, a lawyer of no mean order, an anthropologist by initial training and an accomplished political personage like Oswald Gaskell Harding should seek the "diversion" of questing for an understanding of the human person. Could this have derived from a yearning based on many decades of practicing law in society and among human beings? Could it be that there is a gap between the political efflorescence of ideas and the implementational praxis within society? Or could the need have arisen from something more profound – a feeling that there is something lacking in the parlance of law, politics, anthropology, teaching and social engagement to which his life has been devoted that only the philosophical quest could meet? Or could it be that there is a need to know more not just about the self, but about the ultimate reality, ultimate source of being and possibly, also, the ultimate end of being that drives religious, quasi-religious, and even the non-religious needs to an investigation of matters transient and transcendent?

Whatever the final "true" answer or answers to these questions may be, we may never find out for sure. But what is clear is that the reason why the final answer(s) to the(se) question(s) may not be accessible may not be because the jury is on recess, but it may be (and may have been) that the answers are not finally determinable by one person. Surely, it will not be because those who have addressed their minds to these matters have not attempted to provide answers. Clearly, not because Dr. Harding has not tried, as the evidence is right here in this volume, documenting the blending of a careful legal mind, exhibiting a critical political predilection with an astute philosophical mien, to investigate one of the most pressing issues for the human being.

The body-mind problem is an aspect of metaphysics which require us to provide an answer for the nature of the human person. Human beings are hard to cure of what David Hume has called "habit and custom". Once formed, habit and custom guide our relationship with our universe and with our fellow human beings. Thus, human beings are habituated to regarding the person as a combination of matter and mind, mental and physical, and material and spiritual in most cultures. Even when science and technology show that we may need to revise our views about what we have supposed for such a long period of time, there often remain a time lag between the discovery of the new (probably more accurate information) and their seepage into collective consciousness for general acknowledgement and acceptance as commonsense truth. This accounts for the fascination of Cartesian interactionism, different forms of dualism and various forms of religiosity – conceiving of the person in terms of a combination of some material and spiritual element called "soul". It can also account for why incongruent positions and arguments are often elucidated in novel and intricate ways to provide a justification for accepting and maintaining old customs.

It seems that humankind is now attempting to make up for centuries of neglect for the subjective coefficient of knowledge of the universe and reality. In various forums, the effort is being made to unravel the extra-rational and the extra-empirical. The West has been neglectful of the possibility of some irascible (not just irrational) force that permeates and animates the material universe(s) and has been for too long spiteful of other societies that attempt to live harmoniously with these ill-understood aspects of the multiverse that we simply encapsulate in the concept "nature". But mere atonement is not going to do it. A penitence that is cheeky and miasmic would rather obfuscate the issues.

What do we mean by the above? An emotion laden universe has for long disregarded the fact that the selection of scientific options to pursue itself is not as rational as we may wish. Obviously, emotion and the subjective coefficient of science and episteme are erroneously spitefully and disrespectfully derogated at our own peril. Now that we have come through a circuitous route to acknowledge that one way or another every injustice demands some reparation, we have to beware of pandering to a reparation syndrome which a minority of the vocally aggrieved can unleash for their own selfish gain. It is in this sense that the tempered and sophisticated approach adopted by Dr. Harding in the following pages in dealing with the body-mind problem becomes salutary.

After competently and critically surveying the literature on the body-mind problem in Western Philosophy, Harding adopts what one can call a futuristic way of seeking a solution to the problem. Well, almost futuristic, as many traditional societies have often conjectured, for various reasons, that a human person is capable of existing at various planes at one and the same time, and also at different times – including the possibility of survival of bodily or physical demise. Could the fact that matter does not ever totally go out of existence regardless of the changing of states have to do with the possibility of survival? Or does genetic and hereditary transmission of cellular transmission through DNA coding of each human cell, whereby each cell has the potential of becoming the whole from which it derives existence mean such survival? Or is such a possibility in the form of holographic interpretation the solution to the yearnings of humanity for eternity? These are very testy questions to which Harding amply suggests answers in this well written book. While by nature, philosophers are the sort of human beings who never believe in the finality of solutions, and while by nature, philosophical problems are essentially insoluble, the trajectories of thought pursued by Harding here are creative and well reasoned to make the vistas presented very tempting to even the most skeptical as it marries scholarship with scientific currency in elucidating a solution to the body-mind problem.

There is an added bonus to what Harding has offered us here. For students being introduced for the first time to the metaphysical problem of body and mind, there is ample interesting rudimentary material for study. For the advanced researcher in matters pertaining to the nature of the mind, consciousness, theories of the mind, out of body existence, near death experience and holography, there is a rewarding but non-convoluted presentation of ideas in a simple, elegant and stimulatingly interesting manner. The general reader is not left out of the loop, be he or she curious or old and interested in contemplating what is next after earthly living is over, as the issues treated are done in a very simple and accessible manner.

The plausibility of the overall thesis canvassed in this volume is creatively and convincingly evident in the arguments provided. There is no doubt that what is presented here will serve to generate more discussion, deviating from the often sterile abstraction of mainstream studies in philosophy of mind which in many instances inadvertently send the reader into spasms of incredulity. With the currency of the bibliographic documentation provided, coupled with detailed notes in the form of acknowledgement of sources of various ideas, it is clear, in my view, that Dr. Harding has provided indications as to further ideas for critical investigations of the issues that he has raised and ably discussed in this very original book. This is an effort that is as outstanding as the author.

Dr. John Ayotunde Isola Bewaji
University of the West Indies, Mona Campus
August 2005

INTRODUCTION

Science has removed many of life's ancient mysteries, it has chased demons and evil spirits out of the explanation of many natural and human phenomena. We now have a much better understanding of, for example, human behaviour and the processes that drive it. But the problem of consciousness remains unsolved. There is much evidence of a nexus between the mind and the brain, therefore, there exist good reasons to accept that consciousness arises from physical systems such as brains, but we still do not know how it occurs, why it exists and why it is even needed.

Recent studies in cognitive science and neuroscience have offered explanations of how the brain processes environmental stimuli and integrates information, but these are really peripheral to the problem of consciousness. There are persons who prefer to deny the existence of consciousness or say that it is an illusion, but the problem will not go away as we know more, directly, about consciousness than any other phenomenon. Its existence can hardly be seriously denied, but as to what it is, well, that is another matter.

I am here concerned with the matter of consciousness because of my concern with Near-Death Experience (NDE) and Out-Of-Body Experience (OBE), all of which I hold to be a part of the consciousness reality, in much the same way as David Chalmers (1996). I apprehend consciousness to be a natural phenomenon and subject to natural laws. In similar fashion, I take NDE and OBE to be natural phenomena and subject to natural laws. Consequently, there ought to be some scientific theory which governs consciousness and explains these phenomena, whether at the moment they are capable of being suitably formed or not. Although I speak of natural laws, I do not mean that the natural laws concerning these phenomena will be just like laws in other domain. They may be different in kind.[1]

Just as with consciousness, this phenomenon lies at the crossroads of science and philosophy, and certainly is a legitimate study for the philosophy of mind as it is for science. The problem, however, is that it is not open to investigation by the usual or everyday scientific method, if for no reason other than the difficulty of observing it or setting up a controlled experiment to monitor it. In short, outside of the subjective experience the data is not easy to come by. This does not mean that external data is not relevant, but before it can even be accepted, there has to be some uniform philosophical understanding of the issues involved.[2]

Though, the problems of NDE and OBE may be scientific problems, they require some philosophical methods of conceptualisation and understanding before we can arrive at solutions to them. The approach here is not to attempt to overturn contemporary science but to broaden our picture of the natural world. It is a broadened scientific perspective that will allow for a naturalistic theory of NDE – the type urged in this essay. In embarking upon the investigation, I was guided by my own inclination, which is *studied agnosticism*, or what Raymond Moody (1996 285), calls 'non-belief', which he distinguishes from belief and disbelief. The conclusions reached have reinforced my inclination.

This book consists of four parts. In part one, I describe the phenomenon of NDE and state why it is a problem and why we cannot ignore it. Chapter one is an introduction to NDE. It reviews the major works of the literature written on the subject and outlines both categories of NDE, namely, deathbed visions and life threatening cases. Chapter two develops an argument for the acceptance of NDE, in the absence of countervailing evidence, as an authentic phenomenon of personal experience. It examines the adequacies of competing arguments for and against the core experience and suggests that what is required is a comprehensive inter-disciplinary theory of NDE. Part one ends with chapter three which gives an account of the possibility of disembodied minds, which must be addressed if the core experience of NDE is conceivable. It signposts the use of holographic theory to further explore NDE.

Part two focuses on the philosophical explanation of the phenomenon, by interpreting its core experience in scientific terms and by using some of the postulates of the holographic theory. Chapter four explains the nature of scientific paradigms, how they are changed and why they are changed. It argues that:

(a) the Newtonian mechanistic model of the universe is inadequate,
(b) there are new paradigms which offer a better understanding of reality, and

(c) there is a need for a paradigm shift.

The holographic theory is offered as a workable model. Chapter five moves along the discussion with the exploration of the concept of a holographic universe, its voluntary nature, its new insights into the fundamental problems as the ordering and organising principles of reality, the distribution of information in the cosmos and in the brain, the nature of memory, the mechanisms of perception and the relationship between the whole and its parts. It discusses the views of reality in general and consciousness in particular as postulated by Karl Pribram and David Bohm. Bohm describes reality and consciousness as one unbroken and coherent whole that is involved in an unending process of change which he calls the *holomovement*.

Chapter six seeks to state the solution to the problem by applying the holographic model to NDE and OBE. In a holographic universe, location is an illusion, everything is non-local, including consciousness, which makes NDE believable. The plasticity of form in holography is similar to the form of the body in OBE, and there occurs a blurring of the vision between past and future, which is sometimes common during such an experience. The experience of going through a dark tunnel is posited as the process of adjustment of consciousness from one plane of reality to another, the moving is awareness itself, or mind without a body, moving through the gateway to holographic or four-dimensional consciousness.

Having accepted OBE as a probable authentic and real experience, a haunting question arises. What is it that is out of the body looking back at the body, and how does it see? Firstly, can this be regarded as seeing in the usual sense as what is understood as seeing, when the eyes remain in the physical body? Secondly, if it is not seeing in the usual sense how does this perception take place? Chapter seven argues that out-of-body or disembodied seeing is independent of ophthalmic vision and in support of this contention cites the case of a blind person whose OBEs match the core experience of sighted persons. Discussions of the physicalist's theory of W. D. Hart and the transcendental awareness theory of Ring and Cooper, are offered as possible explanations of how non-ophthalmic vision may take place.

An understanding of the problem of consciousness and the established theories of the mind is a necessary prerequisite to understanding the phenomenon of NDE. In Chapter eight, I examine the criteria of consciousness and seek to distinguish the domain of the conscious from the unconscious and the non-conscious. It is necessary, also, to consider whether consciousness is a real phenomenon with a coherence of its conceptual foundation or a supernatural mystery. The ontology of consciousness is still open to debate, but the phenomenal aspects of consciousness remain the most difficult. Consciousness as a super-ordinate term, as conceived by Flanagan (1977: 97), is meant to cover all mental states, events, and processes that are experienced and therefore would apply to NDE.

The central problem of philosophy of mind continues to be the problem of giving an accurate account of the relationship between the mind and the body. Chapter nine surveys the various theories of the mind put forward by philosophers, over the years who have sought to tackle the problem.

There seems little or nothing in our physical or functional nature, which will allow us to understand or explain our subjective experience. This has been referred to as the "explanatory gap" (Levine 1983: 354-361). None of the theories which have been examined have been able to close the gap, or even come close to doing so, though the *Dual or Double Aspect theory* offers some insight. At the end, we are still unclear as to where the place of consciousness resides in an entirely physical world. Yet, any successful physical theory of the mind must account for its subjective nature, so the mind-body problem lingers on.

Part Four, chapter ten makes concluding remarks on our changing world view. It points out the realignment of some of our most basic assumptions and beliefs about the way things are supposed to be, the shift from seeing a Newtonian mechanistic universe with no mind or will of its own to an intelligent ever evolving one; a reality where human beings are in the middle affecting it as they experience it. Attention is drawn to some philosophical consequences of quantum mechanics, and the point is made that it is against the changing world-view of reality, emerging as it does from various areas of new paradigm science, that the holographic model for investigating NDE becomes tenable.[3]

It may be that the mind-body problem is unsolvable because of a continuing fundamental conceptual error, that is, the perpetuation of a traditional distinction which is made between animate and inanimate, between organic and inorganic, between mind and body, a distinction which may be false. In the emerging world-view, the new order is envisioned as a single seamless whole, of which the manifest world is but one aspect.

The ultimate nature of physical reality is an individual whole in perpetual flux. The material world, as we know it, is only a small wave-like excitation on top of an immense background. This undivided whole comprises parts that emerge in a constant flow and change, which Bohm calls the *holo-*

movement. The holomovement has two coexisting interpenetrating orders of reality: (a) the physical manifestation of energy in bounded time and space, which is the manifest or explicate order, that is, the material world as we perceive it through our senses, and (b) the physically transcendent order of pure energy which is infinite and absolute, that is, the implicate order.[4] The material flows from the higher implicate order which may always be beyond direct sensory experience (Bohm, 1980: 177).

The emerging concept of reality is one that is both dynamic and holographic in nature. Every portion of the flow contains the entire flow, just as each small part of a hologram contains information about the entire image; each subunit of the universe, such as human beings, in some sense contains the whole. The universe, in turn, subsumes each part. This perspective of simultaneous interrelatedness and interpenetration of all phenomena has been called the *holonomic paradigm* (Wade 1996:8). It is in this holonomic or holographic world that the transpersonal consciousness of NDE has been studied and explained.

CONTENTS

PART ONE: NEAR-DEATH EXPERIENCE

CHAPTER 1   Near-Death Experience (NDE) 2
CHAPTER 2   Scepticism and Empiricism 17
CHAPTER 3   The Disembodied Self 28

PART TWO: A HOLOGRAPHIC APPROACH

CHAPTER 4   New Paradigms and the Mechanistic Universe 46
CHAPTER 5   The Holographic Universe 54
CHAPTER 6   A Holographic Explanation of NDE and OBE 71
CHAPTER 7   Non-Ophthalmic Vision 89

PART THREE: CONSCIOUSNESS AND THE NATURE OF THE MIND

CHAPTER 8   Problems of Consciousness 108
                8.1 Introduction 108
                8.2 What is Consciousness? 109
                8.3 Consciousness Puzzle 113
                8.4 Overview of Theoretical Issues 116
                8.5 Non-Naturalism 118
                8.6 Naturalism 120

	8.7	Non-Mental Naturalism 121
	8.8	Eliminative Naturalism 123
	8.9	Constructive Naturalism 125
	8.10	Naturalistic Dualism 127
	8.11	Summary 130

CHAPTER 9 Theories of the Mind 132
    9.1 Introduction 132
    9.2 Dualism 132
    9.3 Idealism 134
    9.4 Materialism 137
    9.5 Phenomenology 146
    9.6 Dual Aspect Theory 152
    9.7 Double Aspect Principle 162
    9.8 Event Ontology/Holographic Reality 164

PART FOUR: EVALUATION AND CONCLUSION

CHAPTER 10 Evaluation and Summary 168

CHAPTER 11 Conclusion 185

NOTES AND REFERENCES 189

BIBLIOGRAPHY 216

ARTICLES 225

APPENDIX I Comments by Dr. Hugh Vaughn 229

INDEX 231

PART ONE:
Near Death Experience

Chapter 1

NEAR DEATH EXPERIENCE (NDE)

1.1 Introduction

Mankind in the modern computerized and scientific age is still unable to let go the dreams and visions of a spirit world that held sway in the infancy of the human race. The question of a life after death looms as large as ever in the thoughts of men. Some make short shrift of the question, for, in their view, consciousness is but a biological by-product of brain events and as such perishes with the body, which, after biological death, is known to rot and decay. Yet, to others, the thought lingers like a half-remembered melody: is death really the extinction of human personality or does it allow for some continuity of consciousness?

Anything which appears to determine the question will no doubt attract attention. A series of phenomena surrounding near-death seems, at first blush, to offer some answers, but on reflection, does it? It might be that it raises more questions than it answers. The investigations into these phenomena, which have become known collectively as near-death experiences (NDEs), have opened up many avenues of interesting research.

There have been anecdotal reports from ancient days of *anabiosis*. Plato in *The Republic* (Book X) recounts the story of a Greek soldier, Er, who went away to a battle in which many Greeks were killed. His body was among the dead on a funeral pyre to be burned. After some time, his body revived. Er describes what he had seen on his journey to the realms beyond. First of all, he had an out-of-body experience and went to a place where there were "openings" or "passage ways", leading from earth into the realms of the afterlife. Here, the other souls were stopped and judged by divine beings, who could see at a glance all the things that the soul had done while in its earthly life. Er was not judged, instead he was told to go back to inform mankind what the other world was like. Finally, he said that he was ignorant of how he was returned to his physical body.

This story exhibits many of the elements of modern NDE: the out-of-body experience, the "openings" or "passage ways" (the tunnel), divine beings seeing at a glance what the soul had done (life review). Like modern experiencers, he was told to return to earth with a purpose, and not knowing how he had returned to his body.

1.2 Literature Review

For the purpose of this study, however, I propose to deal only with contemporary NDE studies. The contemporary studies began in the early sixties and intensified in recent times, especially since the inception of the **International Association of Near-Death Studies** (IANDS) in December, 1980.

In 1961, internationally known psychologist, Carl G. Jung, published an account of his own near-death experience in *Memories, Dreams, Reflections*, in which he stated:

> The visions and experiences were utterly real...They all had a quality of absolute objectivity...I can describe the experience only as the ecstasy of a non-temporal state in which present, past and future are one. Everything that happens in time has been brought together into a concrete whole... The experience might best be defined as a state of feeling, but one which cannot be produced by imagination.[1]

He goes on to disclose that a good many of his principal works were written only after he had his NDE, which gave him courage to undertake new formulations.

The current resurgence of interest in death-related phenomena, however, seems to have been rekindled by the publication of the work of psychiatrist and thanatologist, Elizabeth Kübler-Ross, in one of the most famous psychological studies of the late twentieth century, *On Death and Dying (1970)*. This study, which grew out of an interdisciplinary seminar on death, addressed the problems of the terminally ill and their families.

Although it cannot be said that the study was a systematic scientific account of her findings, by her countless interviews and conversations, Kübler-Ross has conveyed an understanding of how imminent death affects patients and their families. She summarized what she had learnt from dying patients in terms of their coping mechanisms at the time of terminal illness, which she classified as the five stages of death and which she first explored in this research. These five stages are:

(a) denial and isolation,
(b) anger,
(c) bargaining,
(d) depression and
(e) acceptance.

Kübler-Ross' study shows remarkable sensitivity and appreciation of the functioning of the human mind. For example, on the denial of death, Kübler-Ross states:

> ... in our consciousness, death is never possible in regard to ourselves. It is inconceivable for our consciousness to imagine an actual ending of our own life here on earth, and if this life of ours has to end, the ending is always attributed to a malicious intervention from the outside by someone else.[2]

As the human spirit composes itself for the terminal nature of its existence, it goes through an experience which she describes as follows:

> There is a time in a patient's life when the pain ceases to be, when the mind slips off into a dreamless state, when the need for food becomes minimal and the awareness of the environment all but disappears into darkness...watching a peaceful death of a human being reminds us of a falling star; one of a million lights in a vast sky that flares up for a brief moment only to disappear into the endless night forever...few of us live beyond our three scores and ten years, yet in that brief time each of us create and live a unique biography and weave ourselves into the fabric of human history.[3]

Fast on the heels of *On Death and Dying* came Raymond Moody's *Life After Life (1975)*, which could be regarded as an instant popular success. It was subsequently translated into thirty languages. *Life After Life* was a ground-breaking study of more than one hundred persons who had experienced 'clinical death' and were revived.

Moody does not claim that his work constituted a scientific study nor does he claim to have proven, in technical terms, that there is *life after death*. He does assert, however, that this phenomenon, which he christened near-death experiences (NDE) has great significance not only in the academic fields of psychology, psychiatry, medicine, philosophy and theology, but also for the way in which we live our daily lives.

His hope was for his book to draw attention to the phenomenon and at the same time, help to create a more receptive public attitude towards it. His hope was realized, for his book did set the stage for the receptivity to the 'survival view' and the significance of the phenomenon which was the catalyst for the scientific studies which were to follow.

Osis and Haraldsson investigated the death-bed visions of over one thousand patients as reported by physicians and nurses and published the findings in their well received book *At The Hour of Death (1977)*. There are two cardinal points about this study. Firstly, the data was collected from American and Indian, Hindu and Christian patients, to examine the paranormal experience of dying, and also to see whether a cross-cultural survey would yield any significant differences.[4] It does not appear from these investigations that death-bed visions vary much with religion or cultural backgrounds, but are more likely to be influenced by the depth and authenticity of a belief system.

Secondly, it approached the study on the basis of a scientific evaluation. It is the first scientific study of NDE on an international scale. The study concentrated on NDE and on whether the patient died or recovered. Many other researchers focused entirely on cases of near-death survivors which would undoubtedly result in a severe selection bias in the data, since only patients who did not really die were studied. The emphasis was placed on phenomena which exhibited apparent concerns about entering the after life and which might be indicative of post-mortem survival. The more recent studies have shifted emphasis and included concerns of the living, life reviews and precognitive insights of the future. This study has the life-after hypothesis as its main focus.[5]

Kenneth Ring's *Life at Death* (1980) was not a cross-cultural study, but broadened the scientific investigations by not limiting it to death-bed visions.

In a manner of speaking, Ring revisited Moody's work, using a scientific approach and methodology. Ring devised a weighted 'near-death experience index.' *The Weighted Core Experience Index* (WCEI), commonly referred to as 'Core Experiences', was drawn from Moody's fifteen separate elements.[6] The research was based on a statistical analysis of structured interviews with one hundred and two near-death survivors.

The WCEI Scale was later refined by psychiatrist and editor of the *Journal of Near-Death Studies*, Bruce Greyson (1984) to 16 items.[7] The Scale correlated highly with Ring's and achieved a high level of test-reliability. Ring's own findings offer an impressive degree of independent corroboration to Moody's findings, although they have a somewhat different conception of how these near death phenomena are organized (as will be shown later), but there is no substantive disagreement over the form of the core experience itself.

In Chapter II, Ring examines a number of possible interpretations of NDE such as depersonalization, wishful thinking, psychological expectations, dreams or hallucinations, pharmacological explanations, other drugs, physiological and neurological explanations, temporal lobe involvement, cerebral anoxia and other neurological explanations, all of which do not offer him any satisfactory explanation.

He is especially harsh on the 'depersonalization' interpretation advanced by Noyes and Kletti.[8] They had proposed that the prospect of death initiates a defensive psychological reaction, which serves to allow a person to cope with highly stressful, life-threatening situations. From this standpoint, phenomena associated with the prospect of impending death, such as a sense of peace and well-being, feelings of bodily detachment, a panoramic life review and mystical transcendence (the core experience) are all to be understood as ego-defensive manoeuvres to insulate the individual from the harsh realities of imminent annihilation, by providing a cocoon of compensatory fantasies and feelings. In short, the perception of death results not in a physical ejection from one's body, but in a psychological detachment from one's (apparent) fate.

To Ring, this is a Freudian interpretation to which aspects of the experience are given neurological underpinning as well as a psycho dynamic rendering.[9] Despite its surface plausibility, according to Ring, there are several difficulties with Noyes and Kletti's position that argue for its rejection. Firstly, the classic description of depersonalization given differs in many ways from the psychological state of near-death survivors. Secondly, the depersonalization interpretation offers no explanation to the perception of a deceased relative who the dying person does not know is dead. In his view, this thesis is either unconvincing and/or irrelevant. Furthermore, Noyes and Kletti failed to consider that though stress may indeed trigger a defensive reaction, the transcendental realities that appear to the individual may represent a higher dimension of consciousness and not just a symbolic fantasy rooted in denial. Ring sees this as the tendency of orthodox psychoanalysis towards facile reductionism.

After rejecting a number of possible explanations mentioned above, and presenting his findings from the investigation, Ring offers his own provisional interpretation of the core experience, based on a recent scientific model of consciousness that he feels is capable of handling transcendental experiences. He chose to articulate a scientific framework for the understanding of near-death phenomena. However, he makes it clear that he would not be reticent to speculate about possibilities outside the accepted paradigm of science or contemporary scientific theorizing about states of consciousness which seem inadequate.

His own interpretation of the core experience is that it reflects psychological events associated with a shift in levels of consciousness. A transition is initiated from a state of consciousness rooted in 'this world' sensory impressions to one that is sensitive to the realities of another dimension of existence. When consciousness begins to function independent of the physical body, it becomes capable of awareness of another dimension.[10]

He maintains that aspects of the core experience can be interpreted in scientific terms if one uses some of the postulates of holographic theory.[11] The act of dying involves a gradual shift of consciousness from the ordinary world of experiences to a holographic reality of pure frequencies. So long as one remains tied to the body and to its sensory modalities, holographic reality at best can only be an intellectual construct. The required analysis and examination of this holographic theory cannot be conveniently dealt with here, consequently I shall reserve the arguments for a fuller and more detailed discussion in part two.

Using the refined WCEI scale referred to above, Greyson (1980) found that the depersonalization systems had an extremely low correlation with the rest of the scale, consequently he concluded that NDE is not just a non-specific stress response, but a distinct syndrome.[12]

Another landmark contribution was made to near-death studies by Michael Sabom (1982) with the publication *Recollections of Death: A*

Medical Investigation. After hearing Sarah Kreutziger, a psychiatric social worker, give a talk on the book *Life After Life* by Raymond Moody, Sabom commented: "My indoctrinated scientific mind just couldn't relate seriously to these 'far out' descriptions of after life spirits and such."[13] But Moody had stated at the end of *Life After Life* that what he had done did not constitute a scientific study.

Years of medical training had convinced Sabom that if one pursues the scientific method, most, if not all, of the unanswered questions of the universe would eventually be answered in one form or another, and he was aware that:

> The scientific method of investigation is its systematic collection of objective observation known as 'data'. Only data collected and presented in a rigorous, unbiased manner, however, are eligible for admission into the generally accepted body of scientific knowledge.[14]

As a result of interviews with some of their own patients who had survived close brushes with death, and found that they related experiences which were very similar to those described by Moody, Sabom set out to conduct a scientific study aimed at either verifying or falsifying Moody's findings.

> In the hope of producing an impeccably controlled sample, Sabom and Kreutziger chose samples solely on the basis of their medical records. They did not solicit volunteers through letters or advertisements; in addition they rejected any potential subjects who were considered mentally or emotionally disturbed, and separated the reports of 'prospectively' selected patients from those who had been referred. Finally, they set aside cases involving anesthesia, and were left with a group of seventy-eight victims of cardiac arrest, coma, or accident, twenty-four of whom reported mystical or out-of-the-body states while they were close to death.[15]

In conducting their interviews, they asked each patient normal medical questions about the critical episode, not disclosing their real interest until they asked whether the patient could recall any experiences while unconscious. If the patient asked for some clarification, they would explain.

> I am interested in the experiences and reactions of patients who have survived critical medical illnesses. Some patients have indicated that they have experienced certain events while unconscious and quite ill. I am sincerely interested in any experiences, no matter what they may be.[16]

One of the fundamental features of the NDE was the perceived separation from the body. If the experience progressed, the subject could either remain near-by, looking down upon his or her body, watching the medical procedures or take off to some other realm where they would encounter 'beings' and deceased relatives, and often where their lives would be evaluated. The local out-of-body experience Sabom called 'Autoscopic NDE' and the other world journey 'Transcendental NDE.' There were times when both these experiences were combined.

A group of 116 near-death survivors were given a standardized interview and two death anxiety scales. The subjects ranged in age from 17 to 75. The aim of the study was to get answers to six basic questions about NDE that had arisen out of Moody's book *Life After Life*.

1. Were NDEs really occurring in the patients who had survived an episode of unconsciousness and near death?
2. Did these NDEs follow a consistent pattern or patterns?
3. How often were NDEs in persons revived from a close brush with death?
4. What were the backgrounds of persons reporting on NDE and what were the medical circumstances under which they occurred?
5. Did the content of the NDE vary between groups with different backgrounds or between groups with different near-death situations?
6. Did the NDE *per se* affect the person's death anxiety or after life belief?[17]

The data presented in this study indicate that OBE is a common experience encountered by persons during a NDE. It occurred in 40% of prospectively interviewed near-death survivors. A person's age, sex, race, area of residence, size of home, community, years of education, occupation, religious background or frequency of church attendance did not seem to affect whether a person would encounter an NDE during a near-death crisis event. Prior NDE did not appear to predispose the person subsequently to report an NDE following a crisis event. The type of near-death crisis did not affect whether or not an NDE would occur.

Following the near-death crisis event, persons who had NDE claimed a decrease in their death anxiety and an increase in their after-life beliefs – a response quite different in the death anxieties of persons without an NDE.[18] Moody had noted that many people had later been able to recall specific events that transpired in the vicinity of the physical body at a time when the patient was presumed to be unconscious; more importantly, the recall had consisted of visual details.[19]

Sabom wanted to test whether these events were indeed fact or fantasy. Autoscopic visions could be checked against medical records and doctors recollections and against his own experience.

> I had known from the beginning of my study that the majority of patients, I would be interviewing regarding NDE would have been resuscitated from cardiac arrests. At this stage in my career, I had personally directed and participated in over a hundred such procedures. I know what a resuscitation consisted of and how it would appear to an onlooker. I had been awaiting the moment when a patient would claim to have 'seen' what had taken place in his resuscitation. Upon such an encounter, I had intended to probe meticulously for details, which would not ordinarily be known to non-medical personnel. In essence, I would put both my experience as a trained cardiologist and the description in the medical chart against the professed visual recollections of a lay individual.[20]

Sabom was astonished to find several patients whose reports of what transpired during their period of unconsciousness or 'death' held up to his scrutiny. His data supported the findings of Moody and provided independent, corroborative evidence of visual and auditory perceptions that NDE'ers described as taking place while separated from their bodies. During the autoscopic portion of the NDE, near-death survivors claim to have seen and heard events in the vicinity of their own unconscious physical bodies from a detached elevated position. The details of these perceptions were found by Sabom to be accurate in all instances where corroborating evidence was available.[21]

Sabom concludes that as a physician and scientist he could not say whether NDE represents a glimpse of an after life. For one, the experiences were encountered during the waning moments of life, and the experiencers were not brought back from 'death' but from a point very close to death. These experiences are therefore encounters of near-death and not death itself.[22]

The ultimate question raised by reports of NDE however, is whether a mind-brain split occurs and whether the mind which splits off from the physical brain is, in essence, the 'soul' which continues to exist after the final bodily death.[23] It is here at the point of near-death, according to Sabom, that scientific facts and theories interface with religious doctrines and speculations.[24]

Ring followed his earlier work (1980) with *Heading Towards Omega* (1984). Here, he focuses on the after effects of NDE. The title itself is indicative of where Ring wants to lead his readers. Omega represents an end of life, but end can mean finality or a goal and it is omega as end *point* that has his special meaning. It stands for the aim of human evolution, the ultimate destination towards which humanity is inexorably bound.[25] Omega, by tracing the effects of NDE, seeks to show why NDE's are arguably phenomena whose evolutionary implications must be grasped. Omega suggests that NDE encounters are akin to what others call cosmic consciousness, which may be the outcome of a biological transformation of the human organism that is induced by a release of an energy, called by the Sanskrit name Kundalini. Kundalini arousal seems to give access to the same or similar dimension of consciousness as does the core NDE.

Ring also postulates that it may be that NDE'ers and others who have similar awakenings collectively represent an evolutionary thrust towards higher consciousness for humanity at large. Could it be that NDE itself is an evolutionary mechanism that has the effect of jump-stepping individuals into their next stage of human development by unlocking spiritual potential previously dormant? Are we seeing here a new prototype of man, asked Ring, as he mutates from his pre-NDE personality into a new loving and compassionate individual, a more advanced strain of the human specie striving to come into manifestation?[26] The evolution of *Homo Sapiens* into *Homo Noeticus* brings about a changed psychology based on expression of feelings, not suppression, whose motivation is now cooperative and loving, not competitive and aggressive, and whose psychic abilities are used for benevolent and ethical purposes, not harmful and immoral ones.[27]

Ring is sensitive to the view expressed by John White,[28] that a new form of human life may be appearing on the planet. *Homo Noeticus* is the name

John White gives to the emerging form of humanity. *Noetics* is the term used to mean the study of consciousness. This term, *Homo Noeticus*, accords with the general portrait of NDE'ers drawn by Ring in *Heading Towards Omega* (1985). In this book, he has moved from a collection, analysis, and systematization of NDE data to an extrapolation of an evolutionary thrust. It moves forward to a higher consciousness for all humanity, foreshadowing the birth of a new planetary consciousness as we head towards Omega, the final goal of human evolution.[29]

Melvin Morse, a pediatrician, made his contribution to near-death studies by the publication of his book *Closer to the Light* (1990). What was of special interest was the fact that his research was conducted among children whom one assumes were either unfamiliar with or too young to have inculcated adult views and ideas of death and the after life. He used a control group of one hundred and twenty one children who were critically ill, but not near death. They ranged in age from three to sixteen years of age and were hospitalized in the intensive care unit at a children's hospital. The study group consisted of twelve children "who had looked death in the face"[30]. The questions were carefully structured to be open-ended though addressing specific characteristics of NDE. He recorded first hand accounts of out-of-body movements, telepathic communications and encounters with dear friends and relatives in an after-life.

Morse claims from his study that a person must be on the brink of death to have the symptoms of an NDE. He claims that theories that NDE are the result of drugs or sleep deprivation, or merely bad dreams on the subconscious awareness of surgery must be eliminated. He further claims, after revisiting the work of Wilder Penfield, the "father of neuroscience", that the area he was "mapping" with electrodes which gave 'NDEs' was the Sylvian fissure in the right temporal lobe, located just above the right ear, and that his anatomical conclusion was confirmed by independent investigation made by a group of neurologists from Chile. It is his view that this area close to the right temporal lobe is genetically coded for NDEs. He speculates whether he has discovered the seat of the soul.

Apart from his speculations, the research in *Closer to the Light* of the children's experiences matched closely with the experiences of adults as documented by others (Moody 1975, Ring 1984), except children do not seem to experience life reviews, which form an integral part of the core experience of adults, probably due to their short life span (Morse, 1994 and Serdahely, 1989-1990).

Melvin Morse's sequel *Transformed by the Light* (1992) continues his line of inquiry of children who have had NDE. His sample consisted of one hundred adults who had NDE as children, with fifty patients in each of the five control groups.

The results of Morse's study are that:
(a) compared to the control group, NDE'ers are healthier and have fewer psychosomatic complaints;
(b) psychologically they are happier, they have strong family ties, they have more zest for living, and a greatly diminished fear of death; and
(c) almost all those who have had near-death experiences undergo a significant increase in psychic abilities.

He concludes that:
(a) the light did indeed, transform these people, and
(b) the experience of light is distinctive and perhaps unique, that it does not originate or have its physiological basis in the right temporal lobe, nor in any other region of the brain.

He asserts that it is the "Glow of God" – an assertion not proven by the data.[31]

I now turn to Susan Blackmore's *Dying to Live* (1993) in which she expounds a 'Dying Brain Hypothesis'. This is a recent position in a line of authors who seek to explain the NDE as a purely physiological phenomenon with no other-worldly implications or for survival after death. She asserts that the core experience is as a result of either chemical reactions or the brain's way of dealing with the experience. She maintains that the dissolution of the self accounts for the mystical experiences and after effects. The 'realness' factor, interpreted by our biological organism, the stable tunnel forms, are found in the cortex of the brain. By understanding the role of the limbic system and temporal lobe, she believes that the experience of familiarity, insight and increased psychic experiences after NDE are accounted for with the dying brain hypothesis.

The 'Dying Brain Hypothesis' was also compatible with the reasons for transformative outcomes. Simply forced to think about death, a person can change priorities. Another argument was that, when close to death, an insight takes a form that suggests that the self is only a mental construction, that there was never a solid self and, consequently, there was no one to die.

There never was any real persistent self; a self that makes

conscious choices, a self that observes the objective world at a distance, a self that takes responsibility or is the centre of experience. There never was a separate self who lived through all those experiences, who had all the memories or who made all those decisions. There never was any permanent self and there is no permanent self to survive when the body is gone. There was only a mental model that said there was one.[32]

The person can then let go of the "artificial" construction. Blackmore states that she has no reason to adopt a false hope for the self to survive.

> We are biological organisms, evolved in fascinating ways for no purpose at all and with no end in mind. We are simply here and that is how it is. I have no self and "I" own nothing. There is no one to die. There is just this moment, and now this and now this.[33]

On a review of the literature of the subject, one becomes acutely aware of the similarities of the essence of the various personal stories which are told, so much so that the narratives are now virtually predictable and only the keenest mind can determine whether the minute differences are of any significance.

1.3 Summary

In summary, NDE may be presented in two categories:

(a) Death-bed visions
In these circumstances, the subject is usually ill, perhaps bed-ridden, and suddenly at the hour of death has a vision in which he 'sees' deceased old friends or relatives. The vision may be accompanied by an elated mood and the dying subject remains in a state of "clear wakeful consciousness",[34] and

(b) Life threatening crises
A person not necessarily ill is suddenly brought to the verge of physical death. This situation may be brought about by a car accident, near drowning, a heart attack, a suicide attempt, or some other life

threatening incident. The main common elements found in this type of NDE was summarized by Moody (1975)[35] and largely supported by Ring (1980.[36]

The features of which are:
1. ineffability,
2. hearing the news,
3. feeling of peace and quiet,
4. the noise,
5. the dark tunnel,
6. out of the body,
7. meeting others,
8. the being,
9. the review,
10. the border or limit,
11. coming back,
12. telling others,
13. effect on lives and,
14. new views on death.

Ring describes the main common elements in five stages of a 'prototypical' core experience:

1. euphoric effect
2. an out-of-body state
3. entering darkness
4. seeing an unearthly world of light and
5. entering into the world of light.

At any one of these stages there might occur a "decisional process" where the person "decides to return to life." Often, the subject regrets being brought back to life.

Generally, the features of the two categories of NDE, death-bed visions and close call or resuscitation cases are not dissimilar. In many of the resuscitated cases there are claims that the patient was dead and that there was no display of any vital signs. In some instances, it was alleged there was no heart beat or that the E.E.G. (Electroencephalogram) was flat. But can it be said that such patients were really dead, if during the "death" the organism was capable of being restored to vital functioning? We certainly cannot say this of anyone who has died permanently, except what we are told of the biblical Lazarus.[37]

It is important, however, to differentiate between clinical and biological death because it is possible to be resuscitated from clinical death as in NDE cases. Biological death is irreversible unless one believes in supernatural powers.[38]

Chapter 2

SCEPTICISM AND EMPIRICISM

> *If tickey tickey seh
> shark dey a ribba ba'tam,
> shark di deh*[1].

2.1 Introduction

Scepticism as a critical philosophical attitude has existed from pre-Socratic times to the present. Sceptics have questioned whether any necessary indubitable information can actually be gained about the real nature of things. Some have held that no knowledge beyond immediate experience is possible while some have doubted whether even this much could be definitely known. The objectives of many sceptics were to organize their questioning into systematic sets of arguments aimed at raising doubts. From Sexus Empiricus, (2nd - 3rd Century A.D.) who used Pyrrhonian arguments to cast doubts on claims of knowledge of the naturally non-evident world, to George Santayana's 'animal faith', which he called the process of interpreting the realm of essences,[2] scepticism as a philosophical position runs like a vein of ore through the mountain of western thought. Or, as J.A.I. Bewaji puts it:

> Clearly, universal scepticism has permeated all the critical aspects of philosophical reasoning, giving it the impetus requisite to the formulation of ingenius arguments and doctrines, which, in a typical dialectical manner, subsequently became the issues of contention.[3]

We have been the inheritors of that tradition. Our contemporary society advocates the glorification of doubt. So ingrained is this attitude that to some persons, for one to be accepted as a scholar, one must appear to doubt everything that cannot be "verified" or "proven" or risk your views not being taken seriously or even being ridiculed. Having been schooled in empiricism we have been consumed by the rigidity of verification.

Apart from our inherited scepticism and our fear of accepting as authentic, information that is not currently empirically verifiable, are there genuine grounds for dismissing near-death experiences as untrustworthy or mere illusions? Based on the abundance of evidence, the consistency and universality of the evidence, some of which are from most credible witnesses, by inductive reasoning, ought we not to accept near-death experiences as real phenomena, in the absence of countervailing evidence?

By inductive reasoning, I mean all the cases in which we pass from a particular statement of fact, or set of particular statements of fact, to a generalized factual conclusion that they do not formally entail. In the inference from particular to general, or by analogy, from one particular instance to another, there is an assumption of uniformity in nature and that the future, in appropriate respects, resembles the past, a view which finds favour with Richard Swinburne.

> Richard Swinburne, in his carefully reasoned book *The Evolution of the Soul* (1990), postulates what he describes as the first and most general principle of inductive inference - the *Principle of Credulity*: that in the absence of counterevidence things as they seem to be "seems to be", that is, in the epistemic sense.

The verbs 'seems' and 'appears' constitute an important class of verbs for describing a subject's awareness of the world, and the verbs 'looks', 'sounds', 'feels', 'smells', and 'tastes' are for special senses. There are two crucially different senses of each of these verbs distinguished by Chisholm – the comparative and the epistemic sense.[4]

An object looks like an apple in the comparative sense to John, if it looks to John the way apples normally look, that is, its visual appearance is normal for apples; an object looks like an apple in the epistemic sense to John if, because of the way it looks in the comparative sense John is inclined to believe it is an apple. This he will believe in the absence of further evidence, that is, someone telling him otherwise. Swinburne cites the case of the penny lying on the table which when viewed from an angle looks elliptical in the comparative sense, because it looks the way elliptical things normally look, that is, when viewed from above; it looks round in the epistemic sense to most of us, because of the way it looks in the comparative sense, we are inclined to believe that it is round.

The *Principle of Credulity* states that, if, in the epistemic sense, it seems to John that he is seeing an apple, then he probably is seeing an apple, unless he has a good reason to think that he is subject to an illusion. Such good reason will be the conflict of what seems to him, to be the case, in comparison with other things which seem to be the case. For example, it cannot be an apple if he can put his hands through it, this will be reason enough for supposing that he is subject to an illusion in supposing that he is seeing an apple.

Without this *principle*, there can be no knowledge at all. If you cannot suppose that things are as they seemed to be, unless some further contrary evidence is brought forward, for example, that in the past, in certain respects, things were as they seemed to be, the question will arise as to why you should suppose the later evidence to be reliable. If 'it seems to be' is good enough reason in the latter case, it ought to be good enough reason to start with. And if 'it seems to be' is not good enough reason in the latter case, we are embarked on an infinite regress, and no claim to believe anything with justification will be correct.

It is a slogan of science that we should rely on 'the evidence of our senses', on 'experience'; the principle of credulity crystallizes this slogan more precisely. We should not, however, believe that things are as they seem when there is counter-evidence. There is no avoiding ultimate reliance on the principle of credulity. The rational man is the credulous man – who trusts experience until it is found to mislead him, rather than the sceptic, who refuses to trust experience until it is found not to mislead him.[5]

Swinburne's *Principle of Credulity* is supported by the *Principle of Testimony* – that individuals ought to believe the reports of others about how things seem to them, and so that things were as they report – in the absence of counter-evidence; that is, *ceteris paribus*, the reports of others are probably true. Only if we assume that people normally tell the truth will we ever understand what they are saying. What the principles also expound is that we must assume trustworthiness in the absence of counter-evidence.[6]

Now, if the Principle of Credulity can be applied to NDE cases and OBE's supported by the Principle of Testimony, in the absence of counter evidence, ought we not to take the recollections of resuscitated patients as credulous (especially in view of the considerable congruences between their stories), and as evidence of what the persons stated they had experienced – that they really did? These principles also expound that we must assume trustworthiness in the absence of counter-evidence.

2.2 Consistency and Universality of the Core Phenomena

Over the last twenty years, since Moody's (1975) *Life After Life*, there has been an explosion of published works, theses and articles on NDE. From a review of these writings, what is most impressive is the degree of consistency and universality of the core phenomena. The experiences related come from diverse sources – children and adults, men and women, atheists, agnostics and religious believers, doctors, scientists and the uneducated, whites and blacks, Western and Eastern societies. In report after report, the same message is relayed. The corroboration would be so impressive in a court of law that it would go to the weight of the evidence and by some standard of proof may be accepted as the facts in the case. Any detailed variation of the evidence seem to be influenced by personal life histories, cultural background, a person's belief system and perhaps the circumstances of the nature of the crisis triggering the experience.

Although some of the experiences related are cross-cultural (Osis & Heraldsson – 1990), the cross-cultural differences surfacing so far do not detract from the universality of the phenomenon.[7] They are merely interpretative differences. I am not dismayed by persons saying that they saw the bright light and it was Jesus or that it was Vishnu. It is understandable that in trying to interpret the meaning of their experience it is expressed in culturally familiar terms. The fact that the interpretation of an experience is coloured by cultural reference does not negate the authenticity of the experience.

2.3 Paranormal Material in NDE

Another matter that craves explanation is the paranormal materials sometimes reported in NDEs. The material taken as a whole strongly suggests that there is some substance to the psi - dimension of these experiences. Honorton, in his article *Psi and Internal Attention States*, suggests that altered states of consciousness are psi conducive and NDE situations do generate altered states of consciousness.[8] If this is accepted, it may indicate that NDE's express more than just fantasies or wish fulfillment. If these experiences contain elements of genuine psi, then they are oriented toward objective reality.

However controversial it may be, I would argue that psi in general points to the existence of an alternate, nonsensory reality. A point I will return to, in discussing NDE of blind persons, which seems to confirm the existence of a separate psychological order of reality; if one accepts that the facts about psi cannot be explained in terms of physical theory *(Beloff,* 1980*).*[9]

2.4 Undergoing Changes in Outlook and Attitude

A residual effect of NDE is a modification in the "experiencer's" (a term used to describe persons who have had a NDE) attitude towards life, and a reduction and/or elimination of the fear of death. These transformative experiences are like a religious conversion and seem to be permanent. Experiencers speak of the wonderful gift of unconditional love that sustains them with its qualities of compassion, tolerance and understanding and an 'inner knowing' which provides them with an enhanced view of self and others. There is a new sense of connectedness with life.

These three components of the phenomenon of NDE, namely, its universality and consistency, its paranormal dimension, and its transformative effects must be addressed. It is the unique combination of these components which makes it a challenging matter to explain NDE.[10]

The NDE phenomenon is too well documented to be dismissed or ignored. The searchlight of reason must be brought to bear on it and our available knowledge in the relevant disciplines must provide an understanding, if not, an explanation. Mark Woodhouse suggests that, it is the biomedical scientists' job to propose physiological explanations and to examine the adequacy of various hallucinatory accounts; it is the psychologist's job to research the characteristics of near-death experiences and to assess critically those variables that bear upon the validity of the research; and it is the philosopher's job to examine the logical adequacy of competing arguments and the conceptual and methodological issues that underline those arguments.[11] But I would argue that the philosopher must go further and offer new ways of conceptualizing and providing new conformable explanatory hypotheses approaches to viewing the problem, otherwise his assistance will be of insufficient value.

The validity of the philosopher's contribution consists not in any descriptive or explanatory value which are unlikely to be empirically verifiable in the usual sense, but in the imaginative possibilities, the explorations and the insights which he opens up to the investigator. I shall discuss the imaginative possibilities, explorations and insights in Part Two. For now, let us examine some of the competing arguments.

2.5 Foundation for the Competing Arguments

Some of the difficulties in assessing NDE arise from the predisposition of the assessors. Persons who are inclined to believe in life after death may be sympathetic and lean towards credulity. Those who equate the belief in survival after death with primitive superstition and belief in a magical world are less likely to assess it as a phenomenological datum. Furthermore, the current scientific climate is inimical to any proposal that disparages physicalism and materialism.

Generalizations are dangerous to make regarding any subject, because examples can always be found to contradict the generalization. However, I am bold enough to suggest that, by and large, those who are sceptical of the NDE's are more likely to be persons classified as "materialists". It seems also, though perhaps an over-simplification, that the "dualists" who, because of their acceptance of the possibility of the existence of a soul or mind as separate from the body, can contemplate the possibility of an after-life, may be more inclined to be sympathetic to NDEs.

It will pay to digress momentarily to give a background and to make clear the bases for the competing arguments used in assessing the NDE. These arguments stem largely from the body/mind dualists and the materialists.

The origin of dualism as a philosophical outlook is lost in antiquity. The concept of dualism is to be found in the Book of Genesis in the Bible. Also, from the first to the last, the texts of Pert em hru (*The Egyptian Book of the Dead*) reveal the unaltered belief of the Egyptians in the immortality of the soul, resurrection, and life after death. These beliefs led to the practice of mummification of the dead from about 3100 B.C.[12] The separation of mind (or soul) and body, as a fundamental principle, was also adumbrated by the Hebrew prophets and began to find philosophic formulation in the early pre-Platonic Greek philosophers. Plato himself contrasted the immateriality and immortality of the soul to the body, a view subsequently emphasized by the Neo-Platonist, Plotinus (205-270) and by the Christian St. Augustine (354-430), under whose influence the early church nurtured the basic separation of flesh and spirit, or matter and mind, and which was to dominate the whole of medieval philosophy. This was only modified in the thirteenth century by St. Thomas Aquinas (1225-1274) who was more influenced by Aristotelian ideas. Its modern formulation owed much however, to the deliberate and distinct expression of the doctrine in the first half of the seventeenth century by Descartes, who made the fundamental distinction and assumption of irreducibility between mind and matter, sometimes referred to as 'mind-body dualism'.

For Descartes, the universe has two kinds of "substance", body and mind. By 'substance', he means that which required nothing but itself in order to exist. Only body and mind are substances, and everything in the universe is reducible to one or the other, and each is self-sustaining.[13]

Materialism, which is a narrower version of naturalism, was among the oldest of philosophies found in Greek thought in the seventh century B.C.[14] The naturalists assume no intrinsically unknowable reality and would question the existence of any events which cannot, in principle, be scientifically investigated. The growth and development of modern science since its beginning in the post-medieval period has certainly bolstered and encouraged the materialists' points of view. One of the classic points of view of materialism is that everything which exists is resolvable or reducible in the long run to 'matter'.[15] Early exponents of this philosophy were the Greek philosophers, Leucippus and Democritus in the late fifth and early fourth century B.C.[16] They espoused the view that all things could be reduced by scientific analysis into their material constituents. The ultimate constituents were atoms, which were indivisible. Although, the universe appeared to contain more than was physical or material, atoms and empty spaces were all that existed 'in reality'. Everything else was the product of a subjective, artificial, human way of looking at things.[17]

The general characterization of materialism, in its broadest terms, is that all realities can be 'reduced' to material properties or biological properties undergoing change of motion in space. What we call 'mind' and its activities are, in fact, just complex movements in the brain, general nervous system or other bodily organs. In sum, all phenomena, including psychological phenomena such as desires, hopes, images and social phenomena such as tradition, civilization, nationalism, and so on, are simply disguised forms of a basic physical reality and its casually changing relations.[18] The materialists argue that if all things are conceived in material terms, then there is no need to appeal to any mysterious principles of explanation in order to account for a supposed relation between the material and non-material. This approach, they argue, accords with our experience. We know that all 'mental' phenomena can be changed when physical conditions change. Ideas and emotions are not possible without bodily functioning and no mental events have ever existed except in a body and there can be no thoughts without a brain.

Materialism in a broad sense connotes a commitment to 'matter', the nuts and bolts of the universe, the raw materials of physics. But as our later discussion of quantum physics will show, matter has become increasingly dematerialized of its traditional properties and replaced by the concept of energy in its numerous forms. Matter and energy are no longer seen as 'core-alities'. Matter is but a form of energy and energy is the fundamental reality. Energy is active and material objects are 'materialized' by their becoming. A question now arises: are there any implications of the 'new physics' for NDE?

2.6 Competing Arguments.

2.6.1 Arguments Contra.

The arguments dismissing NDEs run something like this: NDE cannot be accepted as anything more than stories related by persons who had some traumatic experience and almost died. They cannot be scientifically duplicated and tested, their value is purely anecdotal. Furthermore, similar stories have been related by persons who have not been on the point of death. Therefore, it cannot assist to establish any evidence of life after death.

There are medical professionals who dismiss the whole phenomena as simply reflecting signs of disassociation. Patients suffering from psychosis like schizophrenia and organic brain problems, like delirium and dementia, are known to have similar experience. Schizophrenia may involve the 'hearing' of disembodied 'voices', and delirium is brought about by lack of oxygen to the brain causing a chemical imbalance and hallucination. NDE occurs when the brain is starved of oxygen.

The out-of-body experience (OBE) is easily understood in terms of 'autoscopic hallucination' which is the mental projection of one's self into visual space. When this occurs the subject can see a perfectly normal duplicate of himself as he would see another person. The experience of travelling through the tunnel is a recall of the subconscious memory of birth, which would explain the universality of this component of NDE. At a time of severe stress, the mind reverts to a vestigial memory of being forced out of the womb along the birth canal towards the waiting circle of light which is the 'real' world and where often strange beings in white, like doctors and nurses, are waiting and catering to you.[19]

NDE may be as a result of a psychological mechanism that trips in, to make things easier, when an individual's life is on the ebb. This idea of the mind tricking itself is referred to as 'transient depersonalization'.

In death-bed NDE cases, the administering of mind altering drugs, such as Thorazine, Demerol, and Morphine as pain killers to the seriously ill, is a simple explanation for these experiences. And, where these drugs are not administered, the brain can release its own pain killers – endorphins, which are more powerful than morphine and may have similar effects. Of course, the most telling point to make is that none of the subjects in NDE cases are dead, only 'near death'. There has got to be some element of consciousness still surviving in every patient who was pronounced dead, for the brain suffers irreversible damage after only a few minutes without oxygen. It may very well be the NDEs are really a phenomenon of life rather than death.

2.6.2   Arguments Pro.

The arguments sympathetic to NDEs run something like this: experiencers have described meeting deceased relatives or friends who they did not know or could not have known had been dead. During out-of-body experiences, subjects have claimed that they can travel through roofs and walls, through ambulance vehicles into space. In some instances, when they are floating they can recount operating procedure in the hospital theater, watching the medical team at work. In many cases, what was described as taking place was confirmed. In one case, a child recalled seeing an African

American on the operating team who was not on the team that had interviewed her. It was confirmed that this doctor was called in at the last minute owing to the inability of a former team member to be present.

In many cases, it is reported that the patient was medically dead, that is, the heart had stopped beating, EEG monitors were showing flat lines and the pupils of the eyes had ceased to function. Yet, individuals having been reported to have remained in that condition for longer than five minutes (after which, according to present medical knowledge there would have been irreversible brain damage), have had spontaneous revival. In the case of the internationally known philosopher, A. J. Ayer, he was told by his nurse and doctor that his heart had stopped for four minutes and he revived.[20]

Sympathizers do not suggest that NDE is a confirmation of any religious beliefs. Many experiencers have been known to be agnostics and atheists. For example, A. J. Ayer was a noted atheist. NDEs are very distinguishable from mental illnesses. Experiencers are positively motivated after their trauma. They do not exhibit the depression, despair and hopelessness of the sufferers of schizophrenia.

Sympathizers argue that NDEs are not drug-induced fantasies. Usually, drug-produced hallucinations are not at all like typical near-death experiences. In any event, there has to be some electrical activity in the brain for hallucination to occur, but where the EEG is flat, the brain is by definition dead and hallucinatory activities are not theoretically possible.

The type of autoscopic hallucination found in a person with psychiatric disorders such as depression, epilepsy or schizophrenia and "autoscopic NDE" is quite different. Unlike the autoscopic NDE, hallucination consists of the physical body (original) perceiving the projected image (double) with direct interaction between the original and the double, which is perceived as being unreal and which commonly evokes negative emotions.

The suggested link between anoxia and NDEs cannot be sustained. Experiments have shown that oxygen deprivation caused the impairment of both mental and physical abilities resulting in slowness of reasoning, convulsions and memory difficulties; hallucinations did not occur. The quality and undream-like reality of NDE cannot be as a result of oxygen deprivation.

2.6.3 Comment.

The pros and cons continue. Some might say let us blow the whistle and call time out. It is likely that the final results will be a draw in any event. On one side are the sceptics who have given little or no weight to the experiential facts, so diligently researched and presented using scientific methodology, by credible researchers such as Kenneth Ring, Michael Sabom and Osis and McCormick. The sceptics eagerly debunk notions of the after-life, even where none were being positively claimed or actively promoted. On the other side are the researchers who proclaim NDE as a solid coherent phenomenon and reject, on that basis, all criticisms which do not treat with every individual aspect of the phenomenon all at once. Yet, the various and separate explanations, when taken together, might very well constitute a solid comprehensive theory, for NDE may be viewed as a composite of different experiences capable of being interpreted separately as James Alcock has carefully argued.[21]

One feature of NDE however, that seems to create problems for the theoretical antagonists is the paranormal aspect, but it may be agreed that there have not been sufficient credible documented cases to persuade the sceptics. The problem for the objective observer now is not the paucity of explanations available, but, if anything, its surfeit. A comprehensive interdisciplinary theory of NDE which takes into account all the current available knowledge in the fields of medicine, psychology, theoretical physics and consciousness research is needed. So far, this does not appear to be on the horizon.[22]

Chapter 3

THE DISEMBODIED SELF

> *Nothing we imagine*
> *is absolutely impossible*
> *- Hume*[1]

3.1 Introduction

Discussions of personal diachronic identity usually results in a bifurcation between bodily or biological continuity and psychological continuity, and although the simplicity of treating bodily continuity as the basis for personal identity is attractive and a retreat to the accounts of organic identification is very appealing, such an approach would be unhelpful in a discussion of disembodiment. Consequently, this discussion shall be centered on psychological continuity.

Amelie Rorty very succinctly set the stage for a discussion of psychological continuity when she asked,

> What are the conditions for the identity of the reflective, conscious subject of experience, a subject that is not identical with any set of its experiences, memories or traits, but is that which has all of them, and can choose either to identify with them or to reject them as alien?[2]

The psychological approach to identity has generally been presented in terms of the continuity of a person's personality, character, beliefs and personal memory, especially the latter; and survival presented as some particular thing through space and time.

Among the psychological approaches, I would include a view traceable to Plato (C.428-348 BC), that as a soul, a human being is an embodied spirit, a simple unchanging substance that can be freed upon bodily death, to exist eternally in a realm of non-physical and incorruptible ideal forms. But what this is exactly is not clear. If this entity were metaphysical, then it would have to be beyond all appearance and remain a mystery. Furthermore, because it does not help to identify either ourselves or others, we are in no better position to identify our own disembodied self.

Despite the seeming inadequacy of the Platonic approach, some philosophers have attempted to recast it by making it more empirical, in what has been referred to as the *Cartesian Approach*. Renè Descartes (1596-1650) espoused the view that the essence of a person is the mind, a non-physical substance that thinks, imagines, believes and doubts.[3] Because we know our minds, we know who we are with absolute certainty and, consequently, can identify ourselves without any special cues on account of our self awareness. But is this helpful in sign-posting the disembodied self?

John Locke (1632-1704) relied on memory as the criterion for identifying a person and proposed that a person is the sum total of his or her memories.[4] Unlike Descartes, a person was not a substance but a quasi-legal or moral entity which may, at different times, be composed of different substances. A person is a thinking thing that has reason and reflection, and can consider itself as itself. It is the same thinking thing in different times and places. A person may have a different body because his physique may have changed, but he is the same person because his memories extend back through those changes. But if it is accepted that people can and do have faulty memories, then, surely this must be a weakness in this approach. Nevertheless, the concept of memories, as such, would not be incompatible with the disembodied self.

David Hume (1711-1776) is critical of those philosophers who imagine that we are every moment intimately conscious of what we call self, and feel its existence and its continuance in existence, and we are certain both of its perfect identity and simplicity.[5] By identity, he is referring to persistence over time without change and by simplicity, he means existence of an individual thing at a time, as opposed to a collection.

Hume questions whether we do, in fact, have any idea of self and if so, from what impression could this idea be derived? For him, there must be one impression that gives rise to the idea of self, and that impression must continue invariably the same through the whole course of our lives. But there is no impression that is constant and invariable. Therefore, it cannot be from any impression that the idea of self is derived and, consequently, there is no such idea.

But further, what must become of all our particular perceptions which are all different, distinguishable and separable, and have no need of anything to support their existence. In what way do they belong to self and how are they connected with it?

> For my part, when I enter most intimately into what I call myself, I always stumble on some particular perception or other, of heat or cold, light or shade, love or hatred, pain or pleasure. I never can catch myself at any time without a perception, and never can observe anything but the perception.[6]

Hume's point is that no self, whether over time or at a given time, ever shows up in experience as a sensory object. If there were a self in experience, it would be a perceiver but when he looked for a perceiver nothing came even close to it, all he found was perception. He claims that our belief that we experience ourselves as selves is based on mistaking a bundle of perceptions for a perceiver and we really do not perceive a self. The twin errors that we make are: firstly, to reify individual perceptions by treating them as though they were a unifying, underlying permanent substance, and secondly, by projecting activity into something which is passive.

A person may perceive something simple and contained which he calls himself, but man is: 'nothing but a bundle or collection of different perceptions, which succeed each other with an inconceivable rapidity and are in a perpetual flux and movement.'

> There is no single power of the soul which remains unalterably the same...The mind is a kind of theatre, where several perceptions successively make their appearance, pass, repass, glide away, and mingle in an infinite variety of postures and structures.[7]

Thus, perception goes in and out of existence, they are in perpetual flux, and have no causal power whatsoever. Moreover, they have no identity over a very short span of time and no unity except, perhaps, as a result of the external relations between them. In short, for Hume, there could be no perceiver because there is no perception that does anything. We misinterpret, as a substantial perceiver, this perpetual flux of separate elements as if it were an active agent of perceptions, collecting and unifying perceptions into some underlying permanent structure. That is why we think we perceive a self.

> It is evident that the identity which we attribute to human mind, however perfect we imagine it to be, is not able to run the several different perceptions into one, and make them lose their characters of distinction and difference which are essential to them...notwithstanding this distinction and separability, we suppose the whole train of perception to be unified by identity...[8]

If we were to ask ourselves the question concerning the identity of a person, whether we observe some real bond among his perceptions or only feel one among the idea we form of them, Hume would answer for us, that:

> ...understanding never observes any real connection among objects, and that the union of cause and effect, when strictly examined, resolved itself into a customary association of ideas. For from thence it eventually follows, that identity is nothing really belonging to these different perceptions, and unifying them together, but is merely a quality which we attribute to them.[9]

In other words, the identity which we ascribe to the mind of a human being is only a fictitious one. Hume also pointed out the important role that memory plays when we consider the successive existence of a mind or thinking person and how the uninterrupted progress of thought is produced.

> For what is memory but a faculty, by which we raise up the images of past perceptions?... and as an image necessarily resembles its object, must not the frequent placing of these resembling perceptions in the chain of thought make the whole seem like the continuation of one object. In this particular, then, the memory not only discovers the identity, but also contributes to its production, by producing the relation of resemblance among the perception... As memory alone acquaints us with the continuance and extent of this succession of perceptions, it is to be considered, upon that account chiefly, as the source of personal identity. Had we no memory we never should have any notion of causation, nor consequently of that chain of causes and effects which constitute our-self, or person.[10]

In the end, Hume fails to recognize that there must be something that misperceives perceptions for a self. If there is misperception, then there must have been a 'misperceiver'. It is no wonder that, in the appendix of his *Treatise*, he confesses, saying,

> But upon a more strict review of the section concerning personal identity I find myself involv'd in such a labyrinth that I must confess, I neither know how to render them consistent.[11]

Immanuel Kant (1724-1804) comes to rescue Hume from his labyrinth with the 'transcendental self', but we will, in the long run, have to decide whether his approach to the problem illuminates more than it obscures. Kant recognizes the existence of the self though not as something you can experience, but as something that makes the having of an experience possible, and yet not a substance.

> In all judgments, I am the <u>determining</u> subject of that relation which constitute a judgment. But that the I which thinks, must be considered as in thought a <u>subject</u> and as a thing which cannot be predicate to thought, is an apodictic and <u>identical</u> proposition. But this proposition does not signify that I, as an object, am, for myself, <u>a self-subsistent being or a substance</u>. ...Our critique would be an investigation utterly superfluous if there existed a possibility of proving a priori, that all thinking being are in themselves simple substances, as such, therefore possess the inseparable attribute of personality, and are conscious of their existence apart from and unconnected with matter; for we should have taken a step beyond the world of sense, and have penetrated into the sphere of noumena (my emphasis).[12]

Kant claims that our experiences are unified. If our experiences are unified, something must account for their unity. Like Descartes, he claims that an "I think" accompanies every one of our experiences. It is:

> ...the vehicle of all conceptions in general and consequently of transcendental conceptions also, and that is therefore regarded as a transcendental conception...although it can have no particular claim to be so ranked, in as much as its

only use is to indicate that all thought is accompanied by consciousness.[13]

Unlike Descartes, however, he did not unify this "I think" as a *res cogitans* – a thinking thing or substance. For him, the 'Ego is but the consciousness of my thought.'[14]

Kant claims that the self exists outside or beyond the phenomena. It is transcendental. It is this transcendental self that makes possible the unification of the phenomena called experience. In his view, Hume erred when he proceeded as though experience could exist by themselves independently of experiencers. The 'having' of experiences logically presupposes that they belong to someone. The reason why Hume could not find an experiencer, claims Kant, is that it is nowhere in experience, that is, nowhere in the phenomenal world. It is transcendental.

What matters in perceiving identity is not transcendental selves or the retention of a particular metaphysical substance in which experiences are embedded, according to those who espouse the relational views of personal identity, but rather the continuity of our physical structures or psychological structure, including memories, beliefs, character traits and so on. The continuity of our physical or psychological structure is not as a result of the persistence of any elements out of which they are composed, but rather the persistence of a pattern or patterns of relationship among the elements. These structures, it is said, although they might not be immediately apparent within any one element of experience, could nevertheless be experienced or explained scientifically. The suggestion being that they could be found within experience or explained in terms of elements that can be understood scientifically. The question arises however, that, since these elements out of which our physical and psychological structures are composed are constantly changing, how can self and identity emerge out of these impermanent elements? The answer is, presumably, on the basis of the relations among them; but if this is so, then we require much greater analysis of these relations.[15]

The core philosophical problem about selves is to establish whether they exist or not, and if they do, what their nature is. The Cartesian approach indicated that because we know our minds, we know ourselves with absolute certainty. That 'I exist' is every 'I's' most certain knowledge. 'I' and certainty are linked. Though we have the feeling of certainty that we are ourselves or have selves, we have difficulties in describing the nature of a self or what a self is. Whatever it is, it has the ability to distinguish itself and its surrounding environment and between self and other. The distinguished editors of *Self and Identity* explain it in this way,

> Strictly speaking, it is not the organism as a whole but a distinguishing mechanism (or mechanisms) within the organism that distinguishes between self and other. This mechanism distinguishes parts of the organism from other parts and the organism as a whole from other organisms. Eventually, at least in humans, the distinguisher itself – presumably the brain or some part of it – also tries to distinguish itself from the organism within which it makes distinctions.[16]

But this surely begs the question for what or who is the "distinguisher", what is it that is doing the distinguishing, what is this self-regulating, self-separating mechanism? This sounds like Gilbert Ryle's 'Ghost in the Machine'.[17] The editors continue:

> In making this crucial move it often reifies itself as a separate thing, that is, in distinguishing between self and the organism in which it is housed – it says not only 'I am a self,' but also "I am the self that has this organism." Such reification is part and parcel of the brains construction of a self-concept existing apart from both brain and organism.[18]

In my view, this is a healthy example of attempting to explain the obscure by the more obscure. The very act of reifying itself as a separate thing concretizes the subject of the reification and acknowledges its real existence and manifestation.

In any event, how did the process of self-reification begin, if it did at all, and when? If we attempt to trace its genesis by seeking an explanation through some evolutionary route, we will be faced with the inevitable problem of when in time did the appearance of self-recognition and awareness occur. Further, where out of the void, did it come from when there were no forms of consciousness? And even if this were established, it is not at all self-evident that this would either dismiss or negate the 'substance self' of Descartes or Kant's 'transcendental self'.

Moreover, what is the level of development required in consciousness for there to be selfhood and at what level in the complexities of the evolutionary process does it occur? Simply put, when do selves first make their appearance? When and how this happened is indeed difficult to ascertain, but why it should happen is even more perplexing.

Anthony Quinton, (1962) in his article "The Soul", re-examines the soul theory of Plato and Descartes in which the soul is an ethereal but nonetheless physical entity capable of independent existence.[19] Their theory is identified with the view that in each person there is to be found a spiritual substance which is the subject of his mental states and bearer of his personal identity. Of course, the existence of a spiritual substance is logically distinct from its being the criterion of personal identity and consequently the arguments against the substance theory of personal identity in no way refutes the proposition that there can be no conscious state that is not the state of some subject.

Quinton identifies three main weaknesses of the spiritual substance theory as a criterion of identity. Firstly, it is regressive in just the same way as is an account of identity of a material object through time in terms of its physical components. How is the identity of the identifier through time to be established? Secondly, what is the observable mental entity that can effectively serve as a criterion in this case? The only plausible candidate is that dim inchoate background, largely composed of organic sensations, which envelops the mental states occupying the focus of attention. The organic background is a relatively unchanging environment for the more dramatic episodes of conscious life to stand out against. Even if its comparatively undisturbed persistence of character suggests it as a criterion, its vagueness makes it even less accessible to public application than the general run of mental criteria and leaves it with little power to distinguish between one person and another. Finally, it is held that the spiritual substance is nevertheless of a permanent and unalterable constituent of a person's conscious life. Thus, it follows that it must be unobservable and as such is useless for the purpose of identification.

To concede that the spiritual substance cannot be the criterion of personal identity, and that it cannot be identified with any observable part of a person's mental life, does not mean that it does not exist. If, however, the spiritual substance is something distinct from both the related series of mental states or the body or from both, as some believe, then it ought not properly to be called the soul, for it could not exist without any states at all, and even if it could, it would be an emotionally useless form of survival of bodily death. Spiritual substance cannot be the criterion of personal identity, and it may or may not be presupposed by the existence of conscious mental states.

Whether as part, or as pre-supposition of our mental life, it should not be identified with the soul when this is conceived as the non-bodily aspect of a person. The well-founded conviction that there is no spiritual substance in the first sense and widespread doubt as to its existence in the second should not be allowed to obscure the issue of whether there is a unitary, non-bodily aspect to a person and, if there is, whether it is the fundamental and more important aspect. Locke saw that spiritual substance could not account for personal identity, yet he clearly believed in the soul as the connected sequence of a person's conscious states, and regarded this sequence as what a person essentially was, and held it to be capable of existing independently of the body.[20]

3.2 Empirical Concept of the Soul

Quinton poses the question whether there can be an empirical concept of the soul which, like Locke's concept, interprets it as a sequence of mental states logically distinct from the body and that is neutral with regard to the problem of the subject. It is undeniable that among the facts that involve a person, there is a class that is describable as mental. But would it be adequate to describe the soul as the temporarily extended totality of mental states and events that belong to a person? How can we speak of something logically distinct from the body when that substance involves some reference to a particular human being. This notion of the soul could have no application to mental states that were not articulated with bodies. The soul, then, must be a series of mental states which over time is identifiable by virtue of the properties and relations of these mental states themselves.

Quinton sets out to construct an empirical concept of the soul. He begins by creating an identifiable unit which he calls a *soul-phase*. A soul-phase is a set of contemporaneous mental states belonging to the same momentary consciousness. Two soul-phases belong to the same soul, if they are connected by a continuous character and memory path. Two soul-phases are directly continuous if they are temporally juxtaposed, if the character revealed by the constituents of each is closely similar, and if the latter contains recollections of some elements of the former. Two soul-phases are indirectly continuous and connected by a continuous character and memory path if there is a series of soul-phases all of whose members are directly continuous with their immediate predecessors and successors in the series, and if the original soul-phases are the two end points of the series. There is an analogy with this criterion and the one by means of which material objects, including human bodies, are identified. Two object-phases belong to the same object if they are connected by a continuous quality and position path. Direct continuity in this case obtains between two temporally juxtaposed object-phases which are closely similar in qualities and are in the same position or in close neighbouring positions. Indirect continuity is once again the ancestor of direct continuity. There is no limit to the amount of difference in position allowed by the criterion to two indirectly continuous object-phases, but in normal discourse, a limit is set to the amount of qualitative difference allowed by the requirement that the two phases be objects of the same kind. Character, in the mental case, corresponds to quality in the physical and memory to spatial position. In the light of this, the soul can then be defined empirically as a series of mental states connected by continuity of character and memory.[21]

Even if the most extreme and reductive version of logical behaviourism were correct, even if a person's mental state were simply and solely behavioural disposition, actual or potential, his character, a complex property of these dispositions, and his memory, a particular disposition to make first person statements in the past tense without inference or reliance on testimony, the empirical concept of the soul would still apply to something distinct from any particular human body, through some body or other, not necessarily human perhaps, would be required to manifest the appropriate dispositions in its behaviour and speech. In other words, even an extreme, reductive, logical behaviourism is perfectly compatible with reincarnation, with the manifestation by one body of the character and memories that were previously manifested by another body that no longer exists.

It could be argued that the soul, as defined by Quinton, and the body cannot be clearly distinguished, since the possession of some sorts of character trait requires the possession of an appropriate sort of body, and a very large number of character traits seem to presume nothing about the age, sex, build and general physical condition of their host. Even if this were an empirically well founded point, it would not be relevant, for it would merely show that the possession of a given trait of character required the possession of an appropriate *kind* of body and not the possession of a particular body.[22] The soul defined as a series of mental states connected by continuity of character and memory, is the essential constituent of personality. According to

Quinton, it is not only logically distinct from any particular human body with which it is associated; it is also what a person fundamentally is.

Can the soul exist in an entirely disembodied state or must the soul be associated with some human body? Quinton claims that even where personal characteristics are not associated with any sort of body in the physiological sense, they are associated with a body in the epistemological sense. In other words, it is an essential part of the story that the soul in question have physical manifestations.[23]

In Quinton's approach, strictly disembodied existence is conceivable, in the sense that it is conceivable that there can be circumstances in which there could be good reason to claim that a soul existed in a disembodied state. Could this be what obtains in an out-of-body experience?

P. F. Strawson, in *Individuals* (1993) also allows for disembodied existence. To him, the concept of a person is logically prior to that of individual consciousness. Therefore, the concept of a person is not to be analysed as that of an animated body or of an embodied "anima". By this, he does not mean that the concept of a pure individual consciousness might not have a logical secondary existence, if one thinks, or finds it desirable. But we speak of a dead person – a body – and in the same secondary way we might at least think of a disembodied person. He makes the point that a person is not an embodied ego, *but an ego might be a disembodied person*, retaining the logical benefit of individuality for having been a person.[24] Since the concept of pure individual consciousness could not exist as a primary concept, to be used in the explanation of the concept of a person, then for Strawson there would be no mind-body problem, as traditionally conceived.

To Strawson, the concept of a person is to be understood as the concept of a type of entity such that predicates ascribing states of consciousness and predicates ascribing corporeal characteristics and a physical situation as equally applicable to an individual entity of that type.[25] In reinforcing his argument, that 'pure individual consciousness' could not exist as a primary concept to be used in the explanation of the concept of a person, though it might have a logical secondary existence, he states:

> Thus, from within our actual conceptual scheme, each of us can quite intelligibly conceive of his or her individual survival of bodily death. The effort of imagination is not even great. One has simply to think of oneself as having thoughts and memories as at present, visual and auditory experiences

largely as at present, even, perhaps – though this involves certain complications – some quasi – tactual and organic sensations as at present, whilst (a) having no perceptions of a body related to one's experience as one's own body is, and (b) having no power of initiating changes in the physical conditions of the world, such as one at present does with one's hands, shoulder, feet and vocal chords.[26]

Of course, condition (a) must be expanded by adding that no one else exhibits reactions indicating that he perceives a body at the point which one's body would be occupying, if one were seeing and hearing in an embodied state, from the point from which one is seeing and hearing in a disembodied state. Strawson recognizes also that it is possible to imagine condition (a) being fulfilled, in both its parts, without condition (b) being fulfilled.[27]

Indeed, this would be a rather vulgar fancy, in the words of Strawson, in the class of the table tapping spirits with familiar voices. But suppose disembodiment is taken strictly in the sense that one imagines both (a) and (b) above to be fulfilled, then according to Strawson, two consequences would follow. The first is that the strictly solitary disembodied individual is strictly solitary, and it must remain for him indeed an utterly empty, though not meaningless speculation, as to whether there are any other members of his class. The other is that in order to retain his idea of himself as an individual, he must always think of himself as disembodied, as a former person. That is to say, he must contrive still to have the idea of himself as a member of a class or type of entities with whom, however, he is now debarred from entering into any of those transactions the past fact of which was the condition of his having any idea of himself at all.[28]

Strawson paints a bleak picture of an individual's disembodied existence, solitary, lonely and forlorn. Since he has, as it were, no personal life of his own to lead, he must live much in the memories of the personal life he did lead; or he might, when this living in the past loses its appeal, achieves some kind of attenuated vicarious personal existence by taking a certain kind of interest in the human affairs of which he is now a mute and invisible witness – much like a kind of spectator at a play, or perhaps even more like a ghost.

In proportion, as the memories fade and the vicarious living palls, to that degree his concept of himself as an individual becomes attenuated.[29] At the limit of attenuation there is, according to Strawson, from the point of view of his survival as an individual, no difference between the continuance of experience and its cessation. Disembodied survival, on such terms as these, does seem unattractive. Perhaps it is for this reason that the orthodox have wisely insisted on the resurrection of the body.[30]

Conditions (a) and (b) above are reminiscent of the experience of a person who has had an out of body experience and was "a mute and invisible witness to human affairs." A relevant question here is whether there is any continued existence of a person's conscious life in a disembodied form after the death of the body? If consciousness were to continue to experience mental events without a body, then that would suggest that mental events are not just some by-product of bodily processes. This would refute epiphenomenalism but would still not be evidence that this disembodied consciousness could affect the physical. Even if this were so, that in itself would not establish mind-body interaction, for it may very well be that consciousness could affect the physical body only when in a disembodied state, not when a person has a body.

Such survival of consciousness after the death of the body is certainly imaginable, at least in one's own case. We might then follow Hume in saying, '...nothing we imagine is absolutely impossible' (see note[1]), or put differently, what you can imagine is possible.

But if possibility is to remain objective, according to W. D. Hart, then Hume's principle should be taken not metaphysically but epistemologically. That is:

> It is not that possibilities are, for example, the images we form when we visualize. The idea is rather that imagination is to knowledge of (mere) possibility as perception is to knowledge of actuality.[31]

The analogy claims only that imagination is sufficient for knowledge of possibility, not that it is necessary. According to Hart, "For some of the arcana of say, contemporary physics may be too arcane to have been seen or even imagined, and yet for all that may be actual and so possible."[32]

How, if at all, does one get from Hume's principle to dualism? Hume's principle says that what you can imagine is possible. Dualism says, that you can be disembodied. So in an argument for dualism, there is the premise that you could be disembodied.

But as a disembodied person should be immaterial, it is you in your mental dimension that should persist through disembodiment. You have, in effect, three mental dimensions:

(a) Those faculties that are conduits from the material world, namely the five senses – sight, hearing, smell, taste and touch.

(b) The intra-psychic functions or so-called higher faculties. These include propositional attitudes specified by verbs such as – believes, desires, thinks, wonders, dreams and so on, followed usually by the word 'that'; and

(c) The conduits from the mind to the world, of which the central examples are actions such as locomotion, rearranging your organization – change of attitude and manipulating objects – usually outside the body.

Hart concentrates more on (a) and (c) above, rather than (b). Descartes is often accused of concentrating too much on (b), especially on the intellectual propositional attitude in particular.[33]

If we take perception as derived from the five senses, starting with sight, can one imagine seeing while disembodied? Sight requires visual experience, and we have imagined having visual experience while disembodied. Of course, we must know what sight is, and that whatever it is, you can imagine having it even if you are disembodied. It is a necessary condition of sight that one has visual experience. The three phenomena – sight, visualizing (in the mind's eye), and dreaming, have something in common. The commonality is visual experience; so there is visual experience. Thus, visual experience is common to sight, visualizing and dreaming, but does not suffice for sight.[34] In addition, Hart observes, 'But note that since those who no longer have eyes can visualize, it is possible to have visual experience at a time when one has no eyes.'[35] This would accord with out-of-body experience.

At this point, according to Hart, the tradition adds veridicality. Veridicality is to experience as truth is to thought (predisposition, sentences or statements). A thought is true when the world is as the thinker thinks it to be, and a visual experience is veridical when the world is as it looks to one with the experience. In order for an experience to be veridical, according to Hart, there needs be no substantial connection and no transmission or linkage between the experience and that piece of the world, in virtue of which it is veridical. Veridicality requires only, as it were, a coincident of content, between experience and the world.

Hence, there is no obstacle at all in the way of supposing that a disembodied person's visual experience be veridical, that is, that the world be as it looks to the disembodied person. If that is accepted, then we may suppose that the scene of which he has visual experience is real, that therefore his lines of sight coincide with real lines in genuine space, and that, consequently, the region of convergence of those lines determines a real place in space for part of him or her to occupy.[36] In other words, the tradition distinguishes sight from visualizing and dreaming by veridicality. But as veridicality is a bare conjunctive property, if our disembodied person with veridical visual experience is to see what makes his visual experience veridical, that experience should be caused by what makes it veridical.

But H. P. Grice showed that veridical visual experience is not sufficient for sight, since the world could be as one visualizes it to be, but only by accident.[37] More than the bare coincidence required by veridicality is necessary for sight. In short, we may say that veridical visual experience is sight only if it is caused by that in virtue of which it is veridical.

It has been argued above that mental events do have physical effects and vice versa, so the argument for interaction is accepted. But here comes the age old question again, how could there be causal commerce between immaterial disembodied people and the physical objects they see? On reflection, it seems that the problem of interaction is more about the nature of mind and matter than about the nature of causation. If we return to Hume, he explains causation in terms of temporal priority, spatial contiguity, and constant conjunction. Contiguity certainly requires location. Suppose we could locate a disembodied person's visual experience, bearing in mind that visual experience is always along lines of sight. In visualizing fantasies, these subjective lines of sight need not coincide with real lines in space, but when visual experience is veridical, they will, and the point, or small region of their conveyance is a subjectively described place where the disembodied person's visual experience lies.[38]

The key to Hume's theory of causation is constant conjunction, (the 'besiding' of this and that) by which he intended bare conjunction. But bare constant conjunction between physical and mental event types (or vice versa) seems no more problematic than between any two types of physical events. Put simply, Hume's intuition is that causation requires no occult powers, (that is, he is against invisible links or flow of unperceived quantities from cause to effect) given spatial contiguity and temporal priority, causation requires only bare conjunction, juxtaposition, between tokens of event types. Once mental events are in space, there are no further obstacles in the way of supposing a bare constant conjunction between certain mental and certain physical events than between two types (like different physical types) of events. So on a Humean view of causation, there exist no problem about supposing that veridical visual experience in the disembodied be caused by that in virtue of which is veridical.[39] If this is so, then there is no interaction problem, but if there is still an interaction problem then we are in need of a better view of causation to understand it. One might well come to the view that Hume's approach makes trivial a difficult problem and may even provide ammunition against his view of causation. Hart does not think that the problem of causal interaction is trivial and wants an understanding of causation that will articulate the severity of that problem adequately.[40]

Hart finds in Quine the 'better view' of causation and one that addresses the severity of the problem,

> Quine argues that causation is the flow of energy. Could any quantity pass between things as different as mind and matter are according to dualism? This formulation seems to do better justice to the interaction problem. But it also suggests a treatment of that problem. Energy (or mass energy) is conserved, and conservation is a quantitative principle. So we need intrinsically psychological quantities... We can give a general account of quantity (satisfied by temperature, mass, length and so on) that is pretty well satisfied by desire, belief, how much it looks to one as if such and such, and other psychological phenomena. Once we have such psychological quantities we may imagine that as light from objects seen reaches the region of convergence along the disembodied person's line of sight, it passes straight through but loses some electromagnetic energy and, at a fixed rate of conversion, that person acquires or is sustained in visual experience of those objects seen. Here is a way to imagine that the disembodied person's veridical visual experience be caused by that in virtue of which it is veridical, and *thus far, that he sees*.[41]

Hart feels that with this, he has solved the interaction problem. The fact that he has not been able to imagine exactly how light energy converts into psychic energy implicit in visual experience does not, in the least, embarrass him. For in his view, physicists are not embarrassed when they fail to tell us how mass turns into energy when an atom bomb goes off.

Hart's version of dualism differs from Descartes's, whose interaction is about how a disembodied person's mind is, for example, acted on by objects that he sees. Moreover, for Descartes, extension is the essence of matter. As a result he seems to put all geometrical properties, including location, under extension. To keep mind immaterial he must deny its location. But for post-Newtonians such as Hart, they accept geometrical objects in regions of space without matter, and so, location does not require physicality, consequently disembodied minds can be somewhere in space, without being thereby embodied. This would allow for out of body experience and make the core experience of NDE believable.

But, Hart goes further:

> When disembodied people see on our model, light loses energy where their visual experience occurs, and if this loss were large enough, we would see where a disembodied person is. From one angle, it might look like a dimming where a part of the disembodied person is. So disembodied people could look like the hazy **holograms** in the haunted house at Disneyland.[42] (my emphasis)

The rediscovery of the possibility of the folklore of ghost or ghostlike effigies is not surprising to Hart for whom dualism is the commonsense solution to the mind-body problem. Hart's approach opens the door for examination, and further exploration, of Near-Death-Experience (NDE) using holographic theory and gives direction and impetus to such examination and exploration, along philosophical lines.

PART TWO:
A Holographic Approach

Chapter 4

NEW PARADIGMS AND THE MECHANISTIC UNIVERSE

4.1 Introduction

Thomas Kuhn, in his famous work, *The Structure of Scientific Revolution* (1970), describes a paradigm in its established usage as an accepted 'mode' or 'pattern'.[1] In its standard application, the paradigm functions by permitting the replication of examples, anyone of which could, in principle, serve to replace it. In grammar, *amo, amas, amat* is a paradigm because it displays the pattern to be used in conjugating a large number of other Latin verbs such as *laudo, laudas, laudat* and so on. He points out, however, that in a science it is rarely an object for replication, but functions rather like an accepted judicial decision in the common law; it is an object for further articulation and speculation under new or more stringent conditions.

One has to recognize that a paradigm is limited both in scope and precision at the time of its first appearance. Paradigms, however, gain their status ultimately because they are more successful than others in solving some problems that have come to be recognized as acute and in need of explanation.

The aim of 'normal science' is not to summon new sorts of phenomena, nor is it usually an objective to invent new theories, in fact some scientists are often downright hostile to those theories invented by others.[2] Instead, normal-scientific research is directed to the articulation of those phenomena and theories that the paradigm already supplies. In other words, the existence of the paradigm sets the problem to be solved.

A paradigm is designed to solve a puzzle, for whose very existence the validity of the paradigm must be assumed, but sometimes, normal science is unable to solve the puzzle. The unsolvable puzzles then become 'anomalies'; that is, the recognition that nature has somehow violated the paradigm-induced expectations that govern normal science. At times, an anomaly will clearly challenge explicit and fundamental generalizations of the paradigm, as in the Copernican revolution. When an anomaly seems to become more than just another puzzle of normal science, one that ought to be solvable by known rules and procedures, but resists the repeated onslaught of the ablest members of the scientific community within whose competence it falls, then a transition to 'crisis' and 'extraordinary science' has begun.[4] The anomaly itself now comes to be more generally recognized as such by the profession.[5]

Put differently, when a paradigm fails to deal with an anomaly, despite repeated efforts, and it cannot be aligned with professional expectations; and the scientific community can no longer evade anomalies that subvert the existing tradition of scientific practice, then begins the extraordinary investigations that lead to a new set of commitments, and a new basis for the practice of science. It is after enough extraordinary science has been completed successfully that a paradigm shift occurs; where the new paradigm replaces the old, and, in time, the new one becomes accepted and is embraced by the practitioners of the old, a transformation of world views occurs and the scientific revolution is completed. It is these extraordinary episodes in which there is a shift of professional commitment that Kuhn refers to as a scientific revolution.[6]

Prior to a paradigm shift and the shift of professional commitment, according to Kuhn, one might expect to find resistance, suppression and scepticism from the acceptors of the prevailing scientific paradigm, for normal science is predicated on the assumption that the scientific community knows what the world is like, and they will defend that assumption. Consequently, normal science often suppresses fundamental novelties because they are necessarily subversive of the basic commitments.[7]

As these practitioners conduct the practice of normal science, and puzzle solving, using the accepted paradigms, there is a tendency to take for granted that the paradigm actually describes how the universe works, and that it can account for all things including the anomalous. In the course of his research, it became increasingly evident to Kuhn that, from a historical perspective, the development of the sciences was far from linear. The history of science is by no means a process of gradual accumulation of data and for-

47

mulation of ever increasingly accurate theories, it has been punctuated with inventions and discoveries and changing paradigms:

> The transition from a paradigm in crisis to a new one from which a new tradition of normal science can emerge is far from a cumulative process, one achieved by an articulation or extension of the old paradigm. Rather it is a reconstruction that changes some of the field from new fundamentals, a reconstruction that changes field's most elementary theoretical generalizations as well as many of its paradigm methods and application.[8]

When the unsolvable puzzles or anomalies lead to a crisis and to extraordinary science or 'non-normal science', scientists often turn to philosophy for answers. Kuhn states:

> It is, I think, particularly in periods of acknowledged crisis that scientists have turned to philosophical analysis as a device for unlocking the riddles of their field. Scientists have not generally needed or wanted to be philosophers. Indeed, normal science usually holds creative philosophy at arms length, and probably for good reasons. To the extent that normal research work can be conducted by using paradigms as a model, rules and assumptions need not be made explicit... [T]he full set of rules sought by philosophical analysis need not even exist. But that is not to say that the research for assumptions (even for non-existent ones) cannot be an effective way to weaken the grip of a tradition upon the mind and to suggest the basis for a new one. It is no accident that the emergence of Newtonian physics in the seventeenth century and of relativity and quantum mechanics in the twentieth century should have been both preceded and accompanied by fundamental philosophical analyses of the *contemporary research* tradition.[9]

Stanislav Grof, in discussing the role of paradigm, in *Beyond the Brain* (1985), adopts Kuhn's revised definition of paradigms as a constellation of beliefs, values, and techniques shared by the members of a given scientific community.[10] He, however, categorizes paradigms into those of basic philosophical nature which are general and encompassing, and others which govern scientific thinking in rather specific and circumscribed areas of research.

The concept of reality is extremely complex and it is not possible to deal with it in totality. Consequently, science does not, and cannot, take into consideration or observe all the variables involved in a particular phenomenon, conduct all possible experiments and perform all the laboratory or clinical tests desired. The problem, therefore, must be reduced to a workable scale to enable the scientist to observe and experiment. No doubt, however, his or her selection will be guided by the leading paradigm of the time. Inevitably, this means that the scientist cannot avoid coming to the table with a definite belief system into his or her province of observation and investigation. As Grof puts it:

> Many factors determine which aspect of a complex phenomenon will be chosen and which of many conceivable experiments will be carried out or conducted first... Observation and experiments can and must drastically reduce and restrict the range of acceptable scientific solutions. However, they cannot in and by themselves fully justify a particular interpretation or a belief system. It is thus, in principle, impossible to practice science without some set of a priori beliefs, fundamental metaphysical assumptions, and answers about the nature of reality and of human knowledge.[11]

Most importantly, paradigms have not only a cognitive but also a normative influence; in addition to being statements about nature and reality, they also define the permissible problem field, determine the acceptable methods of approaching it and set the standards of solution. Under the influence of a paradigm, all the fundamentals of science in a particular area becomes drastically redefined.[12]

Grof maintains that during the last three centuries, Western science has been dominated by the Newtonian-Cartesian paradigm, a system of thought based on the work of Newton and Descartes. Using the Newtonian Mechanistic Model of the universe, at first, gave positive results and impact in scientific progress, but in the course of later developments it lost its revolutionary power and became a serious obstacle for scientific research and development.

4.2 Newton's Mechanistic Universe

Newton's Mechanistic Universe, as described by Grof,[13] is a universe of solid matter, made of atoms, small and indestructible particles that constitute its fundamental building blocks. They are essentially passive and unchangeable; their mass and form always remain constant. Newton gave a precise definition of the force acting between the particles, which he referred to as the force of gravity, and established that it was directly proportionate to the mass involved and indirectly proportionate to the square of their distance. Gravity is seen, in Newton's system, as a rather mysterious entity, and intrinsic attribute to the bodies it acts upon and whose action is exerted instantaneously over distance.

Another essential characteristic in the Newtonian universe is the three-dimensional space of classic Euclidean universe, which is absolute, constant and always at rest. The distinction between matter and empty space is clear and unambiguous. Similarly, time is absolute, autonomous, and independent of the material world. It shows a uniform and unchangeable flow from the past through the present to the future. According to Newton, all physical processes can be reduced to movements of material points that result from the force of gravity acting among them and causing their mutual attraction. Newton was able to describe the dynamics of these forces by means of the new mathematical approach of differential calculus, which he had invented for the purpose.[14]

The resulting image of the universe is that of a gigantic and entirely deterministic clockwork, with particles moving according to eternal and unchangeable laws, and the events and processes in the material world consist of chains of interdependent causes and effects. As a consequence, it should be possible to reconstruct any past situation in the universe and predict everything in its future with absolute certainty. As a basic metaphysical assumption, this represents an essential element of the mechanistic worldview.

Another important influence in the philosophy and history of science in the last two centuries has been Descartes's formulation of the absolute dualism between mind *(res cogitans)* and matter *(res extensa)*, resulting in a belief that the material world could be described objectively, without reference to the human observer. One of the serious neglect of this approach has been the neglect of a holistic approach to human beings, society and life on this planet.

It should be noted, however, that the use of the term 'Newton-Cartesian Paradigm' in the context of Western mechanistic science does a disservice to these two great thinkers, for it omits the concept of God which was an essential element in their philosophies and world views. Newton was a deeply spiritual person who had great interest in astrology, occultism and alchemy.[15] Newton did believe that the universe was material in its nature but felt that God had initially created the material particles, the forces between them, and the laws that governed their motion. The origin of the universe could not be explained from material causes, but having been created, it would continue to function as a machine and could be explained and understood in those terms. Descartes also believed in the objective existence of the world independent of the human observer, but for him, its objectivity was based on its constantly being perceived by God. Conceptual thinking in many disciplines reflects a direct logical extension of the Newtonian-Cartesian model, but minus the divine intelligence which was at the heart of the speculations of these two thinkers. Once that disappeared from the picture, we are left with the systematic and radical materialism which become the new ideological foundation of the modern scientific world-view.

We have seen the development of a modern world-view which has elaborated the image of the universe as an immensely complex mechanical system, an assembly of passive or inert matter, developing with no participation of consciousness or creative intelligence. From the time of the *big bang* through the initial expansion of the galaxies to the creation of the solar system, the cosmic evolution was supposedly governed solely by plain mechanical forces. According to this version of creation, life originated in the primeval ocean, fortuitously, as a result of haphazard chemical reactions. In like manner, the cellular organization of organic matter and its evolution to higher life forms occurred quite mechanically, void of any participation of an intelligent principle, by random genetic mutations with the mechanism of natural selection guaranteeing the survival of the fittest. The result of this was a ramified phylogenetic system of specifics arranged hierarchically with increasing levels of complexity.

Somewhere along the phylogenetic scale, an extraordinary and inexplicable event occurred, the unconscious and inert matter become self-conscious and conscious of its surrounding world. The birth of consciousness remains a mystery and scientists cannot agree on the evolutionary stage at which consciousness appeared, yet it remains an accepted postulate of the materialistic and mechanistic world view that consciousness is limited to living organisms with a highly developed central nervous system, and is an epiphenomenon of physiological processes in the brain.[16]

To challenge this view is not to say that the notion that consciousness is the product of the brain is without a basis, for there has been a vast amount of observations from clinical and experimental neurology, neuro-physiology, and psychiatry which demonstrates beyond doubt that there is a close connection between consciousness and the functioning of the brain. But, surely this is not the same thing as saying that consciousness is produced by the brain.[17] Wilder Penfield, in *The Mystery of the Mind*, expressed deep doubt that consciousness is a product of the brain, and felt that consciousness may even be able to have a separate existence if it could obtain a separate source of energy.[18]

Grof makes the point that contemporary psychiatric theory cannot adequately account for many phenomena which lie beyond the biological realm of the unconscious, such as prenatal and transpersonal experiences. The weaknesses of the old paradigm are evident in dealing with such phenomena as Shamanism, mysticism, religion, the healing ceremonies of preliterate societies, miracles and near-death experiences. The mechanistic science continues to defend its belief systems, often any departure from the perceptual and conceptual congruence of the Newtonian-Cartesian model is labeled 'psychosis'; mystical experiences are reduced to culturally accepted, quasi-psychotic states, primitive superstitions or unresolved childhood conflicts.[19] This approach misses the significance of first hand visionary experiences of alternate realities which I shall discuss later.

The old models have strong inhibiting effects on new thinking and open-minded scientific investigations. This is no more evident than in the reluctance of mainstream psychology and psychiatry to accept a mass of data in near-death experiences and death-bed visions, psychedelic research and modern para-psychological studies.

I concede that the image of the universe created by Western science is a pragmatically useful construct that helps to organize presently available observations and data. Unfortunately, it has been generally mistaken for an accurate and comprehensive description of reality. Grof suggests that, as a result of this epistemological error, perceptual and cognitive congruence with the Newtonian-Cartesian world-view is considered essential for mental health and normalcy, and any departure from this 'accurate perception of reality' is seen as indications of serious psychopathology. In this context, non-ordinary states of consciousness are generally considered to be symptomatic of mental disorders.[20] The very term 'altered states of consciousness' clearly suggest that they represent distortions or illegitimate versions of the correct perceptions of 'objective reality.'

As previously stated, paradigms have not only a cognitive but a normative influence. As such, a paradigm is more than simply a useful theoretical model for science. Its philosophy actually shapes the world by its indirect influence on individuals and society. Newtonian-Cartesian science has, according to Grof, created a very negative image of human beings, "depicting them as biological machines driven by instinctual impulses of a bestial nature," an image which endorses individualism, egoistic emphasis, competition, and the principle of "survival of the fittest" as natural and essentially healthy tendencies, unable to recognize the value and importance of cooperation, synergy and ecological concerns.[21]

After years of clinical work with psychedelics and years of conceptual struggle and confusion, Grof concludes that neither the nature of the L.S.D. experience nor the numerous observations in the course of psychedelic therapy can be adequately explained in terms of the Newtonian-Cartesian mechanistic approach to the universe, nor in terms of the existing neuro-physiological models of the brain. He categorically states, 'There is at present little doubt in my mind that our correct understanding of the universe, of the nature of reality, and particularly of human beings, is superficial, incorrect, and incomplete.'[22]

If it is granted that there is substance in Grof's view, it seems we must now re-examine our present world-view, and see whether any new paradigms will offer a better understanding of the 'anomalies'. The scientific mechanistic – cum – materialistic conception of the universe has limited the direction of the search for a solution to the problem, thus restricting options. It is against a changing view of reality, emerging as it does from various areas of new science, that we will need to examine whether the mechanistic universe will now be superseded by a new model, that is, the holographic universe.

Chapter 5

THE HOLOGRAPHIC UNIVERSE

> *In the heaven of Indra, there is said to be a network of pearls, so arranged that if you look at one, you will see the others reflected in it. In the same way, each object in the world is not merely itself, but involves every other object and, in fact is everything else.*
>
> - *Avatamsaka Sutra*

5.1 Introduction

In 1947, British scientist Dennis Gabor conceived of holography, an ingenious new method for photographically recording a three-dimensional image of a scene.[1] Before that, what we had was Louis Jacques Mandé Daguirre's 'Camera Obscura' (1839). The 'Camera Obscura' was a box fitted with a lens at one end and a slanted mirror at the other. The image was then 'collapsed' onto a planar ground glass screen at the top of the box, where the artist could study it or trace it unto translucent paper.[2] Although Gabor's idea was rather recent, it was still a bit too early, for it needed a special kind of light to fully demonstrate its capabilities, this was a frequency called *coherent* light. The name *laser* was an acronym for the words 'Light Amplification by Stimulated Emission of Radiation', for which an atomic process called 'Stimulated Emission' is responsible.[3]

A hologram records the interference pattern formed by the combination of the reference wave with the light waves issuing from a scene, and when this photographic record is developed and again illuminated with laser light, the original scene is presented to the viewer as a 'reconstituted image'. This image is manifested with such vivid realism that often the viewer reaches out and tries to touch the objects of the scene. In photography, lenses are used and they allow only objects at a certain distance from the camera to be in sharp focus. In the holography process, on the other hand, no lenses are used, and all objects, near and far, are portrayed in its image in extremely sharp focus.[4] Gabor first used the term **hologram**. George Stoke, an American scientist, proposed **holography**, which has become the generally accepted term.[5]

5.2   Holography

In short, holography is three-dimensional lenseless photography, capable of recording unusually realistic images of material objects. The holographic approach emphasizes interference vibratory patterns rather than mechanical interactions and information rather than substance.

Hologram and holography cannot be understood in terms of geometrical optics in which light is treated as discrete particles or protons. The holographic method depends on the superposition principle and on interference patterns of light which requires that light be understood as a wave phenomenon. There is no provision for recording the interference patterns of light in mechanical optics. This, however, is precisely the essence of holography, which is based on interference of pure monochromatic and coherent light, that is, light of a single wavelength with all waves in step.

The reconstructed pictures are three-dimensional and have a vivid realism not unlike the everyday perception of the material world. Unlike modern motion pictures, however, holographic images do not merely simulate tridimensionality, they show genuine spatial characteristics, including authentic parallax. Holography has an incredible capacity for storage of information. It also makes it possible to take a picture of two people or an entire group of persons following sequential exposures, using just one film from the same angle. The subsequent illumination of the developed film will yield a composite image of the couple or the group involved. Occupying the same space, this image thus represents not just one of them but all of them at the same time. These genuinely composite images represent an exquisite model of a certain type of transpersonal experience such as the archetypical image of cosmic man.[6]

When the holographic pictures are taken from different angles, all the individual images can be teased out sequentially and separated replicating the original conditions during exposure. This illustrates another aspect of the visionary experience, that is, that the countless images tend to unfold in a roped sequence from the same area of the experienced field, appearing and disappearing, as if by magic.

The individual holographic pictures can be perceived as separate, at the same time, they are an integral part of a much broader undifferentiated matrix of interference patterns of light which they originate. This fact provides an elegant model for some other types or aspects of transpersonal experience. The relativity of separateness versus oneness is of crucial importance for mystical and non-ordinary state of consciousness. Holography, thus, seems to be an ideal conceptual and teaching device to illustrate this otherwise incomprehensible and paradoxical aspect of non-ordinary states of consciousness.[7]

Holography offers much promise in view of the current scientific understanding of the vibratory nature of the universe, and new insights into such fundamental problems as the ordering and organizing principles of reality and of the central nervous system, the distribution of information in the cosmos and in the brain, the nature of memory, the mechanisms of perception, and the relationship between the whole and its parts.[8] So far as the nature of memory is concerned, perhaps the most interesting properties of holograms are related to 'memory' and information retrieval. An optical hologram has distributed memory, in that, any small part of it large enough to contain the entire diffraction pattern, contains the information of the whole *gestalt*.[9]

Pribram saw the hologram as an exciting model for how the brain may store memory. Perhaps it too deals in interactions, interpreting frequencies, and storing the image, like the hologram, not localized but dispersed throughout the brain.[10]

The phenomenon of distributed memory is of the greatest potential relevance for understanding the fact that in certain special states of mind, the subjects report having access to the information about every aspect of the universe. The brain apparently has a parallel processing capability that suggests a model-like optics, wherein connections are formed by paths traversed by light, in addition to its more digital or linear computer type connections. A distribution pattern similar to that of the hologram also would explain how a specific memory does not have a location but is scattered throughout the brain.[11] The holographic approach makes it possible to imagine how the information mediated from the brain is accessible in every cerebral cell, or how the genetic information about the entire organism is available in every single cell of the body.[12]

In his numerous experiments with rats, focusing on the problem of localization of psychological and physiological functions in various areas of the brain, Karl Lashley, after a search of some thirty years, failed to find the 'engram' – the site and substance of memory. He came to the view that memories were stored in every part of the cortex and that their intensity depended on the total number of intact cortical cells. In his book *Brain Mechanism and Intelligence* (1929), Lashley expressed the opinion that the firing of billions of cerebral neurons results in stable interference patterns that are diffused over the entire cortex and represent the basis of all information of the perceptual system and memory.[13]

Karl Pribram who had participated, as a researcher, in several decades of experimental work in neurosurgery and electrophysiology with his teacher Karl Lashley, became fascinated by some of the properties of optical hologram. He was particularly impressed with its vast storage capacity, aspects of its associative recall, the imaging capability of the sensory system, and especially its distribution of memory storage. Pribram came to realize that a model based on holographic principles would account for many of the seemingly mysterious properties of the brain, including memory.[14] Pribram explains:

> Specific memories are incredibly resistant to brain damage. Removing a hunk of brain tissue or injuring one or another portion of the brain does not excise a particular memory or set of memories. This process of remembering may be disturbed in some general way, or even some aspect of the general process may be disrupted. But never is a single memory trace of some particular experience lost while all else that is memorable is retained. This fact has become well established both through clinical observation in man and through experiments on animals. <u>Thus, in some way or other, memory must become distributed</u> – the experienced input from the senses becomes spread over a sufficient expanse of brain to make the memory of that experience resistant to brain damage.[15] (my emphasis)

The holographic model has now been extended into the world of acoustic phenomena by the revolutionary discoveries of Argentinian-Italian born researcher Zucarelli, interested in the capacity of various organisms to localize sounds in auditory perception.[16] Having analysed the mechanisms by which they arrive at the precise identification of the sources of sound, he concluded that the existing model of hearing cannot account for important characteristics of human acoustic perception. The fact that humans can locate the source of sounds without repositioning the earlobes, and even those individuals whose hearing has been destroyed on one side, suggests that the comparison of the acoustic input in either ear is not the mechanism responsible for the human ability in this area. To explain all the characteristics of spatial hearing adequately, he postulated that human acoustic perception uses holographic principles. This requires the assumption that the human ear is a transmitter, as well as a receiver.[17]

By replicating this mechanism while recording sounds, Zucarelli developed the technology of holographic sound. Holographic recordings have the unusual capacity to reproduce acoustic reality with all its spatial characteristics, so much so, that without visual control, it is virtually impossible to distinguish the perception of recorded phenomena from actual events in the three dimensional world. Further, listening to holographic recordings of events that stimulated other senses tends to induce synesthesia, that is, the corresponding perceptions in other sensory area, for example, listening to someone striking a match may induce a strong smell of burning sulphur or the clipping sound of a pair of scissors might convey a realistic sense of one having a hair-cut.[18]

5.3　The Holographic Universe

In optical holography, the holographic images, the field of light that creates them, and the film that is their generating matrix all exist at the same level of reality, and they can all be simultaneously perceived or detected in the ordinary state of consciousness. Similarly, all the elements of a holographic system are accessible to our senses and instruments in ordinary consciousness. But some scientists are beginning to believe that there is evidence to suggest that our world and the things in it are only ghostly images, projections from a level of reality so beyond our own that it is literally beyond both space and time.[19]

The leading proponents of the holographic view of reality are David Bohm, a former professor of Theoretical Physics at the University of London, a protegé of Einstein and a most respected quantum physicist, who has numerous publications to his credit;[20] and Karl Pribram, Stanford University neurophysiologist and author of the classic neuropsychological textbook *Languages of the Brain* (1971). Bohm's main concern has been with understanding, as a physicist, the nature of reality in general, and of consciousness in particular, as a coherent whole. He seeks answers to a number of questions such as: What is the nature of movement? From his point of view, whenever one thinks of anything, it seems to be apprehended either as static, or a series of static images, yet in actual experience of movement, one senses an unbroken, undivided process of flow, to which the series of static images in thought is related as a series of 'still' photographs might be related to the actuality of a speeding car. What is the relationship of thinking to reality? In his view, thought itself is in an actual process of movement, one can feel a sense of flow in the 'stream of consciousness' not dissimilar to the sense of flow in the movement of matter in general. May not thought itself thus be a part of reality as a whole? ponders Bohm. But then, what could it mean for one part of reality to 'know' another and to what extent would this be possible? Does the content of thought merely give us abstract or simplified 'snapshots' of reality or can it go further, somehow to grasp the very essence of the living movement that we sense in actual experience? Bohm concludes that in reflecting on and pondering the nature of movement, both in thought and in the object of thought, one comes inevitably to the question of wholeness and totality.[21]

After many years of dissatisfaction with standard theories and their inability to satisfactorily explain all the phenomena encountered in quantum physics, Bohm formulated a revolutionary model of the universe that extends the holographic principles into realms that at present are not subject to direct observation and scientific investigation. Bohm described the nature of reality in general, and consciousness in particular, as an unbroken and coherent whole that is involved in an unending process of change. This he designates as the holomovement.[22] The world is in constant flux, and stable structures of any kind are nothing but abstractions; and a describable object, entity or event is considered to be derivative of an undefinable and unknown totality. This universal flux cannot be defined explicitly but can be known only implicitly. In this flow, mind and matter are not separate substances, but rather different aspects of one whole and unbroken movement.[23]

What we perceive directly through our senses and with the help of scientific instruments represent only a fragment of reality of the *unfolded* or *explicate order*. This is a special form contained within, and emerging from, a more general totality of existence, the *enfolded* or *implicate order*, that is its source and generating matrix. In the implicate order, space and time are no longer the dominant factors determining relationship of dependence or independence of different elements. Various aspects of existence are meaningfully related to the whole, serving specific functions for a final purpose rather than being independent building blocks. From this standpoint, the image of the universe resembles that of a living organism whose organs, tissues, and cells sense only in relation to the whole.

In Bohm's theory, it is impossible to draw a sharp and absolute distinction between animate and inanimate matter, for they have a common ground in the holomovement, which is their primary and universal source. Inanimate matter is a relatively autonomous subtotality in which life is 'implicit' but not significantly manifested. In contrast to both idealists and materialists, Bohm suggests that matter and consciousness cannot be explained from or reduced to each other. They are both abstractions from the implicate order, which is their common ground, and which represents an inseparable unity. In Bohm's words,

> Intelligence and material process thus have a single origin, which is ultimately the unknown totality of the universal flux. In a certain sense, this implies that what have been commonly called mind and matter are abstractions from the universal flux, and that both are to be regarded as different and relatively autonomous orders within the one whole movement.[24]

In a very similar way, our knowledge about reality in general, and science in particular, are abstractions from one total flux. Rather than being reflections on reality and its independent descriptions, they are an integral part of the holomovement.

The term 'reality' indicates an unknown and undefinable totality of flux, that is, the ground of all things, and of the process of thought itself, as well as of the movement of intelligent perception.[25] Thought can function in two ways: it can function on its own or it can respond directly to intelligence. When it functions on its own it is the active response of memory in every phase of life. This includes the intellectual, emotional, sensuous, muscular and physical responses of memory; all aspects of one indissoluble process. To treat them separately makes for fragmentation and confusion. All these constitute one process of response of memory to each actual situation, which response in turn leads to a further contribution to memory, thus conditioning the next thought. Thought, considered in this way, as the response of memory, is basically mechanical in its order of operation. Either it is a repetition of some previously existent structure drawn from memory, or else, it is some combination arrangement and organization of these memories into further structures of ideas and concepts, but essentially mechanical.[26]

In this mechanical process, there is no inherent reason why the thought that arises should be relevant or fitting to the actual situation that evokes them. The perception of whether or not any particular thoughts are relevant or fitting requires the operation of a non-mechanical energy, which Bohm calls *intelligence*. Intelligence, which is free, independent, and an unconditioned element originating in the holomovement, is able to perceive a new order in a new structure, not just a modification of what is already known or present in memory. This is the second way in which thought can function by responding directly to intelligence. Bohm cites the case of problem solving, when we suddenly get a flash of understanding and may adopt a new procedure and structure which enables us to solve a problem; such a flash, according to Bohm, is essentially an *act of perception*, rather than a process of thought, though it may later be expressed in thought. What we have here is "perception through the mind" of abstract orders and relationships such as identity and difference, separation and connection, necessity and contingency or cause and effect.

We may put together all the basically mechanical and conditioned responses under one word or symbol, that is thought, and we have distinguished this from the fresh, original and unconditioned response of intelligence in which something new may arise.[27] It has been observed in a wide variety of contexts that thought is inseparable from electrical and chemical activity in the brain and nervous system, and from concomitant tensions and movement of muscles, which indicates that thought is basically a material process.[28]

Given that thought is a material process, one is naturally led to inquire into the relationship between thought and reality. Is the content of thought some kind of reflective correspondence with 'real things', a kind of copy or image, or imitation of things? As Bohm rightly points out, such a question presupposes that we know what is meant by the 'real thing' and by the distinction between reality and thought.

Bohm, who often etymologizes, indicates that the word 'reality' comes from the Latin res which means 'things'. To be real, therefore, is to be a 'thing'. 'Reality' signifies 'thing-hood in general' or 'the quality of being a thing'. Of particular interest is that *res* comes from the verb *reri* meaning 'to think', so that literally *res* is 'what is thought about'.[29] Implicit in this argument is that what is thought about has an existence that is independent of the process of thought. If the thing and the thought about it have their ground in the one undefinable and unknown totality of flux, then the attempt to explain their relationship by supposing that the thought is in reflective correspondence with the thing has no meaning, for both thought and thing are forms abstracted from the total process.

Although, it may be that ultimately thought and thing cannot be properly analyzed as separately existent yet the distinction between what is real and what is mere thought is not only absolutely necessary as a practical matter, but also to even maintain our sanity.

5.4 The Enfolding-Unfolding Universe and Consciousness

The central underlying theme of Bohm's argument is the unbroken wholeness of the totality of existence as an undivided flowing movement without borders. The implicate order is particularly suitable for the understanding of such unbroken wholeness or flowing movement, for in the implicate order the totality of existence is unfolded within each region of space (and time). So, whatever part, element, or aspect we may abstract in thought, this still enfolds the whole and is, therefore, intrinsically related to the totality from which it has been abstracted.

What, however, is the implicate order? Bohm reminds us that the word 'implicate' is based on the verb 'to implicate', which means 'to fold inwards' (as multiplication means 'folding many times') and has the notion of something being 'enfolded' within it. To illustrate the concept, he cites the example of a television broadcast where 'the visual image is translated into a time order which is 'carried' by the radio wave. Thus, the radio wave carries the visual image in an implicate order. The function of the receiver is then to *explicate* this order, to 'unfold' it in the form of a new visual image.[30]

Now, what 'carries' the implicate order is the holomovement, which is an unbroken and undivided totality. At times, we can abstract particular aspects of the holomovement such as light, electrons, sounds and so on, but more generally all forms of the holomovement merge and are inseparable. Thus, in its totality, the holomovement is not limited in any specific way at all. It is not required to conform to any particular order, or to be bounded by any particular measure. Indeed, the *holomovement is undefinable and immeasurable.*[31]

To assist in a general understanding of the implicate order, Bohm offers a vividly descriptive analogy to illustrate certain of its essential features: the reader is asked to imagine a devise consisting of two concentric glass cylinders, with a highly viscous fluid such as glycerine between them, which is arranged in such a way that the outer cylinder can be turned very slowly, so that there is negligible diffusion of the viscous fluid. A droplet of insoluble ink is placed in the fluid, and the outer cylinder is then turned, with the result that the droplet is drawn out into a fine thread-like form that eventually becomes invisible. When the cylinder is turned in the opposite direction, the thread-form draws back and suddenly becomes visible as a droplet essentially the same as the one that was there originally.[32]

When the ink particles have been drawn out into a long thread one can say that they have been enfolded into the glycerine as an egg can be said to be enfolded into a cake. The difference, of course, is that the droplet can be unfolded by reversing the motion of the fluid while there is no way to unfold the egg having undergone an irreversible diffusive mixing. The analogy of such enfoldment and unfoldment to the implicate order introduced in connection with the hologram is sufficient for our purposes and we need not extend it any further as Bohm does by introducing two ink droplets, one red and the other blue – bearing in mind always that this is only an analogy. As an analogy, it has served its purpose.

Basically, the implicate order has to be considered as a process of enfoldment and unfoldment in a higher dimensional space. Only under certain conditions, declares Bohm, that this can be simplified as a process of enfoldment and unfoldment in three dimensions: the ink-in-fluid analogy, and even the hologram is a mere approximation. Indeed, the electromagnetic field, which is the ground of the holographic image, obeys the laws of the quantum theory, and when these are properly applied to the field, it is found that this too, is actually a multidimensional reality which can only, under certain conditions be simplified as a three dimensional reality.[33]

In summary, the implicate order has to be extended into a multidimensional reality. In principle, this reality is one of the unbroken whole, including the entire universe with all its 'fields' and 'particles'. The holomovement enfolds and unfolds in a multidimensional order, the dimensionality of which is effectively infinite. However, relatively independent subtotalities can generally be abstracted, which may be approximated as autonomous. This principle of relative autonomy of subtotalities, which is basic to the holomovement, must now be seen to extend to the multidimensional order of reality.

One of the most important contributions of holography is its ability to help to give a certain immediate perceptual insight into the undivided wholeness that is an essential feature of the modern world-view, emerging from quantum mechanics and relativity theory. At this point, it may be helpful to recall the main contrasting features of relativity and quantum theories. As it has been established, relativity theory requires continuity, strict causality or determinism and locality. Quantum theory, on the other hand, requires non-continuity, non-causality and non-locality. It is apparent, therefore, that the basic concepts of relativity and quantum theories directly contradict each other. Consequently, it is hardly surprising that these two theories have never been unified in a consistent way.[34]

The basic notion of a new theory like the holographic theory will not be found by beginning with those features in which relativity and quantum theories stand in direct contradiction. It is best to begin with what they have basically in common and this is the undivided wholeness, although each comes to such wholeness by different routes. The acceptance of the holographic order means that we must drop the mechanistic order.

Modern natural laws should refer primarily to this undivided wholeness in which everything implicates everything else as suggested by holograms, rather than the analysis into the separate parts as required by the mechanistic order. It was difficult to imagine how Bohm's holographic theory and his ideas about consciousness, thinking, and perception could ever be reconciled with the traditional mechanistic approach of neurophysiology and psychology. However, neurosurgeon, Karl Pribram developed an original and imaginative model of the brain which postulated that certain important aspects of cerebral functioning was based on holographic principles.

5.5 Karl Pribram

In pursuing this avenue of research, Pribram concluded that the holographic process must be seriously considered as an explanatory device of extraordinary power for neurophysiology and psychology. In *Languages of the Brain* (1971), and in a series of articles, he formulated the basic principles of the holographic model of the brain. According to Pribram, the holograms that showed the greatest explanatory power and held the most promise were those that could be expressed in the form of the so-called Fourier transforms. The Fourier theorem holds that any pattern, no matter how complex, can be decomposed into a set of completely regular sine waves. Applying the identical transform then inverts the wave patterns back into the image. Localization of function in the brain depends in a large part on the connections between the brain and peripheral structures; these determine *what* is encoded. The holographic hypothesis addresses the problem of inner connectivity within each system, which determines *how* events become encoded.[35]

In the early 1940's, it was generally believed that memories were localized in specific location in the brain cells, such that memory traces were called *engrams*. There were reasons for this view based on the research by Canadian neurosurgeon, Wilder Penfield, in the 1920's, that specific memories had specific locations in the brain.[36] Research in the 1960's had shown that each brain cell in the visual cortex is geared to respond to a different pattern, some brain cells fire when the eyes see a vertical line, others fire when they see a horizontal line. It appears then, that the brain takes input from these highly specialized cells called feature detectors, and somehow fits them together to provide us with our visual perception of the world. Russell and Karen DeValois in 1979 used Fourier's equations to convert plaid and checkerboard patterns into simple wave-forms. They tested to see how the brain cells in the visual cortex responded to these new wave-form images. They found that the brain cells responded not to the original patterns but to the Fourier translations of the patterns. The only conclusion possible was that the brain was using Fourier mathematics, the same mathematics holography employed, to convert visual images into the Fourier language of waveform.[37] Although not conclusive, it suggested that the brain was like a hologram; it certainly provided evidence to that effect, for it demonstrated that the visual cortex was responding not to patterns but to the frequencies of various wave forms.

Pribram's pilgrimage to formulating the holographic model began with the research of Karl Lashley, neuropsychologist, at the Yerkes Laboratory of Primate Biology, where over thirty years of ongoing research failed to produce any evidence of the engram. Lashley's experiment of removing massive areas of rats' brains, no matter what position of their brains, did not eradicate their memory to run a maze. To Pribram, these findings were astounding, for if memories possessed specific locations in the brain, why did Lashley's surgical plunderings made no effect on them? There seemed only one answer, memories were not localized at specific brain sites, but were somehow spread out or *distributed* throughout the brain as a whole. Even patients who had portions of their brains removed for medical reasons never suffered the loss of specific memories. No one ever came out of surgery with any selective memory loss.[38]

Despite the growing evidence that memories were distributed, Pribram was still puzzled as to how the brain accomplished such feat. In the mid 1960's, he read an article in the *Scientific American* describing the first construction of a hologram. He was not only impressed by it as a dazzling concept, but it seemingly provided a solution to the puzzle with which he had been wrestling.

The three-dimensionality of the hologram, though impressive, was not the only remarkable feature. If a piece of holographic film containing the image of an object is cut in half and then illuminated by a laser, each half will still be found to contain the entire image of the object. Even if the halves are divided again and then again, the entire object can be reconstructed from each small portion of film, even though the images will get hazier as the portions get smaller. The meaning of this is clear, every small fragment of a piece of holographic film contains all the information recorded in the whole.[39]

This was precisely the feature that Pribram needed, for it offered, at last, a way of understanding how memories could be distributed rather than localized in the brain. If a piece of holographic film could contain all the information necessary to create a whole image, then it seems possible for every part of the brain to contain all the information necessary to recall a whole memory.

Memory may not be the only thing that the brain processes holographically. Pribram's research revealed that as much as 98 percent of a cat's optic nerves can be severed without seriously impairing its ability to perform complex visual tasks.[40] This is incompatible with the standard understanding of how the vision works for it was thought that there was a one to one correspondence between the image the eyes see and the way that image is represented in the brain. In other words, when we look at a square, it was believed the electrical activity in our visual cortex also possesses the form of a square. In measuring the electrical activity in the brains of monkeys while they performed various visual tasks, he discovered that not only did no such 'one-to-one correspondence' exist, there was not even a discernable pattern to the sequence in which the electrodes fired. In short, no photographic-like image becomes projected onto the cortical surface.[41]

Like memory, it appeared that vision was also distributed. The 'whole in every part' nature of a hologram certainly seemed to explain how so much of the visual cortex could be removed without affecting the ability to perform visual tasks. If there were some kind of internal hologram, even a small piece of the hologram could still reconstruct the whole of what the eye was seeing. This could also explain the lack of any one-to-one correspondence between the external world and the brain's electrical activity. But what wavelike phenomenon was being used to create such internal holograms? The electrical communications that take place between the brain's nerve cells, or neurons, do not occur alone. Neurons possess branches like little trees, and when an electrical message reaches the end of one of these branches it radiates outwards like a ripple in a pond. Because neurons are so densely packed together these expanding ripples of electricity which are also a wavelike phenomenon are constantly crisscrossing one another.

As other researchers became aware of Pribram's theory, it was soon realized that the distributed nature of memory and vision was not the only neurophysiological puzzle that the holographic model might offer an explanation. This model also explains how our brains can store so many memories in so little space. John Van Newmann, the Hungarian born physicist and mathematician, once calculated that over the course of the average human life span, the brain stores something of the order of 2.8×10^{20} bit of information, an astonishing amount of information. Researchers have long sought an explanation for such a vast capability.

Holograms also possess a fantastic capacity for information storage. By changing the angle at which two lasers strike a piece of photographic film, many different images can be recorded on the same surface. Any image thus recorded can be retrieved by illuminating the film with a laser beam possessing the same angle as the original two beams. Researchers have calculated that by using this method a one-inch-square of film can store the same amount of information in fifty Bibles.⁴²

There are other puzzles that the holographic brain model has been used to solve. For example, our ability to recall and forget. Pieces of holographic film containing multiple images such as those described above, also provide a way of understanding our ability to both recall and forget. When such a piece of film is held in a laser beam and tilted back and forth, the various images it contains appear and disappear on a glittering stream. Perhaps our ability to remember is analogous to a shining laser beam on such a piece of film and calling up a particular image. Likewise, when we are unable to recall something, it may be like shining various beams of a piece of multiple image film, but failing to find the right angle to call up the image/memory for which we are searching.⁴³

Brain researchers have long recognized that the ability to recognize familiar things only seem ordinary but is quite a complex ability. Pieter Van Heerden proposed a type of holography, known as *recognition holography*, which offers a way of understanding this ability. In recognition holography, a holographic image of an object is recorded in the usual manner, save that the laser beam is bounced off a special kind of mirror known as a *focusing mirror* before it is allowed to strike the unexposed film. If a second object, similar but not identical to the first, is bathed in laser light and the light is bounced off the mirror and unto the film after it has been developed, a bright point of light will appear on the film. The brighter and sharper the point of light, the greater the degree of similarity between the first and second objects. If the two objects are completely dissimilar, no point of light will appear. By placing a light-sensitive photocell behind the holographic film, one can actually use the set up as a mechanical recognition system.⁴⁴

A similar technique known as *interference holography* may also explain how we can recognize both the familiar and unfamiliar features of an image such as the face of someone we have not seen for many years. In this technique, an object is viewed through a piece of holographic film containing its image. When this is done, any feature of the object that has changed since its image was originally recorded will reflect light differently. An individual looking through the film is instantly aware of both how the object has changed and how it has remained the same.⁴⁵

To most of us, our feelings of love, hunger and so on are internal realities, the sound of music, the smell of early morning coffee are external realities. But how does our brain enable us to distinguish between the two? Pribram points out that when we look at a person, the image of that person is really on the surface of our retinas, but we do not perceive them as being on our retinas but being in the 'world out-there'. Similarly, when we stub our toe we experience the pain in our toe, but it is actually a neuro-physiological process, taking place somewhere in our brain. How then is our brain able to take the multitude of neurophysiological processes that manifest as our experience, all of which are internal and fool us into thinking that some are internal and some are located outside beyond the confines of the brains?

Creating the illusion that things are located where they are not is the quintessential feature of a hologram. If you look at a hologram it seems to have an extension in space, but if you pass your hand through it you will discover there is nothing there. Despite what your senses may tell you, no instrument will detect the presence of any abnormal energy or substance where the hologram appears to be hovering. This is because the hologram is a *virtual* image, and appears to be what it is not, and possesses no more extension in space than does the three-dimensional reflection of yourself in a mirror.

There is further evidence to establish that the brain is able to fool us into thinking that other inner processes are located outside the body. Physiologist Georg Von Bekesy, carried out a series of experiments with vibrators placed on the knees of blindfolded subjects. By varying the rates at which the instruments vibrated, he discovered that he could make his subjects experience the sensation that a point source of vibration was jumping from one knee to the other, or even feel the point source of vibration in the space between the knees. In fact, this demonstrated that human beings have the ability to apparently experience sensation in spatial locations where they have absolutely no sense receptors.[46]

Pribram believes that Bekesy's work is compatible with the holographic view, and in Bekesy's case, interfering sources of physical vibration enabled the brain to localize some of its experiences beyond the physical boundaries of the body. Perhaps this process might also explain the phantom limb phenomenon, such as the sensation experiences by some amputees that a missing arm or leg is still present. They even feel cramps or tingling in these missing limbs, but may be what they are experiencing, according to Pribram, is the holographic memory of the limb that is still recorded in the interference patterns in the brain.[47]

There are other studies which support Pribram's theory of the brain as a hologram. Paul Pietsch, who experimented with salamanders, urged that if salamanders' feeding behaviour is not confined to any specific location in the brain, then it should not matter how its brain is positioned in its head. This is exactly the conclusion he came to after he sliced, flipped, shuffled, subtracted and even minced the brains of his subjects and discovered that when he replaced what was left of their brains, their behaviour returned to normal.[48]

Berkesy's work demonstrated that our skin is sensitive to frequencies of vibration and even produced some evidence that taste may involve frequency analysis. The German physiologist and physicist, Herman Van Helmholtz, (before 1879), demonstrated that the ear was a frequency analyzer. Some recent research reveals that our sense of smell may be based on what is called osmic frequencies. Pribram's own work had discovered that single neurons in the motor cortex responds selectively to a limited bandwidth of frequencies.[49]

Accepting the validity of these findings, the question now arises, if the picture of reality in our brains is not a picture at all but a hologram, what is it a hologram of? What is the world of objective reality? Perhaps the physical things we think we see about us might not even exist, or at least, not in the way we believe they exist. Was it possible, Pribram wondered, that what the mystics had been saying for centuries was true, reality was *maya*, an illusion, and what was there was really a vast, resonating symphony of wave forms, a "frequency domain" that was transformed into the world as we know it, only *after* it entered our senses.[50]

It became clear to Pribram that the answers to many of his questions were outside the province of his own field. He turned to his eldest son, a physicist, who gave him an intensive course in quantum physics and introduced him to David Bohm. He not only found many answers to his questions, but also discovered that, according to Bohm, the entire universe was a hologram.[51]

Chapter 6

A HOLOGRAPHIC EXPLANATION OF NDE AND OBE

6.1 Introduction

One of the fundamental features of the NDE experience is the perceived separation of the individual from his/her body. If the experience progressed, the subject would either remain near by, looking down upon his or her body, watching the medical procedures or take off to some other realm where they would encounter 'beings' and deceased relatives.

6.2 Out-of-Body Experience

Out-of-Body Experiences, or OBEs, have been reported in history by various individuals from all walks of life and across various societies. Among individuals who have reported having OBEs are Aldous Huxley, D. H. Lawrence, A. J. Ayer and Goethe. The phenomenon has been reported among early Egyptians, North American Indians, the Chinese, the Hindus, the Hebrews and the Moslems, and is still widespread today.[1]

The typical OBE is usually spontaneous and occurs most often during sleep, meditation, anesthesia or life threatening situations. The experience has been described as exhilarating, as the person is able to float over his body and travel or fly to other locations. It is described as a vivid sensation that the mind has separated from the body and one is free from the physical self or body, soaring over tree tops and flying through walls.

Although OBEs tend to be spontaneous, there are many reports of persons who have the ability to leave their body at will. One such famous individual was a broadcasting executive named Robert Monroe. In the late 1950's he began keeping a written journal of his experiences, carefully documenting everything he learned about the out-of-body state. Monroe discovered he could pass through solid objects and travel great distances in a flash, simply by 'thinking' himself there. He found that other people were not aware of his presence when he was in that state, and also discovered that he was not alone in his travels as, occasionally, he bumped into other disembodied travelers. He documented his experiences in two fascinating books, *Journeys Out of the Body* (1971) and *Far Journeys* (1985).

OBEs have also been documented in the lab. Charles Tart was able to get a female subject to correctly identify a five digit number written on a piece of paper that could only be reached if she were floating in an out-of-body state.[2] In experiments conducted by Karlis Osis and Janet Lee Mitchell, several gifted subjects were able to "fly in" from various locations all over the country and correctly describe a number of objects in a room, and an optical illusion that could only be seen when an observer peered through a small window in a special devise.[3]

In a holographic universe, location is itself an illusion, things and objects possess no definite location, everything is non-local, including consciousness. Therefore, although our consciousness appears to be localized in our heads, under certain conditions it can just as easily appear to be localized in the upper corner of the room, or hovering over a green field or floating over a ledge. The idea of non-local consciousness may appear difficult to grasp, but may be more understandable if we use an analogy. In a dream, we may be wandering in a crowd, as at a football match, as we wander about or sit at the football match, our consciousness appears to be localized in the head of the person we are in the dream. But where is our consciousness really? An analysis will reveal that it is actually in everything in the dream, in the crowd at the football match, even in the very space of the dream. In a dream, location is also an illusion because everything, people, objects, space, consciousness, and so on is unfolding out of the deeper and more fundamental reality of the dreamer, our current scientific understanding cannot account for the non-locality of consciousness.[4]

Another holographic feature of the OBE is the plasticity of the form that a person assumes once they are out of the body. After detachment from the physical, OBEers sometimes find themselves in a "ghost-like" body that is an exact replica of their biological body. Some describe this phantom double as naked, others find themselves in bodies fully clothed. There are also reports where people have also perceived themselves as balls of heat, shapeless clouds of energy and even no discernible form at all. This suggests that the replica body is not a replica of a biological body, but is, instead, a kind of hologram that can assume many shapes.[5]

What is really one's true form, if any, when we are in a disembodied state? Robert Monroe suggests that once we drop all such disguises we are a "vibrational patterns [composed] of many interacting and resonating frequencies."[6] This view is remarkably suggestive of something holographic going on and that we, like all things in the holographic universe, are ultimately a frequency phenomenon which our mind converts into various holographic forms. It also adds credence to Valerie Hunt's conclusion that our consciousness is contained not in the brain, but in a plasmic holographic energy field that both permeates and surrounds the physical body.[7]

Retrocognition, or the ability of certain individuals to shift the focus of their attention and literally gaze back into the past, has been confirmed repeatedly by researchers.[8] There are examples of psychics who could psychometrize even the smallest fragment of bone and accurately describe its past.[9] Retrocognition suggests that the past is not lost, but still exists in some form accessible to human perception. Our normal view of the universe makes no allowance for this, but the holographic model does. Bohm's notion that the flow of time is the product of a constant series of unfoldings and enfoldings suggest that as the present enfolds and becomes part of the past, it does not cease to exist, but simply returns to the cosmic storehouse of the implicate.

If, as Bohm suggests, consciousness also has its source in the implicate, this means that the human mind and the holographic record of the past already exist in the same domain, then, perhaps only a shift in the focus of one's attention is all that is needed to access the past. Some psychics, it would appear, have the innate ability to make this shift.[10]

Retrocognition, which is the ability to see into the past, is to be distinguished from memory. Memory is the recollection, the remembering, of past events of one's own experience. Retrocognition is a version of the past where clairvoyants often describe a people, their dwellings, their artifacts, the culture that produced those artifacts, and the landscape of their existence.

Another holographic aspect of OBE is the blurring of the division between past and future that sometimes occurs during such experience, as reported by researchers. Osis and Mitchell reported that when their subject, a well known psychic, "flew in" from out of state and attempted to describe test objects they placed on the table, he had a tendency to describe items that were placed there days later.[11] Perhaps during the OB state one enters a realm of the subtler levels of reality that Bohm speaks about, a region that is closer to the implicate and hence closer to the level of reality in which the distinction between past, present and future ceases to exist. Monroe describes the OB state as a place where time and space no longer properly exist, where thought can be transformed into hologram like forms, and where consciousness is ultimately a pattern of vibrations, or frequencies.[12] Is it that when one enters the OB realm one begins to enter Pribram's frequency domain?

6.3 Out-of-body Projection

PSI has been conceptualized as having two basic capabilities: cognitive information gain and kinetic action. J. B. Rhine (1947)[13] hypothesized that the two aspects of PSI go together, in other words that there is an ESP (Extrasensory Perception) component during PK (Pychokenesis) action and a PK action during ESP.

The fundamental nature of OB processes is, for the most part, unknown and therefore subject to wide variations in theoretical interpretation.[14] There are two main contrasting hypotheses:

(1) The *extrasomatic hypothesis*, which states that during a true OBE, consciousness or a major part of the human personality, is externalized and exist a apart from the physical body.

(2) The *intrasomatic hypothesis*, which states that nothing leaves the body during an OBE; the personality remains a normal, psychophysiological unit in a more or less altered state. Verifiable perceptions during OBEs are attributed to 'ordinary' ESP.

Osis and McCormick express the view that both hypotheses describe some aspects of OBE, but, taken separately would be too rigid to accommodate all information that is now available. The OBE appears to be an event changing process rather than an all-or-non phenomenon.[15]

In some individuals the OB process might even oscillate somewhere between the two extremes of full externalization and full internalization. The OB experiment, according to Osis and McCormick, may at times leave no trace of externalization, while at other times offering indices of having 'been out'. Examples of being out would be perceptual and or kinetic interaction with the environment, or being perceived as an apparition by one or more observers. Total externalization might occur at death,[16] while completely intrasomatic experiences would accompany altered states of hypnotically-induced OB states.

Osis and McCormick assumed a more flexible working hypothesis in which OB projections is conceptualized as a unit that is unchanging in the degree of its perceiving-acting capacity, that can move about and, to varied extents, localize itself in a physical environment. Such a unit would use its ESP for 'seeing' and its PK for action. The primary difference between the internalized mode of the OB state and ordinary psi processes would be the matter of localization, according to Osis and McCormick.[17] During the extrasomatic OBE, PSI might function at a point in space remote from the physical body, a place where the OB projection feels itself to be. The base of normal PSI action is, on the other hand, believed to be at the body. Osis and McCormick assumes the same for intrasomatic OBEs or Tart's 1977 pseudo-OBEs.[18]

If that assumption is accepted, uniting the OB externalization hypotheses with that of ESP and PK activation, certain consequences are predictable; specially, that during the successful identification of visual targets while an individual is reportedly in the extrasomatic OB state, there will be registrable kinetic effects at the location where the experiment feels his consciousness to be. In short, the registrable PK effects at the ostensible location of OB projection will be greater when the target is more 'out' and consequently hits visual targets, than at those times when the subject is less externalized and scores a miss on the perceptual task.

Experiment

In the experiment developed by Osis and McCormick, a selected subject was requested to go out of body and localize himself in a shielded chamber containing strain-gauge sensors, and placed in front of the viewing window of an optical image device which displayed visual targets in the optical image device. The shielded chamber is an 18" cube enclosed in one layer of steel sheeting to provide electromagnetic shielding, and a second layer of electrically shielding material. Both shields are grounded. The chamber is suspended from the ceiling by electric rubber strips which reduce environmental vibration. Within the chamber, suspended from an acrylic strip, are two 9 x 8 metal sensors plates place 8" apart. Extremely sensitive strain-gauges are connected to the sensor plates, in such a way that very little movements or vibrations of the sensor will generate electrical impulses in the strain-gauges. The electrical output of the strain-gauge is pre-amplified 100 times by a custom built shielded amplifier attached to the outside of the cubicle.

The subject was given the overt task of identifying randomly selected targets displayed in the optical image device. Unintentional mechanical effects in the strain-gauge were registered on a Beckman polygraph during the time when the subject was trying to identify the targets. The experiment consisted of 197 trials extended over 20 sessions. The results were 114 hits and 83 misses. A 'hit' is defined as the correct identification of any of the three target aspects: colour of the background (green, blue, red or black) quadrant of the background (upper left, lower left, lower right or upper right) and time drawing of five different images. The final composite picture is not located in its complete form in any part of the apparatus, but appears as an optical illusion, visual only from a location directly in front of the viewing window.

The average strain-gauge activation level for the period immediately following target generation, that is, when the subject was reportedly 'looking' at the target pictures, was significantly higher during trials when he scored hits than during trials when he scored misses. The results were interpreted as conforming to the extrasomatic hypothesis of the out-of-body experience.

Osis and McCormick claim that the results support their original hypotheses that ostensibly unintentional kinetic effects can occur as by-products of normally localized OB, but concede that because of the unprecedented nature of their experiment the interpretation must be very tentative. According to these tentative assumptions, Osis and McCormick posit that the strain-gauge activation level rises not only because the subject scores a hit, but also because increased externalization facilitates both kinetic and perceptual effects.

Though the results of the experiment suggest some conformity with their working hypothesis, those results do not conclusively prove or falsify the concepts of their theory. Admittedly, however, the results of the experiment have some relevance for OB theories and consequently for the holographic approach, in particular with respect to holographic hypotheses dealing with extrasomatic localization of OB projections.

6.4 Near-Death Experience - NDE

Another of the fundamental features of NDE is its suggestion of another level of reality and the questions that it raises about an after life. Does a part of at least some of us go on living after our physical being is dead? Are NDEers actually making visits to an entirely different level of reality? With NDE, is there some sort of encounter with an extra dimensional realm of reality? Are we indeed uncovering some trends that point toward a super parallel universe of some sort? The present scientific community, by and large, seem to have ignored these questions. Perhaps because they have no answer or the current prevailing paradigm of normal science is inadequate. It is against this background that several NDE researchers have pointed out that the holographic model offers some answers. It is this which gives us a way to understand the phenomenon.

In the words of George Gallup Jr., the president of the Gallup Poll,

> A growing number of researchers have been gathering and evaluating the accounts of those who have had strange near-death encounters, and the preliminary results have been highly suggestive of some sort of encounter with an extra dimensional realm of reality. Our own extensive survey is the latest in the studies and is also uncovering some trends that point toward a super parallel universe of some sort.[19]

Professor Kenneth Ring, a professor of psychology and author of *Life at Death* and *Heading Towards Omega*, and an NDE researcher, argues in favour of a holographic explanation of NDE. He recognizes that future research may undermine the nature of this kind of interpretation, or lead to its abandonment altogether. Nevertheless, he submits that at the present rudimentary state of our knowledge, the para-psychological holographic explanation of NDE is the best hope for getting an explanatory handle on this otherwise enigmatic phenomenon.

At the stage of the core NDE where the individual's consciousness is assumed to have split off from the physical body, and is continuing to function independently, events far more puzzling than OBE itself begin to take place; such as travelling through a dark tunnel or void towards a brilliant golden light, or encountering a 'presence' or hearing a 'voice'. According to Ring, these experiences reflect psychological events associated with a shift in the levels of consciousness.

The intermediate stages of the core NDE can be understood as initiating a transition from a state of consciousness rooted in "this world" sensory impressions to one that is sensitive to the realities of another dimension of existence. When consciousness begins to function independent of the physical body, it becomes capable of awareness of another dimension. Let us for ease of reference simply call it now, a fourth dimension.[20]

The elements of the core experience being discussed here are not unique to near-death states, but are potentially available to anyone who learns to operate his consciousness independent of the physical body, according to Ring. So that when one quits his body, either at death or voluntarily (as some persons have learned to do), one's consciousness is free to explore the fourth dimensional world.

It is Ring's view that these aspects of the core experience can be interpreted in scientific terms if one uses some of the postulates of holographic theory, an approach which has its origins in both the neurosciences and physics, and which offers a means to make good theoretical sense of the mystical world-view. In support of this position, Ring adopts Karl Pribram's theory, that the brain itself functions holographically by mathematically analyzing interference wave patterns, so that the images of objects are seen. "Primary reality" itself is said to be composed of frequencies only. Different cells of the brain respond to different frequencies, and the brain functions like a *frequency analyzer*, breaking down complex patterns of frequencies into their components or, as Marilyn Ferguson puts Pribram's theory, "Our brains mathematically construct 'concrete' reality by interpreting frequencies from another dimension, a realm of meaningful pattern primary reality that transcends time and space."[21]

Ring makes the point that to make the connection between near-death experiences and holographic theory we must emphasize those properties that Pribram calls the frequency domain, that is, the primary reality composed of frequencies only. On this matter Pribram said,

> The frequency domain deals with density of occurrences only; time and space are collapsed. *Ordinary* boundaries of space and time, such as locations of any sort, disappear...in a sense, everything is happening all at once, synchronously, but one can read out what is happening into a variety of

coordinates of which space and time are the most helpful in bringing us into the ordinary domain of appearances.[22]

Ring's interpretation of the core experience does seem to embrace a mystical conception, but Pribram himself states that:

> As a way of looking at consciousness, holographic theory is much closer to mystical and Eastern philosophy. It will take a while for people to become comfortable with an order of reality other than the world of appearances. But it seems to me that some of the mystical experiences people have described for millennia begin to make some scientific sense. They bespeak the possibility of tapping into that order of reality that is behind the world of appearances... Spiritual insights fit the descriptions of this domain. They're made perfectly plausible by the invention of the hologram.[23]

Ring, it is clear, assumes that the core experience is a type of mystical experience that leads one into the holographic domain. In this state of consciousness, there is a new order of reality that one becomes sensitive to, that is, a frequency domain, as time and space lose their conventional meaning. The "act of dying", then, involves a gradual shift of consciousness from the ordinary world of appearances to holographic reality of pure frequencies. As Ring puts it:

> Access to this holographic reality becomes experientially available when one's consciousness is freed from its dependence on the physical body. So long as one remains tied to the body and to its sensory modalities, holographic reality at best can only be an intellectual construct. When one comes close to death one experiences it directly, that is why core experiencers (and mystics generally) speak about visions with such certitude and conviction, while those who haven't experienced this realm for themselves are left feeling skeptical or even indifferent.[24]

At the 1989 meeting of the International Association for Near-Death Studies (IANDS), Dr. Elizabeth W. Fenske, a clinical psychologist, in her keynote address, announced that she also believes that NDEs are journeys into a holographic realm of higher frequencies. This also supported Ring's hypothesis that the landscapes, flowers, physical structure that appear in the after-life dimension are fashioned out of interacting (or interfering) thought patterns.[25]

OBEers and NDEers often report that when they are detached from their physical bodies they find themselves in one of two forms, either as a disembodied cloud of energy or as a hologram-like body fashioned by thought. For example, one near-death survivor says that when he first emerged from his body he looked something like a jellyfish and fell lightly to the floor like a soap bubble. Then he quickly expanded into a ghostly three-dimensional image of a naked man. However, the presence of two women in the room so embarrassed him, although there was no indication that they could see him, that this feeling of embarrassment caused him suddenly to become clothed.[26]

The form that a disembodied person assumes seems to be fashioned by thought, that is, created by the mind. J.H.M. Whiteman, who himself had experienced OBE, said that he always felt like a woman trapped in a man's body, and during separation from his body, this sometimes resulted in his finding himself in female form. He also experienced other forms during his OB adventures, including children's bodies, and concluded that beliefs, both conscious and unconscious, were the determining factors in the form this second body assumed.[27]

Monroe agrees that it is our 'thought habits' that create our OB forms by saying, "I suspect that one may modify the Second Body into whatever form is desired."[28] Many of the NDEers who did not construct a hologram-like body for themselves, were not aware of any special form and were simply 'themselves' or 'their mind'. Others described themselves as 'a cloud of colours', 'a mist', 'an energy pattern' or 'an energy field', all terms which suggest some kind of frequency phenomena and would fit in with the notion of 'patterns of unknown vibratory energy enfolded in the greater matrix of the frequency domain'.[29]

Joel Whitton, whose research involved hypnotizing patients and regressing them to between life states, (where they reported all the classic features of NDE), after studying their testimony, came to the conclusion that the shapes and structures one perceives in the after-life dimension are thought-forms created by the mind. In fact, he says, "there is no experience of existence without thought."[30]

6.5 Life Review

The 'life review' is a well-known feature of NDE. It is a phase where a person may experience the whole or selected aspects of his/her life in the form of vivid and nearly instantaneous visual images. These images normally appear in no definite sequence, though on occasion they do, but rather as a simultaneous matrix of impressions. In some instances, they appear to include flash-forwards as well as flash-backs. During this instantaneous and panoramic remembrance, the person relives all the emotions, the joys and the sorrows, that accompany all of the events in their life. They feel the happiness of all the individuals to whom they have been kind and the pain of the persons to whom they have been injurious.

During the life review, thoughts too are replayed with accuracy. Reviews, the faces one saw, things that made one laugh, long forgotten day dreams, all pass through one's mind in a second. Many NDEers use similar adjectives to describe the life review referring to it as an incredibly vivid, wrap-around, three dimensional replay of their entire life.

One NDEer puts it this way, "It's like climbing right inside a movie of your life. Every moment of every year of your life is played back in complete sensory detail. Total, total recall. And it all happens in an instant."[31] Another said:

> The whole thing was really odd. I was there; I was actually seeing these flashbacks; I was actually walking through them, and it was so fast. Yet, it was slow enough that I could take it all in.[32]

Ring refers to the life review as "a holographic phenomenon par excellence." Moody, and even many NDEers themselves use the term 'holographic' when describing the experience.[33] Talbot argues that the life review is holographic not only in its three-dimensionality, but in the amazing capacity for information storage that the process displays. It is also holographic in a third way, it is a moment that contains all other moments. Even the ability to perceive the life review seems holographic in that it is a faculty capable of experiencing something that is paradoxically at once both incredibly rapid and yet slow enough to be witnessed in detail. As one NDEer puts it, "It is the ability to simultaneously comprehend the whole and every part."[34]

6.5.1 Instantaneous Knowledge

A well recognized element found in the narratives of NDEers is the importance of knowledge in the after-life dimension. They relate that the beings whom they see emphasize knowledge and seemed pleased whenever an incident involving knowledge or learning is exposed during the life review. Some report that they were openly counselled to seek out knowledge after their return to their physical bodies, especially knowledge related to self-growth, or knowledge which enhances the ability to help others. Some discovered that in the presence of the 'light' they suddenly had direct access to all knowledge. Some gained their knowledge by asking questions. Others did not even have to ask questions to access an infinite library of information. After their life review, they just suddenly knew everything, all the knowledge there was to know from the beginning of time to the end. One NDEer described the experience by saying:

> You can think of a question and immediately know the answer to it. As simple as that. And it can be any question whatsoever. It can be on a subject you don't know anything about, that you are not in a proper position ever to understand and the light will give you the instantaneous correct answer and make you understand it.[35]

Still others said that, instead of acquiring the knowledge they remembered it, but forgot most of what they recalled as soon as they returned to their physical bodies. There seem to be a universal amnesia among those who have had that experience.[36]

Talbot also argues that this vision of total knowledge in addition to being holographic in a wider sense has another specific holographic characteristic. According to NDEers, during the vision, the information arrives in 'chunks' that register instantaneously in one's thoughts. In other words, rather than being strung out in a linear fashion like words in a sentence or scenes in a movie, all the facts, details, images and pieces of information burst into one's awareness in an instant. Monroe, who has also experienced such instantaneous explosions of information while in the OB state, calls them "thought balls".[37]

While dreaming, it is not unusual to become aware of information in this manner. In a dream, we often find ourselves in a situation and suddenly know all kinds of things about it without being told. Many of us have had a detailed idea or inspiration dawn upon us in a flash. Talbot thinks such experiences are lesser versions of the thought ball effect. These bursts of psychic information which arrive in chunks like the psychological gestalts experienced by individuals during transpersonal experiences, are holographic in the sense that they are instantaneous 'wholes' which our time-oriented minds must struggle with for a moment to unravel and convert into a serial arrangement of parts.[38]

6.6 Emmanuel Swedenborg

Emmanuel Swedenborg, the Swedish mystic, born 1688, a leading mathematician, linguist, astronomer and businessman who wrote books on metallurgy, colour theory, commerce, economics, physics, chemistry, mining, anatomy and also invented prototypes for the airplane and the submarine, sometimes referred to as the Leonardo da Vinci of his era, had the ability to enter deep trances during which he had OBEs. So famous did he become for his out-of-body journeys, that many sought his help, including the Queen of Sweden who, it is reported, asked him to find out why her deceased brother had neglected to respond to a letter she had sent him before his death. Swedenborg promised to consult the deceased brother. He returned with a message which the Queen confessed contained information that only her brother would have known. So impressed was the German philosopher Immanuel Kant with Swedenborg's out-of-body encounters, that he wrote an entire book on Swedenborg entitled *Dreams of a Spirit-Seer*.[39]

Most important about Swedenborg's accounts of the after-life realm was how closely it mirrored the descriptions offered by modern day NDEers: the passing through a dark tunnel, being met by welcoming spirits, beautiful landscapes where time and space no longer exist, the effulgent light that emitted a feeling of love, appearing before beings of light, and being enveloped by an all-compassing peace and serenity.[40]

Swedenborg refers to the holographic thought balls the angels use to communicate and says that they are no different from the portrayals he could see in the 'wave-substance' that surrounds a person. Like NDEers, he describes these telepathic bursts of knowledge as a picture language so dense with information that each image contains a thousand ideas. A communicated series of these portrayals can also be quite lengthy and last up to several hours, in such a sequential arrangement that one can only marvel.[41]

There are many remarks by Swedenborg which could be interpreted as referring to reality's holographic qualities. For instance, he said that although human beings appear to be separate from one another, we are all connected in a cosmic unity. Moreover, each of us is a heaven in miniature, and every person, indeed the entire physical universe is a microcosm of the greater divine reality. As stated earlier, he also believed that underlying visible reality was a wave substance. In fact, several Swedenborg scholars have cited the many parallels between Swedenborg's concept and Bohm and Pribram's theory.[42]

Swedenborg believed that heaven is actually a more fundamental level of reality than our own physical world. It is the archetypal source from which all earthly forms originate, and to which all forms return, a concept not too dissimilar to Bohm's idea of the implicate and explicate order. Finally, let us examine specific phenomena of the core experience using a holographic perspective.

6.7 The Core Experience Using a Holographic Perspective

6.7.1 The Moving Through a Dark Tunnel or Void

According to Itzhak Bentov, author of *Stalking the Wild Pendulum*,[43] the tunnel effect is a psychological phenomenon whereby the consciousness experiences 'motion' from one 'level' to the other. It is the process of adjustment of the consciousness from one plane of reality to another. It is usually felt as movement. This is so only for people for whom this is new. For people who are used to going into the astral or higher levels, this tunnel phenomenon does not happen any more because it becomes habitual.[44]

It seems that what Bentov is saying is that the tunnel or darkness is an intermediate or transitional zone occurring between levels of consciousness. In other words, one's awareness is 'shifting gears' from ordinary waking consciousness to a direct perception of the frequency domain while the shift is taking place the lapse in time is experienced as movement through a dark space. What is being suggested is that 'moving' is awareness itself, or mind without a body, moving through the gateway to holographic or four dimensional consciousness. Bentov implies that when this shift becomes habitual it occurs instantaneously. In summary, tunnel effects are merely the mind's experience of transitions through states of *consciousness*.[45]

The tunnel effect is to be found not only in near-death, but also in out-of-body episodes where a transition in consciousness was subjectively taking place.[46] This suggests that aspects of the core experience may occur whenever consciousness can be detached from the body.

6.7.2 The Brilliant Golden Light

The brilliant golden light is some times seen at the end of the tunnel, at other times it appears independent of the tunnel experience, sometimes people report that it envelopes them. One possible interpretation suggested by Ring is that it represents the 'light' associated with the state of consciousness one enters after death. At this level, when we are no longer constrained by the sensory systems of the physical body, we are more sensitive to a higher range of frequencies which appears as light of extraordinary brilliance and unearthly beauty. The extensive popular literature of *Life After Death* is full of descriptions which accords with this conception of an astral realm.[47]

Raymond Moody, in many of his writings, speaks of a 'being of light', and many NDEers report being aware of a 'presence' or 'voice' in association with the light, with some persons the presence is identified with God. Ring, however, in considering what the light represents when conjoined with the sense of presence or with an unrecognized voice makes a speculative leap and submits that this presence/voice is actually oneself. It is not merely a projection of one's personality, but one's *total self* or what is sometimes called the *higher self*. In his view, the individual personality is but a split off fragment of the total self with which it is reunited at the point of death. During ordinary life, the individual personality functions as though it were a separate entity in a seemingly autonomous way, though it is invisibly tied to the larger self-structure of which it is a part.[48]

What has this to do with the light? Ring speculates even further. He states that this higher self is so awesome and so foreign to one's individualized consciousness that it is perceived as *separate* from oneself, as unmistakably *other*. It manifests itself as a brilliant golden light, but it is actually *oneself* in a higher form that one is seeing. In other words, the golden light is actually a reflection of one's own inherent divine nature and symbolizes the higher self. The light one sees, then, is one's own. The high self, furthermore, has total knowledge of the individual personality, both past and future. That is why, when it is experienced as a voice, it seems to be an 'all knowing' one. That is also why it can initiate a life review and provide a preview of an individual's life events. At this level, information is stored holographically and is experienced holographically.[49]

6.7.3 Decisional Crisis

Another additional feature of the core experience to be considered with the higher self interpretation advanced by Ring is the *decisional crisis*. When one is being told that he/she is being 'sent back' or that 'his/her time has not yet come' this presumably reflects on the 'life program', of that person's life. But then, if the higher self does indeed have total knowledge of the individual personality, both past and future, that knowledge would include, according to Ring, the 'programmed' time of death for the personality. Thus, when an individual is told that he is being 'sent back' or that 'his time has not yet come' this presumably reflects the 'life program' of that person's life.[50]

In discussing the possibility of life after death, Carl Jung, the noted psychiatrist states:

> The psyche at times function outside of the spatio-temporal law of casualty. This indicates that our conception of space and time, and therefore of casualty also, are incomplete. A complete picture of the world would require the addition of still another dimension; only then could the totality of phenomena be given a unified explanation...I have been convinced that at least a part of our psychic existence is characterized by a relativity of space and time. This relativity seems to increase in proportion to the distance from [normal] consciousness, to an absolute condition of *timelessness* and *spacelessness*.[51]

Kenneth Ring is satisfied that here Carl Jung is describing a holographic conception of reality.

6.7.4 The Last Stage of the Core Experience

The last stage of the core experience when one appears to move through the light and into a 'world of light', the individual perceives a realm of surpassing beauty and splendour and sometimes becomes aware of the 'spirits' of deceased relatives or loved ones. This world, in holographic terms is another frequency domain, a realm of 'higher' frequencies. Ring feels that at this point consciousness continues to function holographically so that it interprets these frequencies in object terms. And thus, another "world of appearances" (just as the physical world, according to holographic theory, is a world of appearances) is constructed. At the same time, this world of appearances is fully 'real' (just as our physical world is real); it is just that reality is relative to one's state of consciousness.[52]

At this juncture, it is reasonable to ask in just what sense is this realm a holographic domain? Just where do the landscapes, the flowers, the physical structure and so on come from? And, in what sense are they real? Ring offers an answer as follows:

> I believe that this is a realm that is created by interacting thought structures. These structures or 'thought forms' combine to form patterns, just as interference waves form patterns on a holographic plate. And just as the holographic image appears to be fully real when illuminated by a laser beam, so the images produced by interacting thought-form appear to be real.[53]

An analogy must be taken for what it is, and no more; that is, the process of arguing from similarity in known respects to similarity in other respects. But one might well ask, if the pattern produced on the physical holographic plate is only a meaningless swirl which becomes coherent when a coherent beam of light, in the form of a laser, is used to illuminate the swirl, what then, is the equivalent of the laser on this last realm? Ring is determined that it is the mind itself that is responsible for this, consequently, he reasons as follows, "If the brain functions holographically to give us our picture of reality, then the mind must function similarly when the physical brain can no longer do so."[54]

Of course, it would be much simpler, as Ring points out, if we were to assume as Sir John Eccles and Wilder Penfield appeared to have done, that the mind works through the brain during physical life but is not reducible to brain function.[55] If the mind can be supposed to exist independent of the brain, it could *presumably function holographically without a brain.*

Ring would also apply the holographic interpretation to account for the perception of "spirit-forms", a feature often found in the last-stage experiences and death-bed visions. In the same fashion that object-forms are, theoretically, from a holographic point of view, a function of interacting mind patterns, so too are encounters with 'persons' in 'spirit bodies'. Such "entities", it is thought, are the products of interacting minds attuned to a holographic domain in which thought alone fashions reality. The fact that the communication between near-death survivors and the 'spirit form' is said to be telepathic further strengthens the view that it points to a world of existence in which "thought is king". From this vantage point, it appears that the manifestations in this high order of reality could easily transcend the forms of our sensory world as experienced in NDEs and OBEs.[56] Carl Jung says:

> I can describe the experience only as the ecstasy of a non-temporal state in which present, past and future are one. Everything that happens in time has been brought together into a concrete whole. Nothing was distributed over time, nothing could be measured by temporal concepts... one is interwoven into an indescribable whole yet observes it with complete objectivity.[57]

The heart of this speculative holographic interpretation then, is that the world of light is indeed a mind-created world fashioned of interacting (or interfering) thought patterns. Nevertheless, the world is fully as real-seeming as is our physical world.

Chapter 7

NON-OPHTHALMIC VISION

7.1 Introduction

One of the early assumptions of this book has been the acceptance of out-of-body experience as a probable authentic and real experience. If this is accepted, then an immediate question arises. What is it that is out of the body, looking back at the body? How does it behold the many objects and persons reportedly seen in an operating theatre during an emergency or surgery and with what does it perceive? Is this seeing as we understand it, or some other epistemic phenomena? In what sense is it seeing?

7.2 Seeing

Eyes are the physical organs of the body, which enable a person to receive visual images, which the brain interprets; this is what is understood as seeing. In an out-of-body experience, whatever is doing the seeing cannot be the same physical eyes that are usually closed and remain in the physical body. If it is not seeing in the direct sense, then, one might conjecture that the seeing is more like a vision, in the sense of something perceived vividly in the imagination. But the details reported in many NDE cases and in many out-of-body experiences are highly descriptive, often giving the location of objects, their colour and other details about them. This suggests that we adopt a position of something which is of greater clarity, more concrete than a vision, and not something seen through a thin veil as it is sometimes sceptically described.

Of course, the faculty of imagination has been used to great advantage and with much success by authors, from poets to science-fiction writers, who have created worlds with great clarity and much detail. But imagination has a palpable limitation, it is based on past experience. What it creates is a composite, a collage, or conglomerate of past events. In the words of D. W. Hamlyn, "It would be surprising, to say the least, if imaginative power could produce a 'seeing' that was not constructed from any previous seeings."[1]

If limited to past experience, can a person imagine something totally new and different, something that they have never experienced? For instance, can a person imagine a new colour not based on any or a combination of any of the primary colours within their experience? It would seem plausible that since we have not experienced it, it cannot be imagined nor described, and may be cognitively closed to us. Hume had recognized this problem and held, on empirical grounds, that the simple element of all ideas are always copied from the simple elements of the impressions perceived in experience.[2]

'Seeing' in out-of-body experience is not seeing in a straight-forward sense; it is not produced by the sensitivity of light hitting the retina and triggering nerve impulse via the optic nerve – as the eyes do not come into play. Out-of-body or disembodied seeing is not dependent on ophthalmic vision.

In support of this latter contention the case of Vicky (Umipeg), reported in *Vital Signs* (1944),[3] may prove to be of some assistance. Vicky was born prematurely and weighed one pound, fourteen ounces. She was placed in an airlock incubator where she was given oxygen. Unfortunately, she was given an excess amount of oxygen, which resulted in her becoming blind. The excess oxygen had the effect of destroying her optic nerve. She attended school for the blind where it was reported she could see no light, no shadows, in fact nothing at all. It was also reported that she was unable to even understand the concept of light.

At the age of twelve, Vicky had appendicitis and peritonitis and was placed in intensive care. This was where she experienced her first NDE. Ten years later, at the age of twenty-two, as a result of a car accident she was to experience her second NDE. The narrative of her out-of-body experience does not vary in general terms from the core experience of sighted persons who had undergone similar experiences.[4] Vicky reported seeing her body on a metal table being prepared for surgery. She confesses that she had a difficult time relating to seeing because she had never experienced it. When she reported going through "the tunnel",[5] she stated that she saw people about her, they had shapes to them that were like a body; some were at a distance, but she couldn't say how far because she had no concept of distance. She also reported hearing people singing. It sounded to her like all the hymns that one could ever hear, all being sung at once, and yet one could tell each individual hymn. As a musician, she was astounded that nothing was out of harmony, and that all those hymns could be sung together and not sound terrible.

Vicky describes the tunnel itself as being dark, but as she got towards the end of it all became brilliant. She then experienced a panoramic life review[6] where her whole life history passed before her in a lot of detail. Right at the end of the tunnel where the life review took place, she described seeing flowers that were incredible. The flowers smelled somewhat like jasmine, and the grass was fragrant too.

It was as a result of a car accident in 1973 when her second out-of-body experience occurred. She reported that she was floating above her body, which was lying on the pavement; she saw paramedics who came, cut her dress off, and took her to hospital. At the hospital, she saw a female doctor who was expressing concern about blood being found on her eardrum, which might have affected her hearing. She tried in vain to tell the doctor that she could hear, in fact, she was screaming at the doctor who could not hear her.

Vicky had the recognition of being there before, but things somehow were different now; for one, she did not see her body as clearly in 1963 as in 1973, she never had the experience of shouting at anyone before, and the latter experience was more prolonged. She stated that it was nice to be able to see but it was puzzling still, and she was sort of in shock.

After her second experience of going through the tunnel, she found herself lying on the grass and states:

> Everything was in different shades, and everything was bright. Everybody there was made out of light and I was made out of light. It was like I was aware more of what light actually was...I was able to know what it was like- to see; is what I am trying to say...I know what they mean by light. There were different gradations of brightness in the flowers too. I noticed in more detail. The light was about the whole plant, but was more intense in the actual flowers. And the birds, they were all bright, but some were brighter than others. It was different brightness; that's all I know how to

> describe it as. And different shades. But I don't know if it was colours because I don't know how to relate to colours. But I know it was different shades of light. There were different absences and percentages of light.[7]

If Vicky can see light, she may very well be able to see colours; our contention is not her inability to see but the impossibility of her seeing in the usual manner of seeing, whether in black and white or colour, for she lacked the physical apparatus for so doing.

Ring and Cooper cite the case of Marsha in their study of apparent eyeless vision.[8] Marsha, a 40 year old married woman had a NDE when she was 32 as a result of complications in her pregnancy. Like Vicky, she had been born premature. As a result of her premature birth, she developed a condition of retinopathy of prematurity. Unlike Vicky, however, she had some limited vision in her left eye. She could not read print at all, but could see people, though they appeared blurry. Her vision was extremely poor and she used a guide dog. Ring and Cooper classified Marsha as severely visually impaired.

Marsha's experience also supports the contention that 'seeing' in out-of-body experience is *non-ophthalmic vision*. In reply to a question, "do you have any thoughts on the fact that you had vision during this experience?" She replied:

> ...well, see, it was vision. but I don't think it was my eyes. I don't know how it works because my eyes were back here, and since they are not right and I could see everything right, there had to be a more special vision some how.[9]

Marsha also reported that she could see colours clearly in her experience and that "everything was the way it was supposed to be."[10]

Churchland has set out succinctly the process of seeing colours:

> In creatures with trichromatic vision (i.e. with three types of retinal cone), colour information is coded as a pattern of spiking frequencies across the axonal fibers of the parvocellular subsystem of the optic nerve. The massive cable of axons lead to the second population of cells in a central body called the lateral geniculate nucleus (LGN), whose axonal projections lead in turn to the several areas of visual cortex at the rear of the brains cerebral hemispheres, to Vl,

V2, and ultimately to V4, which area appears to be especially devoted to the processing and representation of colour information... A creature competent to make reliable colour discrimination has there developed a representation of the range of familiar colours, a representation that appears to consist in a specific configuration of weighted synaptic connections meeting the millions of neurons that make up V4... <u>Inputs from the eye will each occasion a specific pattern of activity across these cortical neurons</u>, a pattern or vector that falls within one of those subspaces. In such a pigeonholing, it now appears, does visual recognition of a colour consists... <u>This recognition depends upon the creature possessing a prior representation - a learned configuration of synapses meeting the relevant population of cells - that antecedently partitions the creature's visual taxonomy so it can respond selectively and appropriately to the flux of visual stimulation arriving the retina and LGN.</u>[11] (my emphasis).

It is to be recalled that Vicky's optic nerve has been damaged and she has had no past experience of seeing.[12] She, therefore, has a serious deficiency, for she lacks the complex 'prior representations', a processing framework that deserves to be called 'cognitive'. She is further impoverished, in that there will be no specific pattern of activity across the cortical neurons because there is no input from the eyes.

Our second contention is that Vicky cannot imagine light or colours because she has had no experience of them, or, as Colin McGinn puts it:

> We cannot form concepts of a bat's sonar experience, since we do not ourselves have such experiences (of anything like them) <u>just as congenitally blind people with no visual imagery cannot form concepts of visual experience</u>[13] (my emphasis).

Herbert Feigl, in a classic essay the *"Mental"* and the *"Physical"*, attempts to fit the epistemology of experience into a physicalist frame of reference, and to capture within the framework of physical science the cognitive role of direct acquaintance with experience. According to Feigl, the physicalist framework is essentially objective, but the most remarkable information about a sensory experience appears to be subjective, accessible only to those who can employ a sensory organ of the same type as the one that produces the experience.[14]

Laurence Nemirow, in his article 'Physicalism and the Cognitive Role of Acquaintance', points out that Feigl underestimates the difficulty. He says:

> Even it we grant that a congenitally blind psychologist might triangulate the experience of sight, thus confirming that it occurs and discerning all of its physiological aspects, he would not thereby learn what the experience of seeing is like. <u>Knowledge of what seeing is like cannot be inferred from non-visual sensory inputs</u>... Plainly, there is knowledge of what it's like to see that can be learned, remembered and forgotten, <u>but it eludes those who are uninitiated to the experience of sight</u>.[15] (my emphasis)

In discussing the ability equation (that is, how knowing what it is like may be identified with knowing how to imagine), Nemirow states:

> Specifically, the ability to imagine colour (that is, knowing what the colour- is like) may be communicated to someone who has within his repertoire a description of an action by which visualizing can be accompanied... It is generally, albeit contingently, true that imagining an experience might be accomplished only by (1) imagining the experience itself (2) remembering similar experiences or (3) imagining or remembering similar- experiences and interpolating. So the ability to imagine an experience is describable only as imagining for those who cannot do (2) or (3). Those people might be able to imagine, and imagining might be expressible to them as such. But they cannot be told how if they do not already know. <u>Accordingly, the uninitiated cannot be told what it's like</u>.[16] (my emphasis)

> Vicky, I believe, cannot imagine the experience of seeing, or remember previous experiences of seeing, or imagine or remember similar experiences and interpolate. Since she does not already know, she cannot be told what it is like to see. The ability to imagine a colour or light may be communicated to someone who has within his/her repertoire a

description of an action by which visualizing can be accomplished. In the present case, Vicky has no such repertoire.

How then can we account for Vicky, or any out-of-body, or disembodied mind seeing and yet avoid the occult? In chapter 3, I introduced W. D. Hart's theory outlined in his book, *The Engines of the Soul* (1988),[17] where he puts forward a theory involving the exchange of energy to speculate how disembodied minds can see, and hear and, in fact, experience all the five senses. Nothing in his approach requires visual or other experience to play the epistemic role in which sense data was once cast. In fact, there is no commitment to sense data. Vicky, in a narrow sense, has no eyes, but this would not perturb Hart, who, as I indicated, states: "[N]ote that since those who no longer have eyes can visualize, it is possible to have visual experience at a time when one has no eyes."[18]

7.3 Physical Theory of Experience

Let us now examine his theory in greater detail. In the *Engines of the Soul*, W. D. Hart consistently argued that causation is the flow of energy.[19] However persuasive that argument might be, like Rip Van Winkle aroused from his slumber, psychophysical interactionism is awakened, and the problem now becomes how could energy of some sort flow between matter and disembodied minds?

Hart suggests that we might begin to organize our thoughts by re-examining some of the history of the discussions about the problem.[20] There were people, like Spinoza, who thought that a cause necessitates its effects no less than conjunction necessitates its conjuncts. Hume, on the other hand, would agree that causes do not necessitate their effects, for to him, cause was bare conjunction.[21] Another approach was to be found among the schoolmen that there must be as much reality, neither more nor less, in the cause as in the effect.[22] But it is obvious that existing or being real is not a "stuff" of which there can be more or less. Notwithstanding, there is, even if unwittingly, some value to this view for it indicated that some quantity or other is strictly conserved, it neither comes into being nor vanishes. This quantity should be located at places and times, and capable of change of place with time, that is motion. So when an intuitively specified causal chain of events is genuine, the total quantity should be conserved along the chain and traceable along its path, through space and time; presumably, tracing the quantity's motion along the chain would be a way to explain the events in it. The point may be made another way, by saying that in order for a thorough-going causal explanation to be possible, according to Hart, some localizable and conserved quantity should be traceable along causal chains. Is this a restatement of the schoolmen's maxim, that we know *a priori* that if a thorough-going explanation is to be possible, that some quantity or other must be conserved?

Since conservation principles are quantitative, energy can be conserved only if it is a quantity. Of course, a quantity is not always 'stuff'; noteworthy is the fact that energy, though it is a quantity, is not 'stuff'.

For the sake of clarity, it is always useful to distinguish between quantities and measures. Quantities are objective, and independent of us, but measures are our means of detecting quantities. As Hart puts it, 'metaphysics treats quantities; epistemology treats measures'.[23] We can no more assert that all truths should be knowable than we can guarantee that every quantity should be capable of measurement.

To advance the discussion further, we also need to distinguish between two sorts of conservation principles: global and local. A quantity is globally conserved if, and only if, the total amount of it at any one time is the same as the total at any other time; for a quantity to be locally conserved it must have spatial as well as temporal location. Then the quantity is locally conserved if, and only if, the total amount of it in any given volume varies directly with the net amount of it passing into the volume through the surface.[24]

The idea of the flow of energy arises out of the local conservation of energy. Since energy usually flows along intuitively causal chains, there arises the idea of causation as energy flow. Sight, as Hart repeatedly stated, requires veridical, visual experience caused by that in virtue of which it is veridical.[25] And, as causation is the flow of energy, which is itself a quantitative principle, disembodied people could see only if a quantity flows from what they see to them. And, interestingly, he suggests that there are some quantities intrinsic to a disembodied person. But are there any really psychological quantities, and are there some mental phenomena, which determine quantities of that sort?

Hart argues that there are quantities of belief and desires founded on a normative conception of rational belief and desire.[26] He falls short, however, of claiming that there exists a quantity as psychic energy. For, to support such a claim in purely psychological terms, a quantity conserved through and traceable along almost all naïvely identified wholly intra psychic causal chains would have to be found. Hart is unable to say whether such a quantity exists, but there is a gap which undoubtedly would be filled if there were such a quantity as psychic energy.[27]

Hart pointed out that in the final quarter of the 17th century, Newton was reasonably clear about two quantities: velocity and mass. In school, children were taught that kinetic energy is half the product of mass and the square of velocity ($\frac{1}{2} MV2$), a very elemental combination of the basic quantities. But it took nearly two hundred years for the concept of energy to emerge.[28] We have now had Von Neumann and Morgenstern's articulation of the quantity of desire[29] for more than thirty years. Hart ponders, how long will it take to discern which combination of, perhaps, that quantity and, doubtless other as yet inarticulate quantities will deserve to be distinguished as psychic.[30]

Let us now see where our intellectual excursion with Hart has led us. He has furnished the disembodied person with veridical visual experience, but that was not sufficient to enable such a person to see, for sight requires veridical visual experience caused by that in virtue of which it is veridical, and, perhaps, through the medium of light.[31]

Causation, it was argued is a flow of energy of which requires its conservation, itself a quantitative principle, and that there is intrinsically psychological quantities, for example, belief and desire. The disembodied person has been located at the region of convergence of his lines of sight, that is, those lines along which things seem to him to spread out for him; so seeming, because of his visual experience; and along which they actually do spread out because his experience is veridical.

Hart's thesis involves an exchange of energy between light and psychic energy: when the light arrives from those objects along those lines at that region of convergence, it passes straight through, but loses some of its energy. On the other hand, certain quantities in the disembodied person increase. The disembodied person comes to have enough psychic energy that his visual experience continues because of his having that psychic energy; his visual experiences cause him to have, or to sustain some of his beliefs about the objects of which those experiences are veridical; the psychic energy implicated in the degree of conviction with which he holds or sustains those beliefs comes from the psychic energy, implicated in the veridical visual experience that caused or sustained those beliefs; and the psychic energy implicated in his veridical visual experience comes from the energy lost by the light.[32]

We are required, by Hart, to suppose that when light arriving at the region of convergence loses energy, the disembodied person's visual experience continues, and continues to sustain some of his beliefs about those objects of which his experience is veridical, and that there is a fixed rate of conversion between the quantity of the energy lost by the light and the degree of those convictions he continues to have about those objects. With this, he is comfortable that the causal conditions necessary for sight in disembodied people can, probably, be met.[33]

The core of his thesis is the fixed rate of conversion between the amount of energy lost by the light and the degree of conviction held by the disembodied person. This, of course, could only be so if the fundamental energy, (itself potentially either physical or mental) that had been in the light did not vanish into nothing (which naturally would violate the conservation of energy) but has since transformed and continues as a degree of conviction with its psychic energy. If this is so, then Hart has conceived of a flow of energy from objects in virtue of which visual experience is veridical, initially a flow via the transmission of light and ending past the veridical visual experience of those objects.[34]

Hart extends his thesis by applying similar principles to the other four senses. He sketches a scenario where, from freshly ground coffee aromatic molecules drift near the region of convergence, and lose some of their electrochemical energies binding them together, and the disembodied person undergoes olfactory experiences. The disembodied comes to belief that there is freshly ground coffee nearby and there is a fixed ratio between the amount of conviction that he or she thereby acquires and the electrochemical binding energy lost by the aromatic molecules breaking up. That could be what true belief from veridical olfactory experience caused by that in virtue of which it is veridical might be like in the disembodied, so they could smell. Similarly, when food molecules drift into the region, they lose their electrochemical binding energy and break up. Some of these molecules drift straight out the other side. The disembodied person then has gustatory experiences. These caused him or her to form true belief that there is food in the offing, and there is a fixed ratio between the amount of electrochemical binding energy lost by the molecules breaking up and the amount of conviction he acquires. That could be what true belief from veridical gustatory experience caused by that in virtue of which it is veridical might be like in the disembodied, so they could taste.[35]

In between that region where lines of sight converge, and light loses energy on the one hand, and the region where aromatic molecules break up there is a region where, when sound waves arrive, like the ringing of a bell, they lose vibratory or kinetic energy, but pass straight through. Then the disembodied has an auditory experience just like the one you would have if you heard the ringing of that bell. The remainder of his argument is set out seriatim,[36] and in a like manner, the disembodied could hear.

We have dealt with sight, smelling, tasting and hearing in the disembodied self. To conclude the five senses we have yet to deal with touch. Hart's formula is to speculate about how conservation of energy might apply to the embodied sense with its usual organ, and then to transpose those speculations into the disembodied mode. In all of this, it is not proposed that moving objects would bounce off the disembodied, for that would be to attribute impenetrability by matter to them, and impenetrability by matter is the hallmark of matter. But it would be acceptable, in his thesis, that whenever objects pass through the region occupied by the disembodied person, they lose a fraction of their speed but pass straight through without his acquiring any motion.[37]

No two objects of the same kind can occupy the same place at the same time. This is so, because no two material objects of the same kind can fill the same place at once. But a material object may come to fill the volume of space, occupied by a disembodied person, for the disembodied person is not the same kind as any material objects, he or she lacks a material body.[38] To return to the sense of touch, at the same time as matter passing through the disembodied loses kinetic energy, he has veridical tactual experience and the argument once again is repeated seriatim. All this is very well, but how do we imagine away the organs of touch and what is the relevant region? In response to this problem, Hart requires us to imagine our missing limbs, like the phantom limbs of amputees, indeed an entire phantom body, the region at least over the surface of which one is sensitive is the relevant region. So it is that the sense of touch could survive in a disembodied person.[39]

Sensations, such as itches, pain, tickles, perhaps hunger and the feeling of orgasm are to be distinguished from perceptual experiences. Once you have bought the idea of a phantom body, however, you would have no difficulty imagining a disembodied person having such experiences. But why would we anticipate any such sensations is not clear, for we would not need pain to warn us of any bodily injury or hunger to remind us to fuel the body; unless they are just memories in the disembodied like a touch in a phantom limb?

At the heart of Hart's thesis is the exchange of energy, the core of which is the fixed rate of conversion between the amount of energy lost by the light and the degree of conviction with its psychic energy returned by the disembodied person. The language of energy and conservation is the language of physicalism, or its ontology, or, at least, it suggests that it is ontologically dependent on some physical entity.

7.4 Transcendental Awareness

In contrast to Hart's physicalist thesis of disembodied experience, Ring and Cooper (1977)[40] present a thesis of transcendental awareness. Ring and Cooper's study was designed to investigate whether blind persons report NDE, and if so, whether their NDE are the same or different from sighted persons; and, most importantly, whether the blind, claim to have visual impressions during their NDEs or OBEs. They concluded that their findings were unequivocal in the affirmative. The weakness of the study, as admitted by Ring and Cooper, however, was their inability to fully corroborate the claims of sight through independent evidence, though they presented two illustrative and highly suggestive cases.[41]

My question, 'what is it out of the body looking back at the body and with what is it seeing?'[42] is posed differently by Ring and Cooper thus, 'if it can legitimately be asked that the blind in some sense do see, in precisely what sense would that be?' Before dealing with this specific question, Ring and Cooper raise a preliminary issue, 'Might there be some nonretinal based mechanism that in principle account for the result of their study and thus demonstrate that vision in the blind is indeed only apparent and not actual?'[43] In an attempt to answer this question, the authors consider a number of possibilities which we now examine.

7.4.1 The Dream Hypothesis

One possibility that has often been advanced, in the case of sighted persons, is that their OBE is some kind of dream, perhaps a lucid or exceptionally vivid dream, which has such realistic properties that it is easily misinterpreted and given an ontological status it does not deserve. But what is known about the normal oneiric processes in the blind? In the *Psychology of Blindness* (1975),[44] Kirtley stated that:

1. There are no visual images in the dreams of the congenitally blind,
2. Individuals blind before age 5 also tend not to have visual imagery,
3. Individuals who became sightless before ages 5 to 7 may or may not retain visual imagery, and
4. Most persons who lose their sight after age 7 do retain visual imagery, although its clarity tends to fade with time.

In addition, it appears from research, that the primary sense involved in the dreams of the blind is audition, followed by tactile and kinetic elements.[45]

Ring and Cooper conclude that the visual aspect of NDE in the blind has nothing in common with their usual dreams, it is in a class by itself and not to be conflated with dreams. Consequently, they reject dreams as a possible explanation for the phenomenon.

7.4.2 Retrospective Reconstruction

Another possible explanation is that individuals are not really seeing at that time, but talking afterwards as if they did. In short, they actually reconstruct a plausible account after the fact of what might have been expected to have happened, while they were close to death, which they may have sincerely but erroneously believed that they had witnessed at that time. It might be possible for an NDEer to construct imaginatively a pictorial representation of events during an NDE from a combination of prior expectations, familiarity with hospital conditions, overheard conversations, other sensory cues at the time or even information gleaned afterwards. What appears to be a vision in reality might very well be a product of the mind's inventiveness. Ring and Cooper not only found no significant support for such a hypothesis but a number of cogent reasons to reject it, and, to regard it almost as a kind of all purpose refuge for the sceptically minded, rather like the 'super-ESP' hypothesis in parapsychology, which, in principle, is always capable of explaining away, in a pseudoscientific fashion, findings that threaten to disturb prevailing ideas of the possible.[46]

7.4.3 Blindsight

Lawrence Weiskrantz (1986), studied a curious phenomenon which was later to be called 'blindsight', in which patients suffering from extensive cortical blindness appear able to *see*.[47] For example, in the absence of any visual sensation, patients, if asked to reach for a nearby object, the location of which was not described beforehand, tended to move in the right direction.

In a further attempt to distinguish non-ophthalmic vision, Ring and Cooper examines the phenomenon of blindsight in order to eliminate it. But, it was hardly necessary, for patients typically manifesting the effect cannot verbally describe the object they are alleged to see. In fact, blindsight patients do not claim that they can *see* in any sense.[48]

7.4.4 Skin-Based Vision

The idea that there could be a kind of eyeless back-up system based on a dermal sensitivity is an old one. Accepting that the retina itself is a specialized piece of skin, which through evolution has become a 'vision specialist' for the body. It is, therefore, conceivable that our skin itself might be a residual basis for visual detection, which has become nonfunctional through disuse.[49]

Jules Romains' experiments in skin-based perception was published in *Eyeless Sight: A Study of Extra Retinal Vision and the Paroptic Sense* (1924).[50] The general purpose of the study was to determine whether individuals could *see* without the use of their eyes. He conducted a series of experiments with the subjects blindfolded. In the blindsight experiments, he invited his subjects to describe objects placed in front or behind them. Although Romains considered that many of his subjects performed well and exceeded what would have been possible by chance, he found that several conditions affected the probability of correct identification. Firstly, in the case of blindfolded subjects there had to be light in the room for them to *see*. Secondly, his subjects could not perceive the object or 'read' numbers or letters on a paper when an opaque screen was placed between them and the object. Finally, the greater the area on the skin actually exposed, the more accurate subjects tend to be in their description.[51]

In NDE or out-of-body vision, walls and ceilings were no impediment and skin exposure was of no relevance as subjects were often fully covered with bed sheets. The kind of eye vision encountered by Romains was piecemeal, gradual, with elements of perception coming together slowly, often as a result of laborious effort. In contrast, NDE visual perception seemed immediate, unlearned and not restricted to objects close to the individual. Consequently, Ring and Cooper concluded that Romains' findings, even if valid, had no relevance to their study and depended on different mechanisms.[52]

Having demonstrated that the above theories cannot adequately explain the visions reported in NDEs and OBEs, the authors proposed to seek elsewhere for their answers. Before looking elsewhere, however, they needed to be satisfied that the reports of blind persons seeing during their NDE or OBE can legitimately be called 'true sight'. In other words, is it truly a form of seeing, in any sense analogous to physical sight? Could it be a form of synesthesia where many perceptions, the visual, the auditory, the tactile, were blended into some image in the mind, and a complex multisensory awareness seem to have been involved?

To Ring and Cooper, it is beginning to appear that it is more a matter of the blind knowing, through a still poorly understood mode of generalized awareness based on a variety of sensory impressions, especially tactile ones happening around them.[53] Although the data presented by them does not unequivocally establish that point, from my standpoint, the reports seem to imply that the blind do see in a way akin to physical sight. The response to this observation by Ring and Cooper is that the subjects' experiences may have been coded originally and by the time we encounter them they have long been expressed in a particular linguistic form. And, that form is a language of vision which is rooted in the experiences of sighted persons and therefore biased in favour of visual imagery. Further, because the blind are members of the same linguistic community as sighted persons, they can be expected to phrase their experiences in a language of vision, regardless of its appropriatenes.[54] No hard data are presented for these assertions, only that an examination of language usage by the respondents reveal that they tend to use vision verbs far more casually and loosely than do sighted persons, and that such a finding is supported by other researchers who have studied language in the blind.[55]

Even if it cannot be contended that the blind see in these experiences in any straight-forward way, it has to be conceded that they have access to a kind of expanded supersensory awareness that may not itself be explicable by normal means. Like Vicky, who lacked the physical apparatus for seeing, blind persons have reported seeing what they cannot properly see, (since they have no physically mediated sight), or what they cannot know by other than normal means. Then, "we have clearly identified a phenomenon that threatens to cast a dark shadow on the house of conventional science", according to Ring and Cooper.[56] But this is so in NDE and OBE cases, whether the person is blind or not.

Ring and Cooper offer what they conceive as an important clue about the nature of this non-ophthalmic kind of 'seeing' by citing accounts which demonstrate omni-directional awareness as follows,

> I was not seeing from my **eyes** or from any single point of view. I seemed to be seeing everything from everywhere. There seemed to be eyes in every cell of my body and in every particle surrounding me. I could simultaneously see from straight on, from above, from below, from behind and so on.[57]

The authors contend that this 'three hundred and sixty degree spherical vision' is not simply vision but almost a kind of seeming omniscience that completely transcends what mere seeing could ever afford. It is a distinctive state of consciousness, which they call transcendental awareness. In this type of awareness it is not the eyes that see anything, but rather that the mind itself sees, more in the sense of 'understanding' than of visual perception as such, or alternatively, we might say that it is not the eye that see, but the 'I',[58] What students of OBE, tend to call extrasomatic vision seem, to Ring and Cooper, to be identical with what they have labeled transcendental awareness.

The core of Ring and Cooper's transcendental awareness is that blind persons, like others reporting OBEs and NDES, enter a distinctive state of consciousness, which confers access to a realm of knowledge not available in one's waking state, but like others are forced to translate their experiences into visual metaphors. Put differently, the supersensory kind of knowing that the experience provides becomes seeing when it undergoes the necessity of linguistic transformation. They feel that they have now finally identified the phenomenon and it is now in need of explanation.[59]

Ring and Cooper conclude that the generally accepted theories of human perception and cognition will not, without extraordinary extrapolation, be able to account for transcendental awareness. We need to turn to some recent theoretical developments in *New Paradigm Science* for the explanation we seek.[60] Influenced by development in modern physics, a number of thinkers have developed a variety of theories of consciousness that corresponds to what is called transcendental awareness.

One of the postulates, on the nature of consciousness, in these theories, is that consciousness itself is primary and is the ground of all being:

> All events are phenomena in consciousness. Beyond what we see as immanent reality, there is a transcendental reality; ultimately all reality is comprised of consciousness. The

division of reality into transcendental and immanent is an epiphenomenon of experience.[61]

Secondly, consciousness is non-local. What this implies is that the mind, rather than being located in the individual and bounded by time (birth and death), is fixed neither in time nor in space. In fact, there is only mind.

Thirdly, consciousness is unitary. That is, there is only one consciousness which we call mind. The notion of individual minds is nothing more than a useful fiction, as Dossey puts it, 'The illusion of a separate self and the sensation of an ego that possesses a separate mind'.[62]

Finally, consciousness does and, indeed, must sometimes function independently of the brain. This assumption, of course, would offer an explanation of how the blind may become aware of something that appears to be like visual perception,

> If the mind is non local, it must in some sense be independent of the strictly local brain and body...And if the mind is non-local, unconfined to brains and bodies and thus not entirely dependent on the physical organism, the possibility of survival of bodily death is opened.[63]

Although mind is neither confined to the brain nor a product of it, Ring and Cooper remind us that it may of course, work through the brain to give us representation of the phenomenal world.[64]

According to Goswami (1994), our ordinary perception of time and space came about as a result of a quantum mechanical process whereby, consciousness self-referentially 'collapses' what are called 'possibility waves' so as to give rise to actuality. Hence, he says, "In the Process of collapse, one undivided consciousness sees itself as apparently divided into dualities of life and environment, subject and object."[65]

7.5 Summary

In summary, Ring and Cooper have adumbrated a process that begins with mind fully independent of brain becoming self-referential, that is, becoming identified with consciousness into a dualistic modality that generates the phenomenal world. Accordingly, what is called transcendental awareness, by them, is the beginning of a reversal process which enables the individual, even if temporarily, to experience the world from a perspective independent of brain functioning and the operation of the senses.[66] Such then, is the state of awareness during NDEs and OBEs and specifically in blind persons.

Influenced by the development of modern science, and especially the recent developments of new paradigm science, I sought to find an explanation for out-of-body perception. After examining a variety of theories of consciousness, I conclude that it is plausible that consciousness is primary, unitive, non-local and may at times function independently of the brain. If this is so, out-of-body perception is believable.

PART THREE:
Consciousness and The Nature of the Mind

Chapter 8

PROBLEMS OF CONSCIOUSNESS

> That evanescent thing
> called consciousness.
> **Time Magazine**
> *July 17, 1995 (Cover)*

8.1 Introduction

In this part of the presentation, I felt that a discussion of the problems of consciousness would be useful, if not necessary, as a prerequisite to establishing the context in which to develop an understanding of the phenomenal experience of NDE and OBE. In like manner, a survey of the established theories, put forward over the years by philosophers who have sought to tackle the problem, would provide a valuable backdrop against which to examine and interpret continuing problems associated with the distinction between the mental and the physical.

There is, however, a danger implicit in this approach, and which presents a dilemma; discussions of this type, of necessity, will fall short because they have to be cursory, any in-depth presentation would become voluminous and over-ambitious. On the other hand, one runs the risk of the arguments appearing superficial and shallow. One option available is to be selective as to the theories presented, but would this in all likelihood create an unnecessary bias; or in the alternative to omit these discussions completely? In the final analysis, it was thought that the better choice would be to include some theories of the mind; some major theories have been omitted as they were not thought to advance or detract from the main thesis presented.

This survey is not intended to be decisive or complete, the intention is more modest. The aim is to show the inadequacy of some of the current thinking and why it was necessary to explore a new alternative, *the holographic theory*.

I contend that the current theories of the mind have done little to close the gap between the nature of the mind and its relation to the nature of the physical world, with the exception of the dual aspect theory, about which more will be said. The problem of just how objectivity and subjectivity can be reconciled is still with us.

The hope of the materialists that some physiological discoveries will one day bridge the gap is an act of faith. We must avoid the mistake of thinking that it is simply a matter of scientists not yet knowing enough about the brain function, in physico-chemical terms. It seems clear that more knowledge of the same general kind, that neuroscience currently offers, cannot shed any further light on the fundamental problems that consciousness raises. At best, what one can expect from future research, if it continues in this direction, is a clearer more precise, delineation of the mental and physical events involved. It is my firm conviction that we must change the course of our investigations and research, or run the risk of going the wrong way down an intellectual one-way street that can only lead to an epistemological cul-de-sac. The holographic approach is an attempt to untie the Gordian knot.

8.2 What is Consciousness?

Consciousness, as a pre-theoretic phenomenon, is widespread in nature and commonly found, but its common place has not rendered it any easier to decipher or provide any easy formula to a systematic or scientific study. Nonetheless, we do need to establish a criterion of consciousness to enable us to distinguish the domain of the conscious from the unconscious or non-conscious.

What is consciousness and why is it regarded as a problem? Why do so many writers and researchers shy away from attempting a definition of it? Perhaps, it is because the phenomenon of consciousness does not appear to own clean-cut and well demarcated boundaries and its nature does not readily yield to easy analysis.

The first problem we encounter in the literature is that it offers little guidance as to whether everyone is talking about the same thing when they use the term "consciousness". Even within the same discipline there is a diversity of meaning in the usage of the term consciousness. Ralph Perry expressed the point this way:

> There is no philosophical term at once so popular and so devoid of standard meaning... consciousness confuses everything that is and indefinitely much more, it is small wonder that the definition of it is little attempted. It is not only the ubiquitous familiarity with consciousness that renders attempt to give it a precise characterization or definition unnecessary, the reason is rather the difficulty of the analytic task involved in doing so.[1]

There is also wide variation in our pre-theoretic intuition of how wide spread is the phenomenon of consciousness to be found down the phylogenetic scale. Does it stop at mammals? What about birds, fishes or insects, where is the line of demarcation? Well, the answer to that would depend on whether we include experience of sensations, itches, tingles and so on, as required components of consciousness. Consciousness has also been viewed as a supernatural mystery that will for ever escape any naturalistic explanation; or a natural phenomenon so highly complicated that it will never be understood. In the words of Daniel Dennett:

> Human consciousness is just about the last surviving mystery...There have been other great mysteries: The mystery of the origin of the universe. The mystery of life and reproduction, the mystery of design to be found in nature, the mysteries of time, space and gravity... we do not have the answers to any of these questions...but we do know how to think about them. The mysteries haven't vanished, but they have been tamed...With consciousness, however, we are still in a terrible muddle. Consciousness stands alone today as a topic that often leaves the most sophisticated thinkers tongue-tied and confused.[2]

Colin McGinn does not feel that we will ever solve the mystery. He says:

> We have been trying for a long time to solve the mind-body problem. It has stubbornly resisted our best efforts. The

mystery persists. I think the time has come to admit candidly that we cannot solve the mystery.[3]

Whether mystery or otherwise, is consciousness a real phenomenon and does it have a coherence of its conceptual foundations? The sceptics doubt that consciousness has any coherence of conceptual phenomenon and whether it even merits scientific or philosophical investigation.

Patricia Churchland compares consciousness to the now defunct concept of ether, phlogiston and demonic possessions, concepts that, 'Under suation of a variety of empirical – cum – theoretical forces...lose their integrity and fall apart.'[4] So far as John Searle is concerned, he would not even attempt a definition. He says:

> It is not possible to give a definition of 'consciousness' in terms of necessary and sufficient conditions, nor is it possible to define it in the Aristotelian fashion in the way of genus and differential – though we cannot give a non-circular definition, it is still essential for me to say what I mean by the notion.[5]

And what he means by consciousness, he illustrates by examples, 'When I wake up from a dreamless sleep, I enter a state of consciousness, a state that continues as long as I am awake. When I go to sleep or am put under a general anesthetic or die, conscious states cease.'[6]

Searle's description of consciousness is reminiscent of American Psychologist, George Trumbell Ladd, who approached the concept of consciousness in the following manner, 'What we are when we are awake, as contrasted with what we are when we sink into a profound and perfectly dreamless sleep or receive an over-powering blow upon the head – that it is to be conscious.'[7]

This commonsensical approach has also been used by psychologist George Stout, who simply declared: 'What is consciousness? Properly speaking, definition is impossible. Everybody knows what consciousness is because everybody is conscious.'[8] In a similar vein, William James starts out his assertion that,

> The first and foremost concrete fact, which everyone will affirm to belong to his inner experience is the fact that consciousness, of some sort, goes on. 'States of mind' succeed each other in him...'Personal Consciousness' is one of the

terms in question. Its meaning we know so long as no one asks us to define it, but to give a concrete account of it is the most difficult of philosophic tasks.[9]

Nowhere in his two volumes, *Principles of Psychology* does he give a definition of consciousness.[10] According to James, consciousness was a phenomenon too familiar to be given a definition. He was convinced (Vol. I) that everyone took themselves to be possessors of conscious states that were accessible by introspection.[11]

Sigmund Freud can be added to the list of consciousness researchers who regarded consciousness as not in need of any definition, for everybody is familiar with it. He says, 'What we mean by consciousness, we need not discuss; it is beyond all doubt.'[12] Or as Crick and Koch put it, 'Everyone has a rough idea of what is meant by consciousness.'[13]

On the other hand, Katherine Wilkes, would have no semantic problems, for given her way, she would dispense with the concept of consciousness, 'Science can dispose with the concept of consciousness and lose thereby none of its comprehensiveness and explanatory power.'[14] For her, 'consciousness' can be used as a sort of dummy-term like 'thing' useful only for the flexibility that is essential by its lack of specific content.'[15] This is an eliminativist stance, for she sees the definition of consciousness as worthless and defunct, and the phenomenon itself as may actually be non-existent.

This is different from what Owen Flanagan calls the new mysterianism.[16] For those who think that consciousness is mysterious are committed, at least, to its existence however evasive it might be to scientific investigation of philosophical analysis. To Owen Flanagan, who calls his view constructive naturalism:

> Consciousness exists, and it would be a mistake to eliminate talk of it because it names such a multiplicity of things. The right attitude is to deliver the concept from its ghostly past and provide it with a credible naturalistic analysis... it will be our proudest achievement if we can demystify consciousness.[17]

From the preceding discussions, it is evident that there is no consensus on what the term 'consciousness' means. Nor is it immediately clear whether there is a single well defined 'problem of consciousness' within philosophy. One problem of consciousness which may emerge from this however, is the fact that the term consciousness which has been used as a single unified concept is really a composite of several concepts, each with its own intrinsic problem. Perhaps consciousness would best be treated as a cluster concept, for there are just too many connotations that go under the term; and it seems purposeless to try to specify a single concept that would cover all aspects of consciousness. The difficulty, it appears, after looking at the historical analysis of the problem is the qualitative or phenomenal aspect of consciousness or qualia. The disagreements about the concept of consciousness rage over not only particular accounts of consciousness, but also whether there is any naturalistic explanation of consciousness that can be given. These disagreements exist partly due to the difficulty of the nature of the phenomenon but also on account of the lack of conceptual clarity surrounding the notion of consciousness.[18]

8.3 Consciousness Puzzle

Güven Güzeldere asks the question, why does consciousness keep appearing as an unsolved puzzle for philosophy, psychology and neuroscience? In searching for an answer he points to George Miller's concept 'turning a tool on itself', for perhaps the unique difficulty involved in the understanding of consciousness stems from the fact that consciousness is both the phenomenon we try to investigate and the very tool we need to use to pursue the investigation, as, according to him, 'Turning a tool on itself may be as futile as trying to soar off the ground by the tug at one's bootstraps.'[19]

Further, Miller says, 'Perhaps we become confused because whenever we are thinking about consciousness, we are surrounded by it and can only imagine what consciousness is not. The fish, someone has said, will be the last to discover water.'[20] This is an intriguing observation, as Güzeldere points out, for one cannot directly take the picture of a camera by using the camera itself. Keith Gunderson makes a similar point that, 'Just as the eye does not, cannot see itself in its own visual field, so too, the self will never, in its inventory-taking of the world, find itself in the world in the manner in which it finds other people and things.'[21]

But should these considerations apply to the study of consciousness using consciousness itself? It may be that this sort of "recursive impossibility"[22] in the self-study of tools applies to the phenomenon of self-conscious, where one attempts to study one's own consciousness by introspection. But it is not obvious to Güzeldere that this analogy should hold with the study of consciousness in general by other conscious being.[23]

Güzeldere suggests that a principle reason underlying the confusion and seeming mystery surrounding the concept and the phenomenon of consciousness lies in the presence of two influential, equally attractive pretheoretic characterizations, namely:

(a) 'Consciousness is as consciousness does', that is the causal characterization, it takes the causal role consciousness plays in the general economy of our mental lives as basic.

(b) Consciousness is as consciousness seems', that is the phenomenal characterization, it takes as fundamental the way our mental lives seem (or feels) to us, that is the phenomenal qualities that we typically associate with our perceptions, pains, tickles and other mental states.[24]

These two characterizations not only shape the methods with which consciousness is studied, according to Güzeldere, but more fundamentally, shape the way the problems to be studied are defined and delineated. He feels that more times, these two characterizations are taken to be mutually exclusive for explanatory purposes, and this has the undesirable consequence often to deadlock debates on consciousness. It is the notion that if the characterization of consciousness is causal, then it has to be *essentially*, non-phenomenal, and if it is phenomenal, then it is *essentially* non-causal. This Güzeldere calls the 'segregationalist intuition' as contrasted with the 'integrationist intuition', which maintains that what consciousness does, *qua* consciousness, cannot be characterized in the absence of how consciousness seems. More importantly, how consciousness seems cannot be conceptualized in the absence of what consciousness does.[25] Güzeldere's objective is to marry the accounts based on the causal and the phenomenal characterization into a single unified account.

Another explanation to the seemingly unsolved puzzle of consciousness offered by Guzeldere is the recognition of the curious duality inherent in the epistemic study of the phenomenon. This is a duality not needed to be inherent in the ontological nature of the phenomenon itself or its properties. The ontology of consciousness is still open to debate. But so far as the epistemology of consciousness goes, there appears to be a genuine asymmetry between the mode of access to the facts of one's own consciousness and the mode of access to the facts about others' conscious state. It is this asymmetry from the first-person perspective versus the third-person perspective that forms the basis for the important distinction between systematic approaches to consciousness.[26] We all seem to have a 'privileged' way of knowing about our own thoughts, feelings and sensations. There is a special way in which one's experiences are present to one, in an immediate, direct way not available to anyone else. But, there seem to be no ordinary way to peek into the inner lives of others – their pains, their sensations or to directly observe their consciousness. In that, it appears that there is an epistemic impossibility for anyone to have direct access to the qualia of others, that is, to share their first-person perspective.

Firsthand exploration of the consciousness of others seems to be out of the reach of ordinary scientific methods, others' experience being neither observable nor non-inferentially verified. Epistemic duality seems inherent in the study of consciousness.[27]

> It is true that the enterprise of approaching consciousness within a scientific discipline has traditionally been very problematic, largely due to the inadequacy of the scientific third-person perspective all by itself as a penetrating tool for the study of the phenomenal character of consciousnes.[28]

As Güzeldere has stated, however, it is those properties of consciousness that has to do with its phenomenal aspect, problems such as the irreducibility of consciousness, the status of its relation to its physical underpinnings, its immanent subjectivity which are the real culprits. On the matter of subjectivity, Searle had this to say,

> Conscious mental states and processes have a special feature not possessed by other natural phenomena, namely subjectivity. It is this feature of consciousness that makes its study so recalcitrant to the conventional methods of biological and psychological research, and most puzzling to philosophical analysis.[29]

8.4 Overview of Theoretical Issues

Although we know what it is to be conscious, and at times we are even conscious of being conscious, or, as Bertrand Russell puts it, 'We are not only aware of being aware of them,' it does not mean that we know what consciousness is.[30] The physiological inputs into the senses are passively received without any particular effort but they do require a definite and active interpretation for them to be meaningful and understood. The brain along with the rest of the nervous system comprise what Priest calls our 'environment transformer,' which processes sense-data, thus facilitating perception.[31]

But perceiving involves more than being aware of the sense-data or being conscious of them. There is a state when the mind knows both that it is thinking and what it is thinking. It is an awareness of one's own mental state.

We may not know what consciousness is, but we certainly know what it is not. Consciousness is not physical. It has no size or shape, nor texture, nor solidity. It is ethereal, invisible and possesses an ineffable relation between the percipient and the objects perceived. There are not only sensations but there are also the feelings of them. These are all acts of awareness of consciousness. So, the existence and nature of consciousness is not captured by the mere physical description of the world.

In the continuing struggle to solve the puzzle of consciousness, philosophers have choreographed a dance of words, on the one hand, categorically denying its existence and on the other proclaiming it. Stephen Priest unequivocally declares that consciousness does not exist. He concedes that experience exists, but once all the experiences a person is having have been itemized, there is nothing at all to be captured by 'consciousness'. Consciousness is nothing over and above experience. In this connection, he makes three points:

1. All the familiar phenomenological facts about us can be captured adequately by mentioning only experience,

2. The onus is on the advocate of consciousness to prove that it exists, and

3. In his view, two famous facts about consciousness may be explained; firstly, its ethereal and invisible nature and sec-

ondly, the ineffability of the concept are both explained by the fact that there is no such thing as consciousness. It follows logically, therefore, that there no longer need be any philosophical problem between consciousness and the brain.[32]

So, in one fell swoop, the mind-body problem is solved, if we accept Priest's argument.

Diametrically opposed to Priest is Owen Flanagan, who proclaims the existence of consciousness, thus:

> There exist conscious mental states, events and processes that have the property of being conscious. Consciousness has depth, hidden structure, hidden and possibly multiple functions, and hidden natural and cultural history. Consciousness has a first-person phenomenal surface structure. But...the subjective aspects of consciousness do not exhaust the properties of consciousness...Part of the hidden structure of conscious mental states involves their neural realization. Conscious mental states supervene in brain states.[33]

Consciousness, for Flanagan, is a super-ordinate term meant to cover all mental states, events, and processes that are experienced – all the states that there is something it is like for the subject of them to be in.[34] For him, there should be theories for what exists, for what is real, and especially so when what interests us is ubiquitous. Since consciousness exists, and it has depth and hidden structure and it is ubiquitous, it suggests the need for a theory. The theory Flanagan proposes to defend is "Constructive Naturalism" which will be discussed below.

So wide and varied are the theoretical positions expressed in the literature concerning the problems of consciousness that any coherent presentation requires a taxonomic approach. The classification used here is based on non-naturalism and the various forms of naturalism.[35] Naturalism in the philosophy of mind is the thesis that every property of mind can be explained in broadly physical terms and that the mind-brain relation is a natural one. Non-naturalism, on the other hand, is the view that consciousness is not a natural phenomenon and therefore cannot be understood in naturalistic terms.

It may seem appropriate to conclude that 'natural' contrasts with 'supernatural', but in terms of the current debates in philosophy of mind, which centres around the possibility of explaining mental phenomena as part of the natural order, it is the non-natural which has become the contrasting notion. But that is not to say that a position of non-naturalism is a commitment to things supernatural. It appears that some non-naturalists think that consciousness can be explained if it is recognized as a power of a non-physical substance or as a compound of non-physical properties.

8.5 Non-Naturalism

Prominent among the non-naturalists are Popper and Eccles (1977), for whom everything in existence and in experience is subsumed in one or other of three worlds. World 1 is the world of physical objects and states, World 2 is the world of states of consciousness and subjective knowledge, and World 3 is the world of man-made culture, comprising the whole of objective knowledge. Between these three worlds, there is interaction.

The mind-brain problem, for Popper and Eccles, is defined in terms of the three major components that are generally recognized for World 2, namely:

1) the outer sense which relates specifically to the perceptions given immediately by the inputs of the sense organs: visual, auditory, tactile, smell, taste, pain, etc;

(b) the inner sense which comprises a wide variety of cognitive experiences: thoughts, memories, intentions, imaginings, emotions, feelings, dreams; and

(c) at the core of World 2 there is the self or the ego that is the basis of personal identity and continuity which each of us experience throughout our lifetime, spanning the diurnal gaps of consciousness in sleep. Each day consciousness returns with its continuity essentially unbroken by the hours of unconsciousness in sleep.[36]

Popper and Eccles offer a dualist interactionist explanation of the self-conscious mind and the brain. Their thesis is that the self-conscious mind is an independent entity that is actively engaged in reading out from the multitude of active centres in the modules of the liaison areas of the dominant cerebral hemisphere.[37] The self-conscious mind selects from these centres according to its attention and from moment to moment integrates its selection to give unity even to the most transient experiences. The self-conscious mind also acts upon the neural centres modifying the dynamic spatio-temporal patterns of neural events. Thus, the self-conscious mind exercises a superior interpretive and controlling role upon the neural events.

A key component of the hypothesis is that the unity of conscious experience is provided by the self-conscious mind and not by the neural machinery of the liaison areas of the cerebral hemisphere. This treatment of the self-conscious mind in relationship to the brain, it is felt, gives an opportunity for an effective interpretation of sleep and dream and unconscious states. During sleep, the self-conscious mind finds that there is nothing to read out – all modules are closed to it, suddenly it is deprived of data and this is unconsciousness; hence, "Reading nothing gives nothing."[38]

In sum, the central component of this dualist theory is that primacy is given to the self-conscious mind. It proposes that the self-conscious mind is actively engaged in searching for brain events that are of its present interest, but it is also the integrating agent building the unity of conscious experience from all the diversity of brain events. Even more importantly, it is given the role of actively modifying the brain event according to its interest and desire, and the scanning operation by which its searches can be envisaged as having an active role in selection.

Popper and Eccles maintain that their hypothesis belongs to science because it is based on empirical data and is objectively testable. Although it has yet to be subjected to empirical testing it is not refuted by any existing knowledge. When asked where this self-conscious mind was located, the reply is that it is unanswerable in principle. It is like asking where the feelings of love or hate, joy or fear are located or such values as truth, goodness and beauty, which apply to mental appraisals. Abstract concepts such as in mathematics have no location *per se*, but can be materialized, as it were in specific examples or denominations. Similarly, a location of the self-conscious mind appears when its actions become materialized in its interactions with the liaison brain.

8.6 Naturalism

Principled Agnosticism

Thomas Nagel grapples with the problem of how a person transcends his particular point of view and conceive of the world as a whole, that is, how a person combine his perspective inside the world with an objective view of the same world including himself and his view.[39] He states that objectivity is a method of understanding. It is beliefs and attitudes that are objective in the primary sense. To acquire a more objective understanding of some aspect of life or the world, we step back from our initial view of it and form a new conception, which has that view and its relation to the world as its object. In other words, we place ourselves in the world that is to be understood. We do not understand what it would mean to give an objective account of subjectivity.

Although conscious experience is a widespread phenomenon it is very difficult to say in general what provides evidence of it. The fact that an organism has conscious experience at all, according to Nagel, means basically that there is something it is like to be that organism. Fundamentally, an organism has conscious mental states if and only if there is something that it is like to be that organism. This may be called the subjective character of experience and not captured by any revised reductive analyses of the mental. That is not to say that conscious mental states and events cause behaviour. While the physical basis of mind explain many things, it is not possible to include the phenomenological features of experience.

Nagel illustrates the relationship between the subjective and the objective and between the pour-soi and en-soi by citing the case of bats in his celebrated article "What it is like to be a bat".[40] According to Nagel, the essence of the belief that bats have experience is that there is something that it is like to be a bat. We know that bats (microchioptera) perceive the external world primarily by sonar, or echolocation, detecting the reflections from objects within range of their own rapid, subtly modulated high frequency shrieks. Their brains are designed to correlate the outgoing impulses, with the subsequent echoes, and the information thus acquired enables bats to make precise discriminations of distance, size, shape, motion and texture comparable to those we make by vision. But bat sonar, though clearly a form of perception, is not similar in operation to any sense we possess, and there is no reason to suppose that it is subjectively like anything we can experience or imagine.

This appears to create difficulties for the notion of what it is like to be a bat.

Nagel has pointed out that conscious states such as pain states, visual experiences, and so on, are such that it is like something for the subjects of the states to be in them. His point is that such states are subjective. To fully understand them, one must understand what it is like to be them, but one can only do that by taking up the experiential point of view of a subject in them.

To Nagel, consciousness may be explainable only by appeal to as yet undiscovered fundamental non-mental, non-physical properties that he labels "proto-mental properties", the idea being that experiential points of view might be constituted by proto-mental properties together with physical properties.[41]

Nagel, while giving full recognition to the physical basis of mind, realizes that it is not possible to exclude the phenomenological features of experience. He struggles continuously with the relationship between the subjective and the objective. He realizes that we do not understand what it would mean to give an objective account of subjectivity. Ned Block attributes the view to Nagel that though there may be important differences between a naturalistic explanation of consciousness and naturalistic explanations of other phenomena, there is no persuasive reason to regard consciousness as non-naturalistic or unexplainable in naturalistic terms.[42] Perhaps his position is somewhere between naturalist and non-naturalist. Since one does not believe a theory one does not even understand, agnosticism is the best policy. Flanagan (1992) dubs this position 'principled agnosticism'.[43]

8.7 Non-Mental Naturalism (New Mysterianism)

Minds are biological products like bodies, and like bodies they come in different shapes and sizes, more or less capacious, more or less suited to certain cognitive tasks. Different species are capable of perceiving different properties of the world and no species are capable of perceiving every property that things might instantiate. But such closure does not reflect adversely in the reality of the properties that are outside the representational capacities in question. A property is no less real for not being reachable from a certain kind of perceiving and conceiving mind.

From this foundation, Colin McGinn (1991) wishes to raise the super structure of his thesis,[44] that:

1) There exists some property of the brain that naturalistically accounts for consciousness;

2) We are cognitively closed with respect to that property but, that

(3) There is no philosophical (as opposed to scientific) mind-body problem.

Strongly resisting the supernatural, McGinn thinks it is undeniable that it must be in virtue of *some* natural property of the brain that organisms are conscious. There just *has* to be some explanation for how brains subserve minds. Consciousness must be a natural phenomenon, naturally arising from certain organization of matter.

Conscious states are simply not potential objects of perception. One cannot see a brain state as a conscious state. In short, consciousness is non-mental with respect to the perception of the brain. The mind-body problem is a *mystery* and not *merely* a problem.

Conscious perceptual experiences have a subjective aspect, for there is something it is like for the subject of such experiences. But it can also be said that perceptual experiences have a world directed aspect. This is what McGinn represents as the two faces of Janus. They point outward to the external world, but they also present a subjective face to their subject. They are of something other than the subject and they are like something for the subject.

Since we cannot give a theory of consciousness, we cannot give a theory of content, since to give the latter, would be to give the former (at least in the case of conscious experiences). Accordingly, theories of content are cognitively closed to us, argues McGinn. About consciousness, there is no objective miracle in how it arises from the brain. It only seems to us that there is because of the veil imposed by cognitive closure. We project our own limitations on to nature. Thus, we make nature appear to contain supernatural facts. McGinn holds the view that in reality there is no metaphysical mind-body problem, there is no ontological anomaly, only an epistemic hiatus.

What about our introspective faculty considered by some as a method of discovering truths, could that not assist us in our quest to understand consciousness? But introspection does not deal in physical concepts. If we wish to find out about the physical background of our conscious states, McGinn indicates that we have to resort to perception of the brain, aided by theory and apparatus. We may introspect from dusk to dawn and will never figure out the physical causes of the conscious events of experience.

Finally, consciousness is as natural as anything else in nature, but it is not given to us to understand the nature of this naturalness. According to McGinn, it remains a mystery how cerebral computations could give rise to consciousness, as to how mere matter could form itself into consciousness.

8.8 Eliminative Naturalism

Human beings are social and reflective creatures who continually engage in a multiplicity of cognitive practices, which adapt them to their social and cultural world. They adjust to this world by employing a number of ordinary psychological notions and practices referred to collectively as Folk Psychology (hereafter FP).

FP can be viewed as a conceptual framework used by ordinary people to understand, explain and predict their own and other people's behaviour and mental status. Eliminative Materialism (Naturalism) is the thesis that our common sense conception of psychological phenomena constitutes a radically false theory, a theory so fundamentally defective that both the principles and ontology of that theory will eventually be displaced, rather than smoothly reduced, by completed neuroscience.[45]

From the eliminativist's point of view, philosophers who propound their explanations and theories in terms of beliefs, desires, hopes, wants, imaginings – subjective things, will be on par with scientists who talked seriously about phlogiston or the ether. Our everyday vocabulary has become the detritus of an absolute FP, full of occult Cartesian entities. Consequently, eliminativists advocate the elimination of our everyday mental vocabulary on the basis that it is unscientific and misleading and hopelessly inadequate and should play no part in any rigorous philosophy of mind.

In sum, eliminativists believe that there is something fundamentally mistaken about common sense conception of the mind, FP, and argue that we should part with all or part of this conception in preference of one which does not engage notions such as belief, experience, sensation and similar terms which are themselves intrinsically fraught with conceptual difficulties as well as resistant to any reduction to natural science.

Among the leading proponents of eliminative materialism (naturalism) is Paul Churchland. A cardinal ingredient in his case for the elimination of FP, has been the assumption that it is a theory. Hence, he says:

> Such an examination will make little sense, however, unless it is first appreciated that the relevant network of common sense concepts does indeed constitute an empirical theory, with all the functions, virtues and perils enacted by the status.[46]

Having elevated FP to an empirical theory, he then proceeds to criticize its inadequacies as follows:

> We must evaluate FP, with regard to its coherence and continuity with fertile well established theories in adjacent and overlapping domains – with evolutionary theory, biology, and neuroscience...A serious inventory of this sort reveals a very troubled situation. When one centers one's attention not on what F.P., can explain, but on what it cannot explain or fails even to address, one discovers that there is a very great deal.[47]

One which would evoke open scepticism is the case of any theory less familiar and dear to us. On the basis of this reasoning, we should expunge from our language or excoriate the word consciousness as being vague, simplistic and unhelpful. Owen Flanagan sums it up this way:

> According to the eliminativists, consciousness is a concept that is simultaneously too simplistic, too vague, and too historically embedded in false and confused theory to perspicuously denote a phenomenon or set of phenomena in need of explanation. Concepts like consciousness, qualia, and subjectivity are unhelpful in setting out the explanatory agenda for a naturalistic theory of mind. Whatever genuine phenomena these concepts inchoately gesture towards will be explained by the science of the mind. But the explanation will proceed best if we eliminate these concepts from the explanatory platter and seek more perspicuous and credible replacements undergirded by a rich neuro-scientific theory.[48]

8.9 Constructive Naturalism

The brain is indeed an information processor, but a conscious information processor.[49] The phenomenology of consciousness and the complex neural activity of the brain seem to belong to these two disparate orders of reality, the subjective and the objective. Owen Flanagan (1992) calls this view of consciousness 'Constructive Naturalism'.[50] With this view, he seeks to establish that consciousness is a natural phenomenon and that philosophers can construct a theory about its nature, forms, roles and origin. In a somewhat eclectic approach, he would blend theories of phenomenology, psychology, cognitive science, neuro-science and evolutionary biology.

Flanagan sees a scientific theory of consciousness in a relatively straightforward sense. To him conscious phenomena constitute legitimate explananda, and conscious events play explanatory roles in certain well-grounded generalizations, and gathering together all the scientific truths about the class of phenomena will constitute the *theory* of consciousness. So the theory of consciousness will be part of the larger, more systematic theory of the mind as a whole, and it is capable of taking on whatever depth the facts require.[51]

Though one might think that it is important to distinguish the question of whether there can be a scientific theory of some phenomena from the question of whether there can be a unified theory of those phenomena, Flanagan feels that even if such a distinction were well grounded it is not especially important, for facts gathered about aspects of the mind are facts about a complex integrated system. The *truths* about perception or memory or consciousness have a unity that derives from there being truths about salient kinds of activity of a unified mental system that is the product of evolutionary processes.

Flanagan expresses the view that there must be truths about consciousness, since consciousness exists, is a natural phenomenon, and is in need of explanation. What sort of unity the theory will possess and what interrelations it will have to other theories within the overall science of the mind is not yet known. But the job is to get on with providing the fine-grain analysis of conscious mental life and see where it leads.

He posits that consciousness is neither miraculous nor terminally mysterious. He remains optimistic about our ability to understand the relation between consciousness and the brain, and feels sure that we can make intelligible the existence of consciousness in the natural world.

His theory is neuro-philosophical, in that it tries to mesh a naturalistic metaphysic of mind with our increasing understanding of how the brain works. Put succinctly, the mind is the brain.[52]

Owen Flanagan asserts that Patricia Churchland's (1986) work is also in the mode of constructive naturalism.[53] She certainly champions the cause for a unified theory of the brain-mind, which is avidly supported by Flanagan (1992). What is needed, according to Patricia Churchland, is a unified theory of how the mind-brain works, how the mind-brain represents whatever it represents and the nature of the computational processes underlying behaviour.

According to Patricia Churchland the idea of a unified theory has been around for some time but it has been vague and remote and seems more of a misty idea towards which science might progress rather than a real conception.[54] Consequently, philosophers have tended to ignore developments in neuro-science and research in the neuro-science has proceeded without much concerns of what philosophers had to say about the nature of knowledge or of mental states. Today, neuro-science has progressed to a point where it can theorize productively about basic principles of whole brain function. Philosophers, on the other hand, have moved away from philosophy as a purely *a priori* discipline. Psychology itself has begun to deepen its understanding of certain mental processes such as memory and visual perception. Work in computer science and computer modeling of network is providing a general sense of how to address the questions of sub-introspective mind-brain processes, and there is a growing sense of the benefits for research in cross-talk. We have now entered a time, therefore, when the idea of a unified theory of how the brain works is no longer remote, according to Churchland. The collective effort to devise such a theory will, of course, be constrained by empirical facts at all levels, including neuro-physiological, ethological and psychological facts and may even be coloured by pretheoretic hunches of what a theory could look like and what are the basic principles of mind-brain operation.[55] Ultimately, Patricia Churchland's objective is to show that neuro-science matters to philosophy. To support this position, she has argued that:

(a) Mental processes are brain processes,

(b) The theoretical framework resulting from co-evolution of neuro-science and philosophy is bound to be superior to folk psychology, and

(c) It is most unlikely that we can devise an adequate theory of mind-brain without knowing a great deal about the structure and organization of nervous systems. The correlative theme is that philosophy also matters to neuro-science because ongoing research must have a synoptic vision within which the immediate research goals make sense.[56]

8.10 Naturalistic Dualism

David Chalmers sets out in search of a fundamental theory of consciousness (Chalmers 1996) using the basic argument that consciousness is not logically supervenient on the physical, and as such materialism is false. Materialism refers to the doctrine that physical facts about the world exhaust all the facts. The failure of logical supervence not only implies that materialism is false but also that there are features of the world over and above the physical features.

The recognition of the failure of materialism leads to a kind of dualism; that there are both physical and non-physical features of the world, and that experience is fundamentally different in kind from any physical feature. The fact that consciousness does not supervene *logically* on the physical, does not mean that it does not supervene at all. For Chalmers, it remains plausible that consciousness supervenes *naturally* on the physical. The argument therefore is for natural supervenience without logical supervenience.

This position leads to a dualism, not Cartesian dualism but instead to a kind of property dualism. Consciousness experience involves properties of an individual that are not entailed by the physical properties of that individual, although that may depend lawfully on those properties. Consciousness then, is a *feature* of the world. By this, he does not mean to suggest that it is a separate "substance". What is known is that there are phenomenal properties in the world that are ontologically independent of physical properties. It remains plausible, however, that consciousness *arises* from a physical basis, even though it is not entailed by that basis.

Chalmers calls his view of consciousness naturalistic dualism. It is naturalistic because it posits that everything is consequence of a network of basic properties and laws, and because it is compatible with all the results of contemporary science. As with naturalistic theories in other domains, his views allow that we can *explain* consciousness in terms of basic natural laws; for there needs be nothing especially transcendent about consciousness; it is just another natural phenomenon.

Although Chalmers calls his view a variety of dualism, he does admit that it could turn out to be a kind of monism:

> Perhaps the physical and the phenomenal will turn out to be the two aspects of a single encompassing kind, in something like the way matter and energy turn out to be two aspects of a single kind.[57]

This certainly is the formulation of a dual aspect or double aspect theory. It proposes two sets of mutually irreducible properties, physical and phenomenal. We have no idea about the intrinsic properties of the physical. It may be, according to Chalmers, that some of the intrinsic properties of the physical are themselves a variety of phenomenal property as suggested by Russell.[58]

Is this a retreat to panpsychism? For, if phenomenal properties are fundamental presumably they might be widespread, though not a necessary consequence. Chalmers suggests an alternative, that is, the relevant properties may be proto-phenomenal. In such a case, the mere instantiation of such a property would not entail experience, but the instantiation of numerous such properties could do so jointly. He further intuits that if there are intrinsic properties of the physical, it is instantiations of these properties that physical causation ultimately relates. If there are phenomenal properties, then there is phenomenal causation; and if these are proto-phenomenal properties, then phenomenal properties inherit causal relevance by their supervenient status. In either case, Chalmers believes that the phenomenology of experience in human agents may inherit causal relevance from the causal role of the intrinsic properties of the physical.[59]

I would agree that despite the declaration of naturalistic dualism, Chalmers' position is closely aligned to a type of monism, (though not a brand of materialists monism) unlike materialism, he takes phenomenal or proto-phenomenal properties as fundamental. The thesis of naturalistic dualism upholds that the world is not supervienient on the mind of an observer, but rather consists in a vast casual network of phenomenal properties underlying the physical laws that science postulates. The basic properties of the world are neither physical nor phenomenal, but the physical and the phenomenal are constructed out of them. This surely is another instance of expression of a dual aspect theory, not too remote from Russell's neutral monism. Chalmers states that from their extrinsic relations, the physical is constructed.[60] This seems to be very much like a re-statement of Bohm's implicate and explicate order.

In any discussion of consciousness, it is not unusual that questions are raised as to how consciousness might have evolved on a dualist framework. Did some new element just pop into nature? This poses no problems for Chalmers, for he opines that like the fundamental laws of physics, psycho-physical laws are eternal, having existed since the beginning of time. It may be that in the early stages of the universe there was nothing that satisfied the physical antecedents of the laws, and so there was no consciousness, although this depends on the nature of the law. In any event, as the universe developed, it came to pass that certain physical systems evolved that satisfied the relevant conditions. Once these systems came into existence, conscious experience automatically accompanied them by virtue of the laws in question. If you accept that psycho-physical laws exist and are timeless, as naturalistic dualism maintains, then the evolution of consciousness poses no special problems.[61]

The difficulty with consciousness is to explain the principles in virtue of which consciousness arises from physical systems. After all, consciousness is such a ubiquitous and central feature that it seems that it must have arisen during the evolutionary process for a reason. It is natural to suppose that it arose because of some functions that it serves that could not have been achieved without it. The question is, "could homo sapiens have existed without consciousness? Did it evolve with only homo sapiens or with all hominids?"[62]

Finally, having examined and employed a number of theories, including Wigner's (1961), Everett's (1957, 1973), Bohm's (1952), Chalmers concludes:

> I resisted mind-body dualism for a long time, but I have now come to the point where I accept it, not just as the only tenable view, but as a satisfying view in its own right. It is always possible that I am confused, or that there is a new and radical possibility that I have overlooked; but I can comfortably say that I think dualism is very likely true. I have also raised the possibility of a kind of pan-psychism. Like mind-body dualism; this is initially counter intuitive,

but counter intuitiveness disappears with time. I am unsure whether the view is true or false, but it is at least intellectually appealing, and on reflection, it is not too crazy to be acceptable.[63]

8.11 Summary

Consciousness, in the sense discussed here, is phenomenal consciousness by which I mean subjective experience, the experiential properties of sensations, feelings and perceptive experiences, to which I would add thoughts, wants and emotions. There seems little or nothing in our physical or functional nature, which allows us to understand or explain our subjective experience. This is what has been referred to as the explanatory gap.[64] None of the philosophical theories offered has been able to close the gap. The eliminatavists deny the existence of consciousness as discussed above. Consequently, there can be no 'explanatory gap'. Yet, if we accept a physical theory of mind, it must account for the subjective character of experience. If mental processes are physical processes, then there is something it is like. However, I know of no concept which currently gives such a clue. Physicalism is a difficult position to understand because there is no conception of how it might be true.

There are many unanswered questions about consciousness, not least of which is, how does consciousness develop from the organization of matter? According to Fodor, 'Nobody has the slightest idea how anything material could be conscious.'[65]

What is the place of consciousness in the natural order? Is consciousness physical or can it be explained in physical terms? One of the difficulties with consciousness is to explain how it arises from physical systems. If we speculate that consciousness must have arisen during the evolution process for a reason, what was the reason? Did it arise because of some function that it serves? Can we identify such a function? I repeat the question, *could homo sapiens have survived without consciousness?*

If it is approached from the point of view of evolutionary biology, consciousness appears to have arisen relatively early in evolutionary history (at least, phenomenal consciousness) and is found right across the animal kingdom. It is a fascinating phenomenon. As Sutherland puts it, 'Consciousness is a fascinating but elusive phenomenon. It is impossible to specify what it is, what it does and why it evolved.'[66]

When and where awareness was born still remains a mystery. The real problem, however, is that contemporary science teaches that the world is made up of nothing over and above physical elements, whatever their nature might be, waves or particles. Where does this leave us with respect to the place of consciousness in an entirely physical world? Perhaps consciousness is an emergent aspect of matter or the only true reality, and George Miller might yet have the last word, 'Consciousness is a word worn smoothly by a million tongues. Depending upon the figure of speech chosen, it is a state of being, a substance, a process, a place, an epiphenomenon, an emergent aspect of matter or the only true reality.'[67]

Chapter 9

THEORIES OF THE MIND

9.1 Introduction

As has been indicated, minimally formulated, the central problem of philosophy of mind is providing a clear statement of the relationship between the mental and the physical aspects of the human being; that is, giving an accurate account of the relationship between the mind and the body. In this chapter, a survey of the theories put forward, over the years by philosophers, who have sought to tackle the problem, is presented.

9.2 Dualism

The dualists, led by Plato and Descartes, believe that the mind and physical objects, including the body and the brain, are distinct substances in nature and neither is reducible to the other. According to dualists, the mind is a purely mental, non-material or spiritual substance not extended in space, the essence of which is to think. On the other hand, a physical object is purely material, non-mental, the essence of which is extension in space. In short, no mind is a physical object and no physical object is a mind. A person, however, is a composite of both mind and body.

Descartes's system begins with the method of systematic doubt. We are only to accept as knowledge those things which we cannot doubt. Since the existence of matter could be doubted, Descartes could doubt that he had a body, but he could not doubt his doubting, for that would be self-refuting. He could be certain from the start that he thinks and, therefore, know he exists. This is known as the Cogito argument.[1]

From this argument, it would seem reasonable to conclude that a person is essentially his or her mind but only contingently his or her body, for a person is his or her mind but only has or owns his or her body. If this is so, then arguably, a person's mind may logically continue to exist although the person's body has ceased to exist, but if a person's mind should cease to exist then that person must necessarily cease to exist. So, minds may exist without bodies and bodies may exist without minds.

Some dualists might find solace in Leibniz's law, where if two seemingly distinct things are to turn out to be one and the same thing, then they must share all and only each other's property. If we want to know whether something is the same thing as something else or something entirely distinct from it, we may invoke the following criterion:

1. If X has properties AB & C but not DE & F, and Y has properties DE & F but not AB & C then it follows that X is not Y. If X and Y are to turn out to be one and the same, then X and Y must share all and only each other's properties. This principle is known as Leibniz's Law.[2]
2. If, therefore, the mind has properties which the body lacks and the body has properties which the mind lacks, then it must be the case that the mind is distinct from the body. And it would seem that dualism is true.

Since the existence of our bodies is at least doubtful and that of our minds is not, this suggests that they do not share the same properties, hence they are distinct. It is more than doubtful, however, whether psychological predicates express the type of properties sufficient to establish differences that are subsumed under Liebniz's Law. If minds may exist without bodies and vice versa, then, dualism is a claim to possibility, the claim that you could be disembodied. But it is only an assertion of the possibility of disembodiment, not that there are actually any disembodied people floating about as was argued in chapter 3.

A major problem for dualism is that events occurrences in minds cause events in bodies and those in bodies cause events in minds. Stated differently, there may be mental causes with physical effects and physical causes with mental effects. That is, there is a two-way causal relation between body and mind. This causal relation is referred to as "psycho-physical interactionism" or simply "interactionism." The problem of interactionism is to explain how mind and body can interact causally, if immaterial mind is as different from material body as claimed. What is it then that connects our minds to our brains?

Our intuition or pre-philosophical knowledge does tell us that mind and body do interact. If you have ever had your finger caught in a car door, which is physical, you will experience excruciating pain, which is mental. Being chased by a bull in a pasture will create fear in you, which is mental, and which causes your heart to beat or palpitate faster, which is physical.

The real difficulty is to explain how a non-spatial substance, a mind, may cause effects in a spatial substance, a body, without mediation. As the problem of interaction remains unsolved and the raw facts which stare us in our eyes admit of no explanation, interactionism seems to many philosophers absolutely mysterious. But the problem is far less a problem about causation than it is a problem about the nature of mind and matter.

9.3 Idealism

Idealism is undoubtedly incompatible with dualism, for it is a theory that only mind exists, consequently there can be no duality. The issue however is not monism or dualism but the implication that physical objects do not exist. But on close examination idealists are not denying the existence of physical bodies, they only deny that they exist unperceived or unthought of, and, further, that they are made out of a substance called 'matter'. Thus, idealists negate the essential properties of physical bodies.

The cardinal claim of the idealists is that physical objects do not exist independently of minds. Whatever we commonsensically take to be physical is in fact mental. Unless there are minds, physical objects could not exist. However, as Nicholas Rescher puts it,

> Idealism needs certainly not go as far as to affirm that mind makes or constitutes matter; it is quite enough to maintain, e.g. that all of the characterizing properties of physical existent resemble phenomenal sensory properties in representing dispositions to affect mind-endowed creatures in a cer-

tain sort of way, so that these properties have no standing without reference to minds...It is sometimes said that idealism confuses objects with our knowledge of them and conflates the real with our thought about it...The only reality with which we enquirers can have any cognitive commerce is reality as we conceive it to be. Our only information about reality is via the operation of mind – our only cognitive access to reality is through the mediation of mind-devised models of it...any characterization of the real that we can devise is bound to be a mind constructed one: our only access to information about what is real is through the mediation of mind.[3]

Despite the fact that idealism, at first blush, may seem absurd and manifestly false, it is not incompatible or inconsistent with modern science. Clearly, idealism is incongruous with old Newtonian ideas of matter as a kind of stuff of which the universe is made. But those concepts are no longer in vogue, nothing in modern science as a whole erases idealism. All the statements of physics, biology and even neurology could be true and, at the same time, the statement of idealism could be true as well. The idealist's attack on the concept of matter seems now to have foreshadowed the attack that was to be made by quantum physics. In any event, the whole concept and nature of 'matter' will now have to be re-examined.

In this discussion, it must not be thought that idealism is a simple, coherent, homogeneous theory, for there are radically different kinds of idealism, though I would argue that the common denominator is the view that in some sense reality is ultimately mental. It is not possible here to discuss all the varieties of idealism but it would seem woefully inadequate to even mention the word without the name of the Irish philosopher, Bishop George Berkeley (1685-1753). Berkeley posits that physical objects do not exist over and above ideas, either in the infinite mind of God or ideas in the finite minds of persons. Berkeley is an empiricist, which means for him that all knowledge depends ultimately upon experience. It is not being suggested that empiricism necessarily leads to idealism, for none of the others, of about the same period, Thomas Hobbes, John Locke or David Hume, were idealists.

To Berkeley, not only is knowledge acquired through experience but only experience can be certainly known to exist. Our experiences are all that we are ever directly acquainted with, so belief in anything else cannot be based on direct experience. This is the logical limit of empiricism. Experience does not teach us that physical objects exist unperceived, or that they exist before or after and not just during our perception of them. Most importantly, experience does not teach us that physical objects are material, meaning that they are ultimately composed of a substance called 'matter'.

Matter, says Berkeley, is an "unthinking substance" and "by matter we are to understand an inert, senseless substance, in which extension, figure and motion do actually subsist."[4] How then do we ascertain the existence of such a substance? There are only two routes open to us, the use of the senses or reason. Therefore, if we are to know that matter exists this can only be through observation using one or more of the senses, or by reasoning, the logical exercise of the intellect, or perhaps by a combination of both. We cannot perceive matter through our senses because "by them we have the knowledge only of our sensations, ideas, or those things that are immediately perceived by sense."[5]

If we are to know substance by reasoning, this means logically deducing the fact that substance exists from the fact that we have sense experience, but whatever the character of our experiences, it does not follow from the fact that we have them that they are perceptions of physical substances which exist when they are not perceived. As demonstrated by dreams, it is evident that the supposition of external bodies is not necessary for the producing of our ideas.[6] Since we cannot know that matter exists by either of these two means which are the only means available to us, then we cannot possibly know that matter exists.

According to Berkeley, to say that something exists means nothing more than that it is or that it may be perceived. This he encapsulates in the famous phrase: *esse est percipi* – to be is to be perceived. To illustrate what is meant by exist, when applied to sensible things, he says, "The table I write on I say exists, that is, I see and feel it; and if I were out of my study I should say that it existed – meaning thereby that if I was in my study I might perceive it, or that some other spirit actually does perceive it."[7]

A common argument against the mind – independence of the real is that things in nature would remain substantially the same if there were no minds. But physically things are known to exist only through our perception and are not known with certainty to exist over and above our perception of them. It might even be absurd to suppose that physical things exist independently of our perceptions at all. In any event, what 'things' would remain the same? Certainly, the absence of mind would not change 'things' but the determination of 'things', their identification, their classification, and their characterization, all require mind processing. Perhaps the strongest argument in favour of idealism is that there is no characterization of the real that we can conjure up which is not mind-constructed. Our only access to information about whatever there is that is real is through the mediation of the mind.[8]

9.4 Materialism

Materialism, in contrast to idealism, espouses the view that if something exists then it is physical or material, and whatever we commonsensically take to be mental is in fact physical. This is the antithesis of idealism.

It is to be noted that many philosophers and scientists use the words 'material' or 'physical' interchangeably, likewise, the words 'materialism' and 'physicalism'. Although no generally accepted definition of 'physical' exists it is generally thought that if something is physical it is spatio-temporal and it has shape, size and solidity and is capable of motion. Some materialists maintain that physical things are composed of a substance called 'matter'. So, then, this not only suggest that everything which exist is physical, but also denotes that 'matter' exists.

A materialist is also someone who denies that mental state processes and events exist over and above bodily state processes and events. In sum, materialism denotes the doctrine that whatever exists is either matter or entirely dependent upon matter for its existence. There have been several versions of materialism in the history of philosophy. Unfortunately, only passing reference can be made to them here, as I shall have to emphasize examples of current twentieth-century versions of the mind-brain identity theory.

In passing, reference could be made to Democritus, the Greek philosopher of the fourth century B.C. He maintained that everything is composed of physical objects so minute as to be imperceptible. He called these indivisible and impenetrable objects 'atoms'. Not only do atoms exist, only atoms exist. Everything that exists is either an atom or collection of atoms. This is as clear a statement of materialism as was ever propounded.[9]

Reference could also be made to the English philosopher, Thomas Hobbes (1588-1679), who asserted that everything that exists has physical dimensions of length, depth and breath and is composed of matter. He not only maintained that all other thoughts and sensations are caused by physical objects, but that those very thoughts and sensations are themselves physical. This view is consistent with the thinking that any mental event is literally identical with some event or state in the brain.[10]

Among the current thinkers I shall begin with U. T. Place's (1956) paper *Is Consciousness a Brain Process?*[11] Place contends that consciousness is a brain process but puts this forward as a scientific hypothesis and argues that this cannot be dismissed on logical grounds alone. As a hypothesis, of course, it is an answer to a problem, and we do not know whether it is true or false. It is open to be tested for its truth or falsity, its confirmation or refutation. It is as reasonable a scientific hypothesis, according to Place, as the statement "lightening is a motion of electric charges." He does not claim to have proven the mind-brain identity theory, but rather that he has removed the logical obstacles to its plausibility.

In his defense of the thesis that consciousness is a process in the brain, he does not claim that statements about sensations and mental images are reducible to or analysable into statements about brain processes in the way that 'cognition statements' are analysable into statements about behaviour. For "to say that statements about consciousness are statements about brain processes are manifestly false".[12] He does, however, wish to say that the statement, "consciousness is a process in the brain", is neither self-contradictory nor self-evident and although not necessarily true, it is not necessarily false.

To Place, statements about mental and physical concepts have different meaning. A person can describe sensation and mental imagery like 'image', 'pain' and 'sensation' without knowing about brain processes or that the science of neurology exists. The modes of verification for statements about consciousness and statements about brain processes are qualitatively distinct. This is to say that how we find out that a certain conscious thought or experience is happening and a certain brain process is taking place is radically different. We verify that we are thinking or experiencing by introspection. But introspection, however, will not reveal what is taking place in the brain, this can be accomplished only by empirical observation, according to Place. It seems to me that there clearly exists a severe asymmetry between these two types of verification procedures.

To understand the claim that consciousness is a brain process we need to understand the differences between what Place calls the 'is' of definition and the 'is' of composition. The distinction he has in mind is the difference between the function of the word 'is' in a statement like "red is a colour" and its function in a statement like "his table is an old packing case". In both, these two types of 'is' statements it makes sense to add the qualification and 'nothing else'. In this, they differ from those statements in which the 'is' is an 'is' of predication, for example, "her hat is red and nothing else", is nonsense. The 'is' in the statement – consciousness is a brain process – is the 'is' of identity not the 'is' of predication used to ascribe some property to something.[13] Perhaps the distinction is not far from the use of the Spanish words for is, *est* and *esta*.

The mind-brain identity theory has been posed as a scientific hypothesis that is confirmable or refutable by some scientific observation. But the question must be asked: is consciousness the sort of thing that is subject to empirical observation? There are phenomenological problems that are not experimentally solvable but which are nonetheless serious enough to cause philosophical distress or disquiet.

Place is concerned with the difficulty some physiologists have, that it is not possible to explain mental events by describing processes in the central nervous system. They find it hard to see how consciousness could be a process in the brain, for the mental is not captured by any physical theory. Sir Charles Sherrington had posed the problem as follows:

> The chain of events stretching from the sun's radiation entering the eye to, on the one hand, the contraction of the pupillary muscles, on the other, to the electrical disturbances in the brain cortex are all straight forward steps in a sequence of physical "causation", such as, thanks to science, are intelligible. But in the second serial chain there follows on, or attends, the stage of the brain-cortex reaction an event or set of events quite inexplicable to us, which both as to themselves and as to the causal tie between them and what proceeded them science does not help us; a set of events seemingly incommensurable with any of the events leading up to it...Enough has been said to stress that in the sequence of events a step is reached where a physical situation in the brain leads to a psychical, which however contains no hint of the brain or any other bodily part...The supposition has to be, it would seem, two continuous series of events, one physico-chemical, the other psychical, and at times interaction between them.[14]

If we go through the sequence again, in the words of Priest:

> It is possible to describe in physiological detail light waves contacting a retina and the transmission of an electrical impulse in the brain- cortex, where there are links in a causal chain. But the result of the causal link is something qualitatively different; a visual perception, an experience. There seems to be an abrupt discontinuity between the nature of the physical events and the mental event: the chain of physical events seems to come to an abrupt but unintelligible halt when the mental events occurs.[15]

Can we infer from this that there are in fact two distinct series of events, mental events and physical events? If the answer is yes, then perhaps the dualists may be right after all, or is this merely showing that at the end of one series of events another occurs which is discontinuous from the proceeding.

Place's response to this is that it is simply a logical mistake, which he refers to as the 'phenomenological fallacy'. It is a mistake of supposing that when the subject describes how things look, sound, smell, taste or feel to him, he is describing the actual properties of objects and events.[16] In short, the error is the taking of phenomenological appearances to be entities or events. The example he gives is that when a subject reports a green after image he is asserting the occurrence inside himself of an object which is literally green, it is clear that we have on our hands an entity for which there is no place in the world of physics. There is no green object in the subject's environment corresponding to the description he gives, nor is there anything green in his brain. Brain processes are not the sort of things to which colour concepts can be properly applied.[17]

Neurologists have not yet established that the same sort of mental event is correlated always with the same sort of brain event. If two persons are having the same type of thought, it does not follow that their brains are in the same sort of physical state. There has not been established any one to one correlation. If the mind-brain theory is true, it must be the case that qualitatively similar mental events are each identical with a physical event, but sometimes those physical events are qualitatively dissimilar. So the type-type version of the mind-brain identity theory is untenable.

It has been suggested by Priest that the mind-brain identity theory should be construed as a token-token theory. This means that any mental event is in fact identical with physical event, so that each particular mental event is the same as a particular physical event. This allows the possibility that the mind-brain identity theory is true, despite the fact that it is not always true that similar type of mental events are correlated with similar types of physical event.[18]

Finally, we may note that whatever form of the mind-brain identity theory is accepted, as a form of materialism, it is still highly reductionist. It reduces the mental to the physical and ontologically is held to be "nothing over and above" or "nothing but" the physical. Even if thoughts, moods and emotions are not properties of immaterial substance, they are irreducibly mental properties.

9.4.1   J. J. C. Smart

U. T. Place's thesis that consciousness is a brain process is the point of departure for the development of J. J. C. Smart's psychophysical monism in which he seeks to clarify Place's position, answer objections to it and generally to reposition the thesis.[19] To clarify the position, Smart claims that to state that sensations are brain processes is not the thesis that 'after-image' or 'ache' means the same as 'brain-process of sort X'. It is that in so far as 'after-image' or 'ache' is a report of a process, it is a report of a process that happens to be a brain process. The thesis does not claim that sensation statements can be translated into statements about brain processes nor does it claim that the logic of a sensation statement is the same as that of a brain process statement. Its claim is that in so far as a sensation statement is a report of something, that something is in fact a brain process. Sensations are nothing over and above brain processes.[20]

Smart seems satisfied that 'behaviourism' was satisfactory for an account of most mental concepts but not for that of sensation. To him, it was unsatisfactory to analyse most mental concepts, apart from that of sensation, in terms of disposition in a certain way relative to the belief. Initially, his theory was restricted to sensations which he claimed were identical with brain states.

Smart's defence of his thesis was that it led to theoretical economy and removed the need for "nomological danglers" i.e. things which were exceptions to physical laws:

> So sensations, states of consciousness, do seem to be the one sort of thing left outside the physicalist picture, and for various reasons I just cannot believe that this can be so. That

everything should be explicable in terms of physics...except the occurence of sensations seems to me to be frankly unbelievable. Such sensations would be "nomological danglers" to use Feigl's expression. It is not often realized how odd would be the laws whereby these nomological danglers would dangle...

The above is largely a confession of faith, but it explains why I find Wittgenstein's position (as I construe it) so congenial. For on this view there are, in a sense, no sensations. A man is a vast arrangement of physical particles, but they are not, over and above this, sensations or states of consciousness.[21]

When Smart states that sensation is a brain process or that lightening is an electric discharge, he uses 'is' in the sense of strict identity. He does not mean just that the sensation is somehow spatially or temporally continuous with the brain process or that the lightening is just spatially or temporally continuous with the discharge or that it is like so and so. He makes it clear that the brain-process doctrine asserts identity in the strict sense.

But, if mental states are identical with physical states, then presumably the relevant physical states are various sorts of neural states. Yet, our concepts of mental states such as thinking, sensing and feeling are of course different from our concepts of neural states of whatever sort. Even if a particular pain is the very same states as a neural firing we would identify that state in two different ways, as a pain and as a neural firing. The properties by which we identify pain are mental properties, and those by which we identify neural firing are physical. Are we back to a kind of dualism? Even if we reject a dualism of substance, there seems to be a reappearance at the level of the properties of those states. For the painful qualities of pain and the red quality of visual sensations seem to be irretrievably non-physical. If this is so, then mental states do have non-physical properties, even if mental states are identical with physical states. How, then, can identity theory sustain a rigorous mind-body materialism?

To meet the objection that sensations have phenomenal properties which brain states do not have, Smart invokes the idea of neutral analysis of the ascription of sensation, a concept borrowed from Gilbert Ryle.[22] The argument is that despite initial appearances, the distinctive properties of sensations are neutral as between being mental or physical. For example, when I say I have a sensation of red, I am only saying that I am in some state that resembles in some unspecified way, the state I am in when red objects visually stimulate me.

As long as the aspect of similarity remains unspecified, my description is neutral about whether the properties in virtue of which I pick the state out are mental or physical. My description is therefore topic neutral, that is, neutral about the kind of property it ascribes. If the description seems non-physical, that is because it is non-committal about whether the property it ascribes is physical, and not because it ascribes some non-physical property.[23]

But can a topic-neutral strategy succeed? Topic neutral descriptions are neutral as regards their being mental or physical. Mental descriptions certainly cannot be neutral in that way. In any event, the topic-neutral strategy is not necessary to meet the objection about mental properties being non-physical, for just as mental states may be a particular subgroup of physical states, mental properties of those states may themselves be a subgroup of physical properties. In the final analysis, some might conclude, perhaps unfairly, that Smart's thesis ends like a "shaggy dog story", when he states, "If it is asked what is the difference between those brain processes which, in my view, are experiences and those brain processes which are not, I can only reply that it is at present unknown."[24]

9.4.2 Anomalous Monism

Donald Davidson has been classified as a materialist because of the view he holds that any mental event may in principle be given a true physical description, but his materialism is a kind of materialism, which has to recognize the control we have over our own actions. For him, mental events such as perceiving, rememberings, decisions, and actions resist capture by the nomological net of physical theory. How then, can this fact be reconciled with the causal role of mental events in the physical world? Reconciling this freedom with causal determination seems a special problem.

Assuming that both causal dependence, and the anomalousness, of mental events are undeniable facts, there is some 'apparent contradiction' about mental events which Davidson must dissipate. Firstly, there are at least some mental events, which interact causally with physical events. This he calls the *Principle of Causal Interaction*. Secondly, where there is causality, there must be a law: events related as cause and effect must fall under some strict deterministic laws. This he calls the *Principle of the Nomological Character of Causality*. Thirdly, there are no strict deterministic laws on the basis predicted and explained. This he calls the Anomalism of the Mental, that is, the failure to fall under a law.[25]

Davidson offers a version of the identity of the mental and the physical that shows how the three principles may be reconciled.[26] He argues that there can be no strict psychophysical laws, and that from the other two principles, the truth of a version of the identity theory which identifies at least some mental events can be inferred.

According to Davidson, mental events are identical with physical events.[27] But, what does it mean to say that an event is physical or mental? An event is physical if it is describable in purely physical vocabulary, mental is describable in mental terms.[28] We may call those verbs mental that express propositional attitudes, such as believing, intending, desiring, hoping, perceiving and so on. An alternative characterization of the desired class of mental verbs might be that they are psychological verbs, as used when they create apparently non-extentional contexts.

On the proposed test of the mental, the distinguishing feature of the mental is not that it is private, subjective or immaterial, but that it exhibits what Brentano called intentionality. The German Philosopher, Franz Brentano (1838-1917), claimed that intentionality defines the distinction between the mental and the physical. All and only mental phenomena exhibit intentionality (aboutness), so all thinking is thinking about something, all perceiving is perceiving something even if the object of thought is imaginary.[29] (see section 9.7.1)

In order to make clearer the theories of the relation between mental and physical events that emphasizes the independence of claims about laws and claims of identity, Davidson offers the following classification:

a) Nomological monism, which affirms that the events correlated are one (materialists).

b) Nomological dualism, which comprises various forms of parallelism, interactionism and epiphenomenalism.

c) Anomalous dualism, which combines ontological dualism and the general failure of laws correlating the mental and the physical (Cartesianism).

d) Anomalous monism, which resembles materialism in its

claim that events are physical, but rejects the thesis, usually considered essential to materialism, that mental phenomena can be given purely physical explanations. Anomalous monism shows an ontological bias only in that it allows the possibility that not all events are mental, while insisting that all events are physical.[30]

Although Davidson denies that there are psychophysical laws, nevertheless, he holds the view that mental characteristics are in some sense dependent, or supervenient on physical characteristics. Such supervenience is taken to mean that there cannot be two events alike in all physical respects but differing in some mental respects, or that an object cannot alter in some mental respects without altering in some physical respect. And, he maintains that dependence or supervenience of this kind does not entail reducibility through law or definition. His thesis is rather that the mental is nomologically irreducible. There may be true general statements relating the mental and the physical, statements that have the logical form of a law, but they are not *lawlike* in the strong sense.

There are no strict psychophysical laws because of the disparate commitments of the mental and physical schemes:

(a) It is a feature of physical reality that physical change can be explained by laws that connect it with other changes and conditions physically described;

(b) It is a feature of the mental that the attribution of mental phenomena must be responsible for the background of reasons, beliefs and intention of the individual.

Davidson posits that there cannot be tight connections between the realms, if each is to retain allegiances to its proper source of evidence. The irreducibility of the mental does not derive merely from the seamless nature of the world of thought. Physical theory promises a comprehensive closed system guaranteed to yield a standardized, unique description of every physical event, couched in a vocabulary amenable to law.

It is not plausible that mental concepts alone can provide such a framework simply because the mental does not constitute a closed system. Too much happens to affect the mental that is not itself a systematic part of the mental, according to Davidson.

In conclusion, there are no strict laws at all on the basis of which we can predict and explain mental phenomena. This is Davidson's principle of the Anomalism of the Mental. Finally, the two features of mental events in their relation to the physical are (a) Causal dependence and (b) Nomological independence, when combined they explain the efficiency of thought and purpose in the material world and their freedom from law. Particular mental events can be explained when we know their particular identities, but mental events as a class, Davidson maintains, cannot be explained by physical science.

9.5 Phenomenology

In a strict sense, phenomenology is the study of phenomenon. If we investigate what appears to us when we perceive the world rather than the world that so appears, we are engaged in phenomenology. Phenomenology may be viewed as a formal method of enquiry. It is a practice of observing and characterizing the contents of experience just as they appear to consciousness, with a view to capturing their essential features.

Phenomenology attempts to produce presupposition-less descriptions of the contents of experience without any prior commitment to their objective reality. It is whatever is in consciousness when something is experienced, that is, seen, touched, heard, etc. Put differently, it is an investigation of what appears to us when we perceive the world rather than the world as it appears.

Lest a discussion of phenomenology creates the impression that it is a settled body of teachings, it should be made clear that it does not have a clearly delineated body of doctrines and is neither a school nor a trend in contemporary philosophy. If anything, it should be referred to as the phenomenological views or a movement with various proponents. Speaking of the great variety of conceptions within the phenomenological movement, Merleau-Ponty remarked that the responsible philosopher must recognize that phenomenology may be practiced and identified as a manner or a style of thinking, and that is existed as a movement before arriving at a complete awareness of itself as a philosophy.[31] Nonetheless, it is of sufficient importance to be included among the theories of the mind.

Through principally the writings of Edmund Husserl (1859-1938) phenomenology came to be regarded as a branch of philosophy. But to be faithful to the topic, we ought to begin with a discussion of Husserl's teacher Franz Brentano (1838-1917).

9.5.1 Brentano (1838 -1917)

Perhaps Brentano's starting point is not particularly original where he begins by noting that we possess an intuitive or pre-philosophical distinction between mental and physical, although not in a precise way. "All data of our consciousness are divided into two great classes - the class of physical and the class of mental phenomena."[32]

Brentano concedes that we can distinguish mental from physical phenomena but we are as yet unable to formulate precisely what this distinction consists of. He sets out to clarify the meaning of the two terms by creating an inventory of examples of mental and physical phenomena, mental phenomena:

> Every judgement, every recollection, every expectation, every inference, every conviction or opinion is a mental phenomenon. Also to be included under this term is every emotion; joy, sorrow, fear, hope, courage, despair, act of will, intention, astonishment, admiration, contempt, etc.[33]

This he contrasts with the following physical phenomena:

> A colour, a figure, a landscape which I see, a chord which I hear, warmth, colour, odour which I sense; as well as similar images which appear in the imagination.[34]

The distinction he makes between mental and physical phenomena is roughly one between an act of consciousness and the object towards which that act is directed. An act of awareness is a mental phenomena, but its content or object is physical.

Brentano recognizes that his shopping list of examples does not amount to a definition and that it is necessary to clarify the criterion for the distinction made between mental and physical. He attempts to do so by saying that:

> The term "mental phenomenon" applies to presentations as well as to all phenomena which are based on presentations and every idea or presentation which we acquire through sense perception or imagination is an example of a mental phenomenon...By Presentation, I do not mean that which is presented, but rather the act of presentation.[35]

Brentano is here making a distinction between a mental act and its content. An object of awareness is not the same as the very awareness of it. A presentation then is an act of consciousness.

Central to Brentano's philosophy of mind is the concept of intentionality. "Intentionality" is a technical term which means being "directed towards an object"; it is the property or characteristic of the mental, of being 'of' or 'about' something. Every psychological experience contains an intended object or intentional object which the thought is about or towards which the thought is directed. It does not make sense to talk about there being thinking without there being thinking about something or the other, or about perception without perception of something; where there is desire something is desired. According to the immanent intentionality thesis, the desired object is literally contained within the realm of the mental as opposed to physical or non-psychological phenomena. In fact, from his perspective, it is the intentionality of the psychological that distinguishes mental from physical states,

> This intentional inexistence is characteristic exclusively of mental phenomena. No physical phenomenon exhibits anything like it. We can therefore define mental phenomena by saying that they are those phenomena which contain an object intentionally within themselves.[36]

But may there not be mental phenomena which are not intentional and phenomena which are mental but not intentional? To illustrate, feelings of pleasure or pain certainly do not have intentional objects. Pain is not directed towards an object as perception is, nor are moods seemingly intentional. Brentano's reply to this argument is to say that such mental phenomena in a sense refer to themselves. So then, it would appear that the phenomenon itself is its own intentional object. I am not persuaded by this response. For instance, if one feels happy, is happiness directed at itself? Does it take itself as its intentional object? I do not think so. But in fairness to Brentano, he makes a clear distinction between the object of a mental state and the cause of a mental state. In this case, what one is happy about is not a state of one's brain, even if that is the cause of one's happiness, so cause and intentional object may be distinct. When objections are raised that the phenomena of pleasure and pain are not intentional, it is not at all being claimed that they do not have causes. Brentano, feels however, that more feelings are more intentional than we recognize, for certain feelings undeniably refer to objects. Our language itself indicates this through the expressions it employs.[37] Nonetheless, certain phenomena, for instance, moods do not appear to me to be directly intentional.

What about physical phenomena which might exhibit intentionality? Many physical events are directed at objects. A hunter fires at a deer. Also many biological mechanisms are functional, in the sense of "goal directed". For example, the branches of a tree reaching out for sunlight or its roots seeking water or moisture. Are these not cases of being object directed? If this is the same as 'being directed towards an object' then this would suggest that these phenomena are not exclusively mental.

The doctrine of intentionality makes an important contribution to contemporary non-mechanistic theories of mind. Even where Brentano's immanent intentionality thesis was rejected by philosophers it was generally conceded that there was much merit in his underlying claim that thought is essentially object-directed.

9.5.2   Husserl (1859 -1938)

Through the writings of Edmund Husserl, a student of Brentano, phenomenology came to be regarded as a branch of philosophy. It will be recalled that phenomenology is the description of what is given directly to consciousness without any preconception as to objective reality. Many things are presented to us in various ways and it is Husserl's belief that philosophy should be engaged in precise description of these appearances. It should concern itself with how visual objects are perceived and how they depend on our cognitive activity of seeing, focusing, moving about and on the correlation of seeing with touching and grasping.[38] Husserl himself engaged in many analyses in which he distinguishes between the object given and the subjective conscious activities performed to let it be given. He calls the phenomenological description of the object "noematic analysis" and this phenomenological description of this subjective intention "noetic analysis". The noema is the object as described phenomenologically and the corresponding mental activity is the 'noesis'. The objective and the subjective are correlative but never reducible one to another.[39]

Husserl's formula is to enable us to understand the foundation of all knowledge, and perhaps to discover certain *a priori* structures of consciousness common to all human beings. To achieve this, we have to distinguish between the "natural attitude", which is our ordinary involvement with things around us and with the world, and "the phenomenological attitude" which is the reflective point of view from which we carry out our philosophical analysis of the intentions practiced in the natural attitude, as well as, the objective correlatives of these intentions. When we enter the phenomenological attitude, we put out of service or suspend all the intentions and convictions of the natural attitude. Husserl calls this suspension of belief the "transcendental reduction" or "phenomenological epoché".[40] For phenomenological purposes, the objective reality of the world we believe in is "bracketed" or "reduced" to what we literally think and perceive in the present.

In our human life, we begin in the natural attitude and we move to the phenomenological attitude by 'phenomenological reduction', a 'leading back' from natural beliefs to the reflective consideration of intentions and their objects. So for phenomenological purposes, the objective reality of the world we believe in is 'reduced' to what we literally think and perceive in the present. Perhaps it is hoped to show how the richness of our ordinary world is an achievement of consciousness, for it is constructed out of the series of experiences we actually have.

In discussing intentionality in relation to Brentano,[41] Husserl finds the two criteria used to demarcate mental from physical, useful. For example, the doctrine is either a presentation or based on a presentation, but he has reservations about both criteria. He does not doubt that in perception something is perceived or in imagination something is imagined and so on, but he does not accept that the possession of the characteristic of intentionality is a necessary condition for a phenomenon's counting as mental, even though a large number of mental acts show this feature. There are many mental acts which are not intentional and some phenomena which are in fact mental which Brentano has classified as physical.

> It can be shown that not all 'mental phenomena' in the sense of a possible definition of psychology, are mental phenomena (i.e. mental acts) in Brentano's sense, and that, on the other hand, many genuine 'mental phenomena' fall under Brentano's rubric of 'physical phenomena'.[42]

Husserl thinks that certain sensations are not intentional, they are not 'of' or 'about' anything. *That not all experiences are intentional is proved by sensations and sensational complexes.*[43] He disagreed with his teacher on this point. Brentano thinks all sensations are intentional, Husserl thinks they are not. Brentano thinks all mental acts are intentional, Husserl thinks some are not.

Husserl seems to prefer the intentionality criterion to Brentano's thesis about presentations which he uses to distinguish the mental from the physical. One of the difficulties with the latter is that we need to have had a concept of the mental to understand what presentations are, so there is some circularity here.

Husserl develops his own refinement of the doctrine of intentionality with two separate conceptions of his phenomenological method. He employs the notion of content, and the notion of essence. By content, he means content in a wide psychological sense, so there is a content to what one perceives in the sense of what is perceived; a content to what one thinks in a sense of what one thinks; a content to what one says in the sense of what one says. Clearly, therefore, different perceptual, imaginative and linguistic contents will exist. Consequently, the notion of an intentional object will have to be widened to take account of these contents. Also, *the phenomenological logical assertions we aim at are all meant by us...as assertions of essence.*[44]

The essence of something, of course, is what that thing really is. It is important to Husserl to determine the essences of various mental acts, to discover exactly what it consists in to think, to perceive, to imagine, and so on.

Husserl agrees with Brentano that the intentional object need not have objective or mind-independent reality. He gives the example of god Jupiter who does not exist mind-independently, yet may exist as an object of thought. God Jupiter is not to be found as any component part of his intentional experience. But it has no objective or mind-independent existence either, that is to say, it does not exist extra-mentally nor in fact does it exist at all. Therefore, god Jupiter does not exist mentally or physically. However, this does not prevent god Jupiter from 'being actual', or being 'our idea' and of being a particular mode of mindness.[45] There is a class of entities which are not mental acts, and not physical objects but only intentional objects. They are neither mental nor physical but provide the contents for certain of our mental acts. Of course, there are objects of our mental acts which may exist mind-independently.

Finally, we must examine Husserl's concept of consciousness which he seems to employ in a rather unanalysed way, in which, for example, he uses Brentano's expression "given to consciousness." He operates with the idea of a unity of consciousness or the idea of one's consciousness as a whole.

> Our first concept of consciousness, given an empirical psychological slant, covers the whole stream of experience which makes up the individual mind's real unity, together with all aspects that never enter the constitution of this stream.[46]

But he needs to conceptually distinguish consciousness from the various mental acts of which it is constituted and from consciousness in the sense of "inner perception" or the 'intentional relation'. These are both types of mental acts which are parts of consciousness in the first sense.

Consciousness for Husserl is essentially a series of intentional acts and non-intentional experiences called 'sensations'. The intentional acts he structures into three parts: what experiences, the experience itself and what the experience is of, that is, the ego, the experience and the intentional object.

The first of this tripartite structure is the most difficult to grasp, for therein lies a remarkable ambiguity as ego is both part of the world, as a human being and yet it transcends the world as a cognitive centre that possesses or intends the world. This transcendental ego is not separable from individuals; in fact, it is a dimension of every human being. Further, we each have a transcendental ego since we are all intentional and rational beings.[47]

The transcendental ego, the source of all intentional acts, is constituted through time. It has its own identity, which is different from that of the identity of things or states of affairs. The identity of the ego is built up through the flow of experiences and through memory and anticipation.[48]

Although Husserl did not solve the problem of the status of the ego, if indeed it is capable of solution, he has had a great influence on twentieth century philosophy where his concept of intentionality is seen as a way of dispensing with Cartesian dualism of the mind and the world. His concept of the life-world (Lebenswelt) has been used as a way of integrating science with wider forms of human activity. He claims that scientific and mathematical abstraction has its roots in the pre-scientific world, the world in which we all live. This world has its own structure of appearance, identification, evidence and truth, and the scientific world is established on its basis. One of the tasks of phenomenology is to show how the idealized entities of science draw their sense from the life-world.[49]

9.6 Dual Aspect Theory

The dual aspect or double aspect theory enunciates the view that the mental and the physical are two properties of the same underlying reality, perhaps at a level deeper than either the mental or the physical, but which is intrinsically neither mental nor physical.

It is the doctrine that one thing can have two sets of mutually irreducible essential properties, mental and physical, which are distinct modes of a single substance.

A version of the dual aspect theory is sometimes called 'neutral monism'. Monism because it implies that only one kind of entity exists and neutral because it is neither mental nor physical.

The dual aspect theories attempt to do justice to the mental and physical by avoiding extremes of either an overemphasis or underestimation of one or the other. At the same time, it avoids the metaphysical difficulty of the mind-body dualists who have to explain the causal interaction between dissimilar substances. It is at odds with dualism, idealism and materialism, in that it is a denial of both mental and physical substance, but it is at one with those theories, in that, it is monistic rather than dualistic because its thesis is that only one substance and one kind of entity fundamentally exists.

One deficiency of this theory is the uncertainty of what the 'neutral' entities really are and the equal uncertainty as to what mental and physical properties are. In this connection, it may be instructive to examine some of the arguments of the following philosophers: Benedictus (Baruch) de Spinoza, Bertrand Russell and P.F.Strawson.

9.6.1 Spinoza, Baruch (1632-1677)

Central to Spinoza's theory is that only one substance exists in reality and it may be seen in two important ways, that is, the one world which exists and with which we are acquainted has two essential properties or attributes, thought and extension. Spinoza's concept of substance is not too unlike that of Descartes – res cogitans (mind) and res extensa (body). His ontology, however, consists of substances, their attributes and their modes. In *Ethics*, Spinoza defines 'substance' as what is "in – itself and conceived through itself", 'attribute' as that which "the intellect perceived of a substance as constituting its essence"; and 'mode' as "the affections of a substance, or which is in another through which also it is conceived".[50]

So a substance depends upon nothing except itself for its own existence and nature, no other thing can cause a substance to be or to be what it is. First of all what is, is, it exists. Furthermore what is, is all that there is, therefore, there cannot possibly be anything upon which the totality of existence depends for its own existence. It must follow therefore that all there is depends only upon itself for its own existence. For Spinoza, the only plausible candidate for a substance in this sense is reality as a whole, that is the totality of what exists. Spinoza's solution is that the world system as a whole, the one substance, includes its own explanation. Its existence is part of its essence, it is its own reason for being.[51]

While Descartes had recognized in a strict sense that only God is a substance, (in the sense of that which depends on nothing else for its own existence), he also recognized in a second sense that there are two kinds of substances each with its own principal attribute: extended substance, whose only principal attribute is extension; and minds whose only principal attribute is thought. Spinoza, in contrast, maintained that there is only one substance. The one substance is God, which is "a being absolutely infinite, that is, a substance consisting of an infinity of attributes, of which each expresses an eternal and infinite essence". Of these infinite attributes however, humans can comprehend only two: extension and thought.

Reality may be viewed in two ways for Spinoza, depending on whether we are considering it under the attribute of thought or the attribute of extension. If we think of the world as extended then we should call it 'Nature'. If we think of it as conscious we should call it God. Thus God and nature are two terms denoting a single substance which possesses both mental and physical characteristics. In his world system, substance is reality as a whole, the totality of what exists. The one substance includes its own explanation, its own reason for being. Its existence is part of its essence. It depends upon nothing except itself for its own existence and nature. No other thing can cause a substance to be or to be whatever it is, which means if it has a cause it is the cause of itself *(causa sui)*.

There is a folk saying that if you cannot solve a problem, the next best thing is to dissolve it. Perhaps that is Spinoza's solution to the body/mind problem. He subsumes human beings in his metaphysical picture as parts or aspects of the one substance. Just as one substance may be conceived under the attribute of thought and so be known as 'God', and just as one substance may be conceived under the attribute of extension, and so be known as 'nature', so the individual human being may be conceived as mental or physical and so may be thought of as mind or as a body. The mind and body are one and the same individual, which is conceived now under the attribute of thought, and now under the attribute of extension.[52] If there are not two substances, then the question of causal relations or interactions does not arise, and Spinoza's monism has succeeded in bypassing the issue and dissolving the problem.

To understand in what way human beings are conceived as parts or aspects of God, we need to understand what Spinoza thinks God is. God is the one substance. God is identical with the totality of what exists. God is not the transcendental cause of what is. He is what is. God is equivalent to reality as a whole. God is the infinite substance of which all attributes must be ascribed.[53] All things, then are in a sense 'in' God. If there is nothing that is not in God, then Spinoza can be viewed as a pantheist. Spinoza believes that it makes sense to ascribe characteristics like 'infinite' and 'omnipotent' only to the whole of existence. For, if God were not everything, then there would be something which was not God, thus placing a limitation on his infinity. Likewise, unless God is whatever does, or can do, everything or is the system of existence as a whole, then something less than the whole did everything which happens. It is because everything which happens follows necessarily from the nature of God, that the nature of human beings also follows inevitably from God's essence: the essence of man is constituted by certain modes of attributes of God.[54]

In sum, people are not substances, nor are their minds and bodies substances. They are modes of the two attributes of God and He is the only substance.

9.6.2 Strawson

Strawson accepts the concepts of the 'mental' and the 'physical' but is of the view that our use of these two concepts depends upon our being able to use the more primitive or fundamental concept of a 'person'. His acceptance that persons have both mental and physical properties in no way makes him a dualist, in fact, to him mind-body dualism is conceivable only because it is not true, as will emerge later in this discussion.

He speaks of descriptive metaphysics as the actual structure of our thoughts about the world, which he contrasts with revisionary metaphysics which attempts to produce a better structure or an altered conceptual scheme. He claims that his book is an essay in descriptive metaphysics.[55] As we examine his work, we need to assess whether he is altering and revisiting our concept of a person or simply explicating the concept of a person which we already have.

Strawson begins his discourse on persons by pointing out that each of us distinguishes between himself and the states of himself on one hand, and what is not himself or a state of himself on the other. Our world is distinguished into two mutually exclusive parts. This view elicits certain philosophical responses to a number of questions. How is it possible to draw this distinction? How can it be maintained and are we justified in drawing it the way we do? If we think for a moment about our experience, there are many different items included in it. We have various moods, thoughts and emotions, we perceive physical objects and other people. Yet, to have the idea of oneself we must have the idea of the subject of the experiences, of that which has them. How then can a person have an idea of himself as the subject of experience. For to have the idea at all, it seems that it must be an idea of some particular thing of which he has experience, and which is set over against or contrasted with things of which he has experience, but which are not himself. But if it is just an item within his experience of which he has this idea, how can it be the idea of that which has all of his experiences?[56]

This is the problem of the existence of the subject which needs to be addressed. He noted how we ordinarily talk about ourselves or some of the things we ordinarily ascribe to ourselves: thoughts and feelings, perception and memories, as well as location and physical position. The question then arises, why do we ascribe states of consciousness to the very same thing as we ascribe physical characteristic? Strawson frames the question as follows, "That is, we have not only the question: Why are one's states of consciousness ascribed to anything at all? We have also the question: Why are they ascribed to the very same thing as certain corporeal characteristics, a certain physical situation?"[57]

It might be thought that an answer to both these questions could be found in the unique role which each person's body plays in his experience, particularly his perceptual experience. Strawson however, takes us through a thought experiment to demonstrate that the experience of a single subject could be determined by facts about more than one body and illustrate some of the ways in which each person's body occupies a special position in relation to the person's perceptual experience.[58]

> We may summarize such facts by saying that for each person there is only one body which occupies a certain <u>causal</u> position in relation to that person's perceptual experience, a causal position which in various ways is unique in relation to each of the various kinds of perceptual experiences he has; and – as a further consequence – that this body is also unique for him as an <u>object</u> of the various kinds of perceptual experience which he has. We also noted that this complex uniqueness of the single body appeared to be a contingent matter, or rather a cluster of contingent matters; for it

seems that we can imagine many peculiar combinations of dependence and independence of aspects of our perceptual experience on facts about different bodies.[59]

This approach of Strawson, allows him to make the relationship between experience and a particular body a causal one rather than a logical one, and the relation between a particular person and a particular body a contingent one, not a necessary one. By this approach, he has also avoided the problem of 'having' or 'owning' a body which is fraught with philosophical complexities.

There are two other concepts of the self which Strawson considers. The first is the Cartesian, that is, a view credited to Descartes and those who support his views. Basically, as we have seen in section 9.2, this is the view that a person comprises two and only two distinct substances. One is the bearer of mental properties and the other is the bearer of physical properties, and no property of one is a property of the other. In other words, the two substances are of different types, each with its own appropriate types of states and properties, and none of the properties or states can be a property or state of the other. States of consciousness belong to one of these substances and not the other. In sum, one is the bearer of mental properties and the other the bearer of physical properties.

The second concept is the so-called "no-ownership" or "no-subject" doctrine of the self. According to Strawson it may be, though not conclusive, that both Ludwig Wittgenstein and the logical positivist Moritz Schlick embraced the no-ownership theories at one time.[60] The "no-ownership" theorist may be presumed to start his explanation with the facts of the sort which illustrate the unique causal position of a certain material body in a person's experience. The uniqueness of this body is sufficient to give rise to the idea that one's experiences can be ascribed to some particular individual thing, can be said to be possessed by, or owned by, that thing.[61] But it is a mistake to think that one's states of consciousness are 'ascribed' to anything at all – with, perhaps the possible exception of one's body:

> Only those things whose ownership is logically transferable can be owned at all. So experiences are not owned by anything except in the dubious sense of being causally depended on the state of a particular body; this is at least a genuine relationship to a thing, in that they might have stood in it to another thing.[62]

We can now examine Strawson's own definite account of what a person is and how he proposes to deal with anticipated criticism. By the concept of a person Strawson means, "the concept of a type of entity such that both predicates ascribing states of consciousness and predicates ascribing corporeal characteristics, a physical situation etc., are equally applicable to a single individual of that single type."[63]

He reiterates that the concept of a person is 'logically primitive', logically primitive with regard to the concept of the individual consciousness. We could not identify individual consciousness unless we already had the prior notion of the whole person. A person possesses both mental and physical properties, for the concept of a person is logically prior to that of individual consciousness. The thought of a person as comprised of a mental or physical substance is an outgrowth of the thought of oneself as a whole person (See Chap3).

To Strawson, the whole person is the subject of consciousness and it is an error to think that there is pure consciousness:

> ...the concept of the pure individual consciousness – the pure ego - is a concept that cannot exist; or, at least, cannot exist as a primary concept in terms of which the concept of a person can be explained or analysed. It can only exist, if at all, as a secondary, non-primitive concept, which itself is to be explained, analysed, in terms of the concept of a person.[64]

To really appreciate Strawson's concept of person we need to understand the distinction he makes between two kinds of predicates. Firstly, there are those which we ascribe to ordinary physical objects or material bodies: 'M-predicates'. Secondly, there are those which consist of all the other predicates which apply to persons: 'P-predicates'. P-predicates are various, they include things like 'smiling', 'is going for a walk', 'is in pain', 'believes in God' and so on. M-predicates are perhaps more straight forward, and they include things like 'weighs 160 lbs.', 'is in the basement' and so on.[65]

If a P-predicate applies to something, then that thing is conscious whether it directly ascribes states of consciousness such as 'is in pain' or others which are not directly ascribed such as 'is smiling', if the predicate truly applies then what it is ascribed to is capable of consciousness. P-predicates imply possession of consciousness.[66]

It cannot be that we learn how to ascribe P-predicates only from our own case, otherwise that would violate Strawson's thesis. But what that means is that we must be able to make third person ascriptions, which would depend on observing other person's behaviour. *What I have said is that one ascribes P-predicates to others on the strength of observation of their behaviour.*[67]

Strawson has a 'criterion' under which it is appropriate to use a certain predicate. In the case of the third person ascription using P-predicates, the criteria are behavioural. For example, if we take the P-predicate 'is in pain' it is impossible to acquire the use of this expression from one's own case. One needs, in addition, acquaintance with the pain behaviour of others. This provides 'criteria' for the use of 'is in pain'. Strawson is not insensitive to the fact that in certain cases there might be pain but no pain behaviour or pain behaviour but no pain; but this could not always be so otherwise the predicate could have no meaning.[68]

This thinking is the very antithesis of Cartesianism for it makes third person ascriptions conditions for first person ascriptions. In the Cartesian perspective, psychological concepts first take on one's own case then they are extrapolated to third person cases.[69]

In sum, Strawson's philosophy of mind recognizes the use of the two concepts of 'mental' and 'physical' but defends the position that their use depends upon our being able to use the more primitive or fundamental concept of a person. The concept of a person predates or precedes the distinction of 'mental' or 'physical'. Unless we were already seized of the concept of the whole person we could not have consciousness as something distinct from the body. Our making the mental/physical distinction in our thought and language depends logically upon our prior acquaintance with the whole person.

9.6.3 Russell, Bertrand (1872-1970)

To Russell, ultimately or fundamentally, the universe is composed of events spatio-temporal events - with specific durations and extensions. Some of these events are describable in one of two ways, either mental or physical. A physical event is an object of study for physics and a mental event is an object of study for psychology. Like Spinoza, Russell holds that mind and matter are two aspects of some more fundamental underlying reality. He calls his theory 'neutral monism'.

In *An Outline of Philosophy*, Russell outlines his position as follows:

> Popular metaphysics divides the world into mind and mat-

ter, and a human being into soul and body. Some – the materialists – have said that matter alone is real and mind is an illusion. Many – the idealists – have taken the opposite view, that mind alone is real and that matter is an illusion. The view which I have suggested is that both mind and matter are structures composed of a more primitive stuff which is neither mental nor material. This view called 'neutral monism' is suggested by Mach's Analysis of Sensation...[70]

Russell assails the traditional notions of mind and matter with his thesis that *everything in the world is composed of events*.[71] In his account of matter, 'a piece of matter like a space time point, is to be constructed out of events'.[72] Clearly, something is a logical construction if it can be reduced to that thing. This is to say that matter is a logical construction out of events or what matter is may be totally explained using the language of events. By stating that physical objects are logical constructions out of events, Russell wishes to be consistent with physics. He knows fully well, however, that physicists use quite different conceptions of matter for different explanatory purposes.

He is interested principally in the two possible theories used to explain atomic structure, the Heisenberg matrix mechanic and the DeBroglie-Schrodinger wave mechanics theories. These theories logically imply one another and there is no contradiction in them in the mathematical language, but when they are translated into natural language it becomes apparent that they imply rather different ontologies.

On the Heisenberg theory, a piece of matter is a centre for the emission of radiations and although radiations exist, what they radiate from does not exist, like a mathematical point which is postulated for explanatory purposes, like the centre of a geometrician's circle. It follows therefore that matter is as fictitious as the theoretical constructs of the mathematicians. With the concept of radiating energy, we are now much closer to Russell for we have adopted an event ontology.

On the other theory, matter is analysed as wave motions. Matter is now the motions of energy waves, which are themselves nothing over and above the changing state of energy. The result of all this is that wave motions are as much events as radiation, either way Russell's event ontology finds support.

This is an intellectual onslaught on the traditional concept of matter as impenetrable and indestructible and the external causes of sensations. In subatomic physics, particles may collide under certain conditions and annihilate one another and totally cease to exist – so much for the indestructible nature of matter. If these subatomic particles are logical constructions out of events then one can understand their disappearance simply by noting that certain processes or events have ceased. The upshot of this is that Russell, if his theory is valid, has destroyed the idea that matter is a substance because he has demonstrated that matter depends on events. Thus, *matter has ceased to be a 'thing' and has become merely a mathematical characteristic of the relation between complicated logical structures composed of events.*[73] If these arguments are accepted, it would follow that the idea that matter is an indestructible, permanent and substantial cause of our sensations will have to be abandoned.

Russell is no less critical of the traditional concept of mind as he is of matter. He makes the point that the concept of mind is unclear and lacks precise definition. The traditionally accepted distinguishing characteristics of mind viz. perception, introspection, memory and knowledge are defective. Perceptions may be mental but what does their mentality consist of? Their being mental is no more than their capability of entering into causal relations, the nature of which may be studied by psychologists not physicists. If it is accepted that perceptions are mental, there is still uncertainty as to what else may be included under, or excluded from the definition. This is so, because we have no clear definition of 'mental' according to Russell. But whatever else precepts are, they are events which are consistent with his ontology.

Perhaps memories are mental and their existence is bound up essentially with what minds are. Russell, however, would reject this suggestion, for in his view, it is possible to explain what memory is in largely physical terms, in terms of the theory of conditioned reflexes.[74] To Russell then, 'memory' is really a biological concept which may be used to characterize certain living systems, including some that are not minds. He may be right if the word can be used to denote the retention and transmission of, for example, genetic information. Introspection, on Russell's account, collapses into a kind of knowledge, a kind of knowledge by acquaintance or by direct perception. He calls these contents of perception 'sense data', but he is quite clear in his writings that they are neither mental nor physical.[75] However, so far as we may introspectively know what we are perceiving we are directly acquainted with sense data and this is a kind of knowing.

To understand Russell's neutral monism we need to bear in mind that any of the event called 'mental' may also be given a physical description, and described either in terms of psychology or physics. 'Sense data' are not intrinsically mental or physical. They may be either mental or physical, depending on the sorts of relations they enter into with other events. The 'datum' is a datum equally for physics and for psychology, according to Russell, and is "neutral" between mental and physical descriptions. It is the "meeting point" of physics and psychology.[76] Events, in themselves, are neither mental nor physical, as, "'mind' and 'mental' are merely approximate concepts, giving a convenient shorthand for certain approximate causal laws. In a completed science, the word 'mind' and the word 'matter' would both disappear, and would be replaced by causal laws concerning events"[77]

9.7 The Double Aspect Principle

Chalmers' treatment of information brings out a critical link between the physical and the phenomenal. He defines an information space as an abstract space consisting in a number of states and a basic structure of *difference* relation between these states.[78] They are not part of the concrete physical or phenomenal world. But information can be found in both the physical and phenomenal world according to Chambers.[79] Whenever an information space is realized phenomenally, the same information is realized physically. And when an experience realizes an information state, the same information state is relayed in the experience's physical substate.[80] It is not known how these states are coded, and therefore it is not known how the information space is physically realized. Chalmers, however, concludes that:

> It need not be the case that information is encoded *locally*, in a small structure of neighbouring neurons, for example. It is quite possible for information to be physically realized in a holistic fashion, as one finds for example with certain **holographic forms** of information storage. (my emphasis)[81]

He also suggests that this double life of information spaces corresponds to a duality at a deep level, and further that this double realization is the key to the fundamental connection between physical processes and conscious experience.

As a basic principle, information (in the actual world) has two aspects: a physical and a phenomenal aspect. Whenever there is a phenomenal state, it realizes an information state, an information state is also realized in the cognitive system of the brain. Conversely, for at least some physically realized information spaces, whenever an information state is in that space is realized physically, it is also realized phenomenally.[82]

What is going on inside the brain is enough of a mystery that one may be tempted to suppose that consciousness is somewhere "located" in those brain processes, but Chalmers argues that even coming to understand those processes will not alone bring consciousness into the picture. One will never find consciousness within a system on a close examination, and will always be able to understand processing without invoking consciousness. Consciousness is quite distinct from the processing properties of the system.[83]

We need some intrinsic properties to make sense of the physical world, according to Chalmers, and we need to find a place for the intrinsic properties revealed in phenomenology. The suggestion is that information spaces required by physics are themselves grounded in phenomenal or proto-phenomenal properties. Each instantiation of such an information space is in fact a *phenomenal* or proto-phenomenal realization.[84]

The ontology that this approach leads to is truly a double-aspect ontology. According to Chalmers, physics requires information states but cares only about their relations, not their intrinsic nature; phenomenology requires information states but cares only about the intrinsic nature. He postulates a single basic set of information states unifying the two:

> We might say that internal aspects of these states are phenomenal, and the external aspects are physical. Or as a slogan: Experience is information from the inside; physics is information from the outside.[85]

I would venture to suggest that this seems comparable to Bohm's implicate and explicate order. Chalmers agrees that it may also be possible to argue for the superposition principle by applying the double-aspect theory of information and to argue further, that the relevant information embodied in the original physical is also present in the superposition.[86] This theory predicts that even if the world is a giant superposition, there will still be subjects who experience a discrete world.

9.8 Event Ontology/Holographic Reality

Of the theories discussed above, Russell's monism perhaps most closely approximates the holographic approach. The view taken by Russell, as he has stated, is not that of popular metaphysics which divides the world into mind and matter, and a human being into soul and body, but the view that both mind and matter are structures composed of a more primitive stuff which is neither mental nor material. This I equate with the holomovement.

To Russell, everything in the world is composed of events, and physical objects are logical construction out of events. Events are neither mental nor physical. Russell's theory seeks to undermine the idea that matter is a substance, because matter depends on events, and a substance depends upon nothing except itself for its own existence and nature. If matter is not a substance, then it follows that, the idea of matter as being indestructible, permanent and the external cause of our sensations will have to be abandoned. Perhaps, it may be suggested, that the world of event ontology is not unlike a hologram.

If what exists is not fundamentally material, then, in Russell's view it is not fundamentally mental either. Although the traditional view of mental is unclear, according to Russell, he accepts that perceptions are mental; but their being mental is their capacity of entering into causal relations of the sort which may be studied by psychologists. Whatever else perceptions are, for Russell they are events.

> When we have a percept, just what we perceive...is an event occupying part of the region, which for physics is occupied by the brain...what we perceive is part of the stuff of our brains, not part of the stuff of tables, chairs, sun, moon and stars.[87]

Is consciousness, then, part of the stuff of the brain, or is the brain a creation of consciousness?

Keith Floyd, a psychologist at Virginia Intermont College, has pointed out that if concreteness of reality is but a holographic illusion, it would no longer be true to say that the brain produces consciousness. Rather, it is consciousness that creates the appearance of the brain, as well as the body and whatever else around that we interpret as physical.[88]

When tangible reality is like a holographic image, underlying it is a deep order of existence, a vast and more primary level of reality, that gives birth to all objects and appearance of our physical world. This deeper level of reality is the implicit or enfolded order.

If, as Russell postulates, the universe is composed of events, spatio-temporal events, with specific duration and extension, then such a universe must be dynamic and ever-changing; a universe in which subatomic particles may collide and annihilate one another out of existence. If, they are indeed logical constructions out of events, then their disappearance is understandable because certain processes or events have ceased. An *event ontology* entails constant change.

The holographic reality is a world of constant flux, and stable structures of any kind are abstractions; and a describable object, entity or *event* is a derivative of an unknown totality. In the flow of mind and matter, there are not separate substances, but rather different aspects of one whole and unbroken movement (see chapter 5). The world organized in this frequency domain is a world of *no space, no time, just events*, mind and matter are interdependent and correlated but not causally connected.

The dual aspect theory does not assert the falsity of physicalism but it stops short of postulating a non-physical substance to account for the ontology of the mind. It is an elegant way of unifying the radically disparate elements that gives rise to the mind-body problem.

PART FOUR:
Evaluation & Conclusion

Chapter 10

EVALUATION AND SUMMARY

> Up to the 20th century, 'reality' was everything humans could touch, smell, see and hear. Since the initial production of the chart of electromagnetic spectrum in 1930, humans have learned that what they can touch, smell, see and hear is less than one-millionth of reality.
>
> **Buckminster Fuller**[1]

10.1 A Changing World-View

An assertion that we live in a time of considerable and constant change is likely to go unchallenged. But it is the focus of that stated change which is the critical issue and which may be contentious. Popular parlance speaks of the computer age and the "information explosion", of globalization and the global village; these are expressions of external and social changes. But what of the internal and psycho-spiritual changes, that is, our changing belief systems, our new assumptions and changing values? In short, what about our changing world view?

Every society, irrespective of its level of development, whether highly industrialized or underdeveloped, attempts to give explanation of, and almost certifies the nature of things and how they work. Societies do express their world-view, which encapsulates their closely held beliefs and assumptions about the many aspects of human reality, whether through myths or metaphors, or legends or scientific theories. This is their cultural paradigm, which determines not only what they see in the world out there, but how they see it.

It currently seems that there is taking place, in the world of ideas, a realignment of some of the most basic assumptions and beliefs about the way things are.[2] There has been a definite movement away from seeing a mechanistic universe with no mind and will of its own, to seeing an intelligent ever evolving one. A movement from a universe where matter is indestructible, objects are solid, time is linear and space is three-dimensional; a universe which is totally deterministic, where everything is connected through chains of cause and effect and the observer reflects more or less accurately this objective reality of a physical world, which exist independently and objectively, to a world with human beings in the middle of reality, affecting it as they experience it, yet not fully objectively separate from it and playing a participatory role in creating it.

In Chapter 4, we discussed the nature of a paradigm as an accepted 'model' or 'pattern'. It is comprised of our closely held beliefs and assumptions about a particular aspect of human reality. Individuals in the same field of endeavour generally share a paradigm, but each of these paradigms is constructed upon a more general and over-arching cultural paradigm, which is a world-view. Any information or data which does not fit in with our world-view or which runs counter to our fundamental beliefs is likely to be jettisoned because they are necessarily subversive of our basic commitments.

There has been in this century, in the Western world, a prevailing scientific world view. At the heart of this scientific world view has been the scientific method; observation, hypothesis, experiments to test theories, results and conclusions.

Russell E. DiCarlo expresses the view that according to this scientific world view, if something cannot be measured, detected, analysed or studied, then for all intents and purposes it does not exist. It is not scientifically real.[3] Harmon Willis makes a similar point when he states:

> According to the world-view of many, many scientists, what is real is only what is physically measurable. All their scientific concepts and theories are derived from that assumption. That implies the use of the physical senses in the usual sense.[4]

He hastens to add, however, that there are others who would say that there are whole realms of other things, including levels of consciousness, which have not been included in traditional science, but which are real in the sense that they produce real effects.

Science does place an overriding importance on knowledge gained through the five senses, but there are other ways of knowing about reality than simply through the agency of physical sciences. For instance, how do we explain intuition, which often comes in a flash of inspiration? The real question is, how much beyond the five senses are we willing to go, to include other things as being a legitimate order of perception? All of us will resist any change to our own internalized assumptions, so it is difficult to accept as legitimate any form of perception that goes beyond our five senses. Yet, this is what the 'new paradigm science'[5] invites us to do.

In non-ordinary states, the material world is experienced as a dynamic process where there are no solid structures and everything is a flow of energy. Everything is perceived as patterns of energy, and behind the patterns of energy, there are patterns of experience. Reality appears to be the result of an incredibly precise orchestration of experience. This is exactly the picture that is now emerging from various areas of new paradigm science. The world we live in is "virtual reality" created by the technology of consciousness. In this century, quantum-relativistic physics has seriously undermined the belief in the tangible and unambiguous nature of our material reality.[6]

10.2 Quantum Physics

Quantum physics, instead of dealing with observables as objective qualities, deals with observables as processes, affected by operators which are driven by human motivations. The observation itself drastically affects the behaviour of the objects which are the consequences of those operators. The 'observer' in classical theory has been replaced by the 'participator' in the new physics.8

Quantum theory helps us to distinguish reality from naïve objectivity, based upon experiments conducted in the subatomic realm. It only predicts probabilities, for subatomic phenomena cannot be observed directly. If Einstein thought that there was a picturable objectivity, a clear and determinate world which was the only form that physical reality could take, he would have been in error. The famous E.P.R. (Einstein-Podolsky-Rosen) experiment (1935) pointed out that when two quantum entities have interact, they retain a certain power to influence each other simultaneously, however widely they separate.[7] This was thought counterintuitive – 'togetherness in separation' and showed an incompleteness of the theory, but such an effect of non-locality is to be found in nature.[8] Even at the fundamental level, the world does not fall apart but reflects a degree of mutual cohesion.

The philosophical implication of quantum mechanics is that all the things in the universe, including human beings, that appear to exist independently are actually parts of one all-encompassing organic pattern, and that no parts of that pattern are ever really separate from it or from each other.[9] In the words of Henry Stapp, 'The new phenomena entail a peculiar kind of macroscopic wholeness, a strange sort of non-separability of macroscopically separated parts of the universe'.[10]

The empirical evidence provided by quantum phenomena demands a radical revision of our ideas about physical reality. For instance, the whole idea of a causal universe has been undermined by Werner Heisenberg's 'uncertainty principle.'[11] Classical physics is based on the assumption that our reality, independently of us, runs its course in space and time according to strict causal laws; not only can it be observed, unnoticed, as it unfolds, but its future can be predicted by applying these causal laws to its initial conditions.[12] Niels Bohr was succinct when he wrote that quantum mechanics, by its essence contains, 'the necessity of a final renunciation of the classical ideal of causality and a radical revision of our attitude towards the problem of physical reality.'[13]

According to the 'uncertainty principle', we cannot measure accurately, at the same time, both the position and the momentum of a moving particle. The more precisely we determine one of these properties, the less we know about the other. If we precisely determine the position of the particle, then, paradoxically there is nothing that we can know about its momentum. If we precisely determine the momentum of the particle, there is no way to determine its position.[14]

10.3 A Philosophically Coherent World-view

There are many-world views as there are individuals, in the sense that every human being has a set of attitudes on a wide range of fundamental matters. A philosophical world-view, however, must be more than this. It needs to be articulate, systematic and coherent, and at least have a metaphysics which articulates the type of entities constituting the universe, and how they relate to each other, and an epistemology which deals with the assessment of human claims to knowledge of these things or to justify belief in them.

A necessary condition for the coherence of a philosophical world-view is the meshing of its metaphysics and its epistemology. The metaphysics should be capable of understanding the existence and the status of subjects like ourselves, who are capable of deploying the normative procedure of epistemology. And, the epistemology should suffice to account for the capability of human beings to achieve something like a good approximation to knowledge of metaphysical principles, in spite of the spatial and temporal limitations of our experience, and the flaws and distortions of our sensory and cognitive apparatus. This meshing Shimony calls the 'closing of the circle'.[15] But how is the closing of the circle to take place? Are we to expect that the positive outcome of experiments will resolve metaphysical problems? It is factual that elementary particle physics and cosmology seem to be making contribution to our metaphysics but it would be premature to attempt to determine the extent. In any event, experimental results, *per se*, without careful conceptual analysis will not allow any elucidation of metaphysical problems.

Shimony postulates that the conjectured stochastic modification of quantum dynamics would contribute greatly to 'the closing of the circle', for it would explain, in principle, how these are definite outcomes of experiments and these outcomes would provide the evidence upon which the immense super structure of physical theory is based.[16] He concedes, however, that physical outcomes of experiments constitute only a necessary but not a sufficient condition for human experience and inference, and considers that the greatest obstacle 'to closing the circle' is the mind-body problem. Can contemporary particle physics help to solve this problem?

There are certain metaphysical innovations of quantum mechanics of which he speaks: objective indefiniteness, objective chance, objective nonepistemic probability (propensity) and objective entanglement that have obvious analogies to some phenomenological features of mentality.[17] It would, however, be somewhat reckless and risky to predict the significance of these analogies. Abner Shimony would, however, conjecture that a world in which these metaphysical principles hold is somehow more hospitable to a dualism of mind and body than a world governed by the metaphysical principles associated with classical physics, but he does not suggest that quantum mechanics by itself provides a resolution to what Whitehead calls 'the bifurcation of nature."[18] I would go no further than to suggest that particle physics might provide a framework within which to seek a solution to the mind-body problem, for the definite physical outcomes of experiments, so far, do not provide a sufficient condition for human experience and inference.

10.4 Organic and Inorganic

In seeking a solution to the mind-body problem, I would explore the relationship between the organic and the inorganic. Traditionally, we separate the world of our experience into organic and non-organic. Organic means living things, and living things process information and respond to it. Non-living things do not have that capacity, and consequently cannot process information and respond to it. But is this dichotomy based on a conceptual prejudice? Physics study the non-living but there is mounting evidence in quantum mechanics which suggest that subatomic "particles" constantly appear to be making decisions based on decisions made elsewhere as demonstrated by the spin correlation experiment.[19] They seem to know instantaneously what decisions are made elsewhere. But a particle is a thing as classically defined and as such cannot process information. A thing has location, it is either here or there, it cannot be both here and there at the same time. Or is it that a subatomic particle is not a thing at all, such as a dust particle? Quantum mechanics views a subatomic particle as "tendencies to exist" or "tendencies to happen". It also suggests that particles may be related with other particles in a dynamic and intimate way that coincides with the definition of organic.[20]

Here the well known double-slit experiment is instructive.[21] The experiment is set up with one side of the double slit screen open, through which a photon is fired and the spot on the photographic plate which the photon lands is marked. It is noticed that the photon lands on an area that would be dark if the second slit were open. That is, if the second slit were open no photons would be recorded in that area. Then, the experiment is repeated with both slits open, now no photons are recorded in the area where the photons hit in the first experiment. Did the photon in the first experiment "know" that the second slit was not open, for the information seems somehow to have been transmitted? Although there does not seem to be a ready answer to this question, some of the speculative answers are fascinating. E. H. Walker speculates that the photons may be conscious.[22] Another speculation on the "knowing" might be to call it synchronicity. Jung's "acausal connecting principle" refers to a non-causal relationship linking two events together in a meaningful way. But meaningful coincidences are unthinkable as pure chance; the more they multiply the greater and more exact the correspondence is;[23] nor does it support hylozoism – the doctrine that all matter has life?[24]

Photons, which are energy, do appear to process information and do act accordingly. Are they therefore organic? And are they conscious? Bacteria and viruses, apparently, have memory and can communicate information to succeeding generations. Are they conscious?

Zukav argues that, according to Western thought, the world has only two essential aspects, one of which is matter-like, the other of which is idea-like. The matter-like aspect is associated with the external world, most of which is the inorganic stuff like rocks and stones and lifeless things, all of which are inanimate stuff and unresponsive.[25] The idea-like aspect is associated with our subjective experiences and abstract thoughts. The philosophies which expound these two aspects are Materialism and Idealism (see sections 9.3 and 9.4). The tension between these two aspects has been fundamental in the philosophy of mind.

The fundamental theoretical quantity in quantum mechanics is the wave function, which is a dynamic description of possible occurrence. But what does it really describe? Is it the physicists' description of reality and is it the best possible description? The crucial question is which of the two aspects does the wave function represent? According to the orthodox view of quantum mechanics, as expounded by Stapp, the wave function represents something that partakes of both idea-like and matter-like characteristics, a view with which Zukav agrees.[26]

If the wave function is thought by physicists to be a complete description of reality, and since that which the wave function describes is idea-like, organic and inorganic, then physical reality must be both idea-like and matter-like and cannot be completely substantive (made of stuff) as it may appear to be. It would, therefore, seem that there is a fusion of the organic and inorganic, and our attempt to separate them are merely constructs designed to facilitate the development and articulation of knowledge. If this is accepted, then it is plausible that consciousness, at the most fundamental levels, is a quantum process.

Roger Penrose, the Oxford mathematician and physicists, had suggested, in the *Emperor's New Mind* (1989), that consciousness is created by some mysterious quantum mechanical phenomenon that takes place in brain cells. He expressed the view that consciousness is not computable, and if consciousness is not computable, then whatever processes in the brain that gives rise to consciousness must also be non-computable.

According to Penrose:

> If this is the case, and consciousness is not computable, then the brain must incorporate a physical process that simply is not covered by the known laws of physics. Consciousness must be rooted in new physics, that is, in laws not yet discovered or formulated and perhaps one ought to search for them in the underworld of quantum mechanics.[27]

If we can experience the most fundamental functions of our psyche, and if they are quantum in nature, then it is possible that the ordinary conception of space and time might not apply to them at all. This seems to be the case in dreams, in LSD trippers and NDE, where time and space collapse.

It has become apparent that consciousness has a very fundamental role in the cosmos. It is not to be regarded, according to Grof, as a side product of inert and inactive matter that somehow appeared in the universe, more or less, accidentally after many millions of years of evolution.[28]

Emerging from various areas of new paradigm science is a picture that consciousness and creative intelligence permeate all of nature and the entire universe has an underlying master blueprint. In transpersonal states of mind, it is even possible to subjectively experience identification with other people, with animals, with plants and even organic materials and processes. It appears then that whatever can be experienced in the every day state of consciousness as an object, has in non-ordinary state of consciousness a subjective correlate.[29] Consciousness is not an epiphenomenon of the neurophysiological processes of the brain or a by-product of matter, according to Grof, but a primary attribute of existence. It is the material reality which is a creation of consciousness. Quantum-relativistic physics has seriously undermined the belief in the tangible and unambiguous nature of our material reality.[30] Grof maintains that modern consciousness research actually has brought ample evidence that there are other experiential dimensions of reality with specific and demonstrable characteristic, and, in his words, material reality is just one "holographic cosmic channel". There are other 'channels' that are equally real or unreal as this one.[31]

10.5 Holographic Approach

It is in this intellectual climate, and against this changing view of reality, emerging as it does from various areas of new paradigm science that invited a holographic approach in this presentation. The theories of neuroscientist, Karl Pribram, and physicist, David Bohm, when taken conjointly, appear to account for transcendental experience and some paranormal events. Their combined theories suggest that altered states of consciousness may be due to a literal attunement to an invisible matrix which generates reality. This process might enable interaction with reality at a primary level, thus accounting for time distortion, rapid learning and the experience with the universe as related by NDE. The hologram is a starting point for a new description of reality, that is, the enfolded or implicate order. Classical reality has focused on secondary manifestations, that is, the unfolded or explicate order, not the source. From this perspective, what we have is a brain employing a holographic process to abstract from a holographic domain, which is a world organized in the frequency domain, a world of no space, no time, just events. Transcendental experiences, such as NDE or OBE, suggest that there is access to the frequency domain which is the primary reality. But inherent in the holographic system is a deep appreciation for non-rational modalities of experience and expression which multiply the difficulties of explanation. An explanation of holographic theory must, perforce, be given entirely in word symbols which of necessity are contextually narrow and confining in scope, and this cannot communicate the ineffable. Our very language, belief system and thought patterns inhibit our understanding ourselves or the universe in a holographic or holistic way.[32]

The holographic paradigm is a system from which arise explanations from various events and activities which we associate with life and consciousness. But it is merely a static recording of movement and abstraction of the holomovement which is the ground of all manifest entities. Bohm prefers to use the term holomovement to describe the holonomic and dynamic nature of reality. The holomovement comprises two coexisting, interpenetrating orders of reality: the physical manifestation of energy in bounded time and space, that is the material world as we perceive it; and, a physically transcendent order of pure energy which Bohm calls the implicate order.[33] The holomovement is a dynamic phenomenon out of which all forms of the material universe flow. The aim of Bohm's approach is to study the order enfolded in this holomovement, not by dealing with the structure of objects but rather with the structure of movement, taking into account both the unity and dynamic nature of the universe. Space and time, too, emerge as forms flowing out of the holomovement. Bohm also regards consciousness as an essential feature of the holomovement. To him, mind and matter are interdependent and correlated but not causally connected.[34]

As the frequency domain is "timeless" and "beyond time and space" the holomovement theories appear to make more plausible psychic and mystical phenomena that transcend the usual space-time relationship. It, therefore, seems a natural tool for the exploration and investigation of NDE. It is not surprising, therefore, that Kenneth Ring was seduced to walk this path. Ring's hypothesis seeks to explain the phenomenon of NDE, using some postulates of holographic theory:

> The core experience of NDE reflects psychological events with a shift in levels of consciousness. In the intermediate stage a transition takes place from a state of consciousness rooted in 'this world' sensory impressions to one that is sensitive to the realities of another dimension of existence. When consciousness begins to function independent of the physical body, it becomes capable of awareness of another dimension...Aspects of the core experience can be interpreted in scientific terms if one uses some of the postulates of holographic theory...The act of dying involves a gradual shift of consciousness from the ordinary world of appearances to a holographic reality of pure frequencies... So long as one remains tied to the body and to its sensory modalities, holographic reality can only be an intellectual construct. When one comes close to death one experiences it directly.[35]

Ring's attempt to articulate a scientific framework for understanding near-death (see section 6.3) by using a holographic approach is met with fierce resistance from Stephen Braude.[36] Braude does not share the general enthusiasm for Ring's holographic approach and castigates him for two sorts of errors:

(a) Those inherent in any attempts to reduce reality to nothing more than a frequency domain, and

(b) Those specific to particular application of the holographic paradigm.[37]

Braude's first assault on the holographic model is that it was both reductionist and atomistic. This is based on his interpretation of the model that:

> Nature reduces to, or is composed essentially of, frequencies forming various interference patterns (the 'primary' level of reality). These frequencies, moreover, are atomic or basic. In the sense that they are the building blocks for our familiar perceptual and experiential reality.[38]

Let us deal with the first complaint. It is, in my view, an over simplification or exaggeration to suggest that the model reduces "reality to nothing more than a frequency domain". Pribram used the concept of the hologram to develop an understanding of the distributed nature of memory and vision and the brain's mechanism for information storage and retrieval. He says:

> I developed a precisely formulated theory based on known neuroanatomy and known neurophysiology that could account for the brain's distributed memory store in holographic terms...Essentially, the theory reads that the brain at one stage of processing performs its analysis in the frequency domain. This is accomplished at the junctions between neurons not within neurons...Aside from their anatomical and physiological specifications, a solid body of evidence has accumulated that the auditory, somatosensory, motor and visual systems of the brain do in fact process, at one or several stages, input from the senses in the frequency domain.[39]

Braude offers no evidence to support his contention that, in the model the frequencies are atomic or basic in the sense that they are building blocks for our perceptual and experiential reality.

Modern physics has shown that the concept of the 'basic building blocks' of matter is no longer tenable. All the 'elementary particles' turn out to be composite structures themselves; nature cannot be reduced to fundamental entities but has to be understood entirely through self-consistency. The universe is seen as a dynamic web of interrelated events. This approach has been called the 'bootstrap' approach in particle physics originated by Geoffrey Chew.[40] The bootstrap philosophy not only abandoned the idea of fundamental building blocks of matter, but also accepts no fundamental entities whatsoever, no fundamental laws, equations or principles.

The bootstrap picture of an interconnected web of relations in which particles are dynamically composed of one another, each of them involving the others, contrary to Braude's thinking, shows great similarities to holographic models. Subatomic particles are dynamic patterns which can only be described as a realistic framework where space and time are fused into a four-dimensional continuum.[41] Ring makes reference to this fourth dimension, thus:

> When consciousness begins to function independent of the physical body, it becomes capable of awareness of another dimension. Let us for ease of reference call it now, a fourth dimension.[42]

The limitations of the hologram analogy (and an analogy is all that it is) was clearly recognized by David Bohm who preferred to use the term holomovement to describe the holonomic and dynamic nature of reality.[43]

Braude's second foray is that the model is committed to two principles:

(a) That there is a preferred parsing of nature into atoms or elements (the frequency domain), items in principle identifiable independently of any description of the ordinary reality which the elements compose; and

(b) That the objects, events, and states of affairs of our familiar reality are simply ordered arrangements or structures mathematically transforms of 'primary' structures composed of these basic particulars.[44]

Once again, Braude does not offer any evidence to explain or justify these conclusions. Pribram, however, does remind us that perhaps the most profound insight gained from holography is the reciprocal relationship between the frequency domain and the image/object domain which is our familiar reality. Images are mental consciousness. They do result from processes involving the brain and the senses in the interactions with the environment and the objects of the reality of appearances. The process of image construction does not involve a reciprocal stage, a transformation into the frequency (holographic) domain. This domain is characteristic not only of brain processing but of physical reality as well. Bohm refers to this as the implicate order.[45] The fact that the holographic domain is reciprocally related to image/object domain does imply that mental operations (such as mathematics) reflect the basic order of the universe.

Braude argues that the elements of an object, event or state of affairs cannot be specified independently of some criteria of relevance. But since these criteria are obviously context-relative features of nature, objects, events etc., they are not constructs out of logically more basic elements. Rather, the elements are abstractions rendered appropriate within a context. Consequently, the holographic model cannot even be applied in those cases where it allegedly has the most plausibility, that is, memory and perception, much less in cases of NDE. According to Braude, thoughts or mental states cannot be mere constructs out of more fundamental elements. The elements of a mental state exist only relative to some context in which a certain parsing or parsings (but not others) will count as appropriate.[46] Braude's argument may very well be valid, but it is a misplaced argument. Where does the model state that objects, events, etc., are constructs out of logically more basic elements? There have been other researches which have supported Pribram's theory of the brain as a hologram: Paul Pietsch (1981) *Experiments with Salamander's brains* and the Fourier 'transforms' which were equations developed to convert images into waves forms and back again.[47] The Fourier 'transforms' suggested that the visual system worked as a kind of frequency analysis. Since frequency is a measure of the number of oscillations a wave undergoes per second, there is a strong suggestion that the brain might be functioning as a hologram does.[48]

During the 1960's, research had shown that each brain cell in the visual cortex was geared to respond to different patterns, some brain cells fire when the eyes see a horizontal line, others fire when the eyes see a vertical line, and so on. Consequently, many researchers concluded that the brain takes input from highly specialized cells called feature detectors, and then somehow fit them together to provide us with our visual perception of the world.

Russell and Karen DeValois (1979) had some reservations about these conclusions and decided to test other assumptions by utilizing the Fourier's equations to convert plaid and checkerboard patterns into simple wave forms. They then tested to see how the brain cells in the visual cortex responded to these new wave-form images. What they discovered was that the brain cells did not respond to the original patterns, but to Fourier's translation of the patterns. This led to one ineluctable conclusion, that is, the brain was using Fourier mathematics, the same mathematics holography employed to convert visual images into Fourier language of wave-forms. Although the DeValoises' experiment did not prove conclusively that the brain behaved as a hologram, it certainly provided corroborating evidence that Pribram's theory was correct.[49] Finally, Ring is chided for not explaining what are thought-structures and interacting thought structures forming interference patterns.[50] But if Braude is correct, would this not be consistent with the reductionistic and atomic criticism which he leveled at the model, for in the original formulation of atoms and the void we were never told what such atoms were or what they could be, we were told only of their relationship to one another. It was much later that we were told of their structure.

Braude is of the view that partisans of the holographic paradigm seem unaware that the construction of an image by means of laser illumination of interference patterns is quite different from a construction of a meaningful image (or image of something).[51] I am not surprised at this conclusion and this simplistic view which he attributes to them, for he does not seem to understand the use of the model, and this, to some extent, is because he is a literalist. Only a literalist would say "what is true of the photo is true of anything at all that represent something".[52]

Braude pairs Ring and Pribram, and metes out to them the same treatment, because Ring's analysis of NDE is modeled after Pribram's holographic analysis of cognitive phenomena, and he accuses both of them of making the same mistakes. But Ring's use of the model goes beyond perception and memory into a holographic universe which treats with transpersonal consciousness. It is somewhat curious, therefore, that Braude at no time discusses or alludes to David Bohm, one of the architects of the holographic model of reality, which Ring adopts when he speculates about a fourth dimension and transpersonal consciousness.

10.6 A Holographic Model of Transpersonal Consciousness

Robert Anderson in his article, "A Holographic Model of Transpersonal Consciousness," distinguishes between personal or individual consciousness and transpersonal or unitive consciousness. Personal consciousness is the experience of multiplicity of things being discrete and separate while transpersonal consciousness is characterized by the experience of unity, the absence of all multiplicity and the complete oneness of everything. In this latter state of consciousness, the boundaries between objects dissolve and the separate and discrete merge into each other, the boundary between the personal self and the external world disappears, and one experiences an all encompassing unity.[53]

Anderson makes the point that it is hard for most Western researchers to see how these two concepts, which are often defined in terms of each other's negation could be anything but mutually exclusive. Furthermore, some of them dismiss transpersonal and cosmic consciousness as non veridical and hallucinatory experience, while some in the Eastern tradition see personal consciousness as mere illusion. In his view, the idea of the hologram provides a concept that can bridge the gap between personal and transpersonal consciousness, though at first, they may appear to be unresolvable.[54]

Experiments suggest how the model of the hologram can prove a link between the two kinds of consciousness. For example, in the double slit experiment described above, each photon seems to contain information about the existence of the slit it does not go through, so that its trajectory taken along with that of the other proton will make up the appropriate distribution.[55] The 'quantum' context thus calls for a new kind of description that does not imply the separability of the 'observed object' and 'observing instrument'. The experimental conditions and the meaning of the experimental results have now to be one whole, in which analysis into autonomously existent elements is not relevant.[56] Also in the E.P.R. paradox (discussed above), where two particles first interact, then go their separate ways after the interaction, this measurement of the momentum of one of the particles will determine a correlated state of momentum for the other particle. A crucial question arises as to what kind of relationship exists between them, bearing in mind, that by hypothesis they no longer causally affect each other. In short, what kind of acausal connection could there be that would account for a change in the other, for it cannot be explained in terms of the propagation of signals as chains of causal influence. An answer can be forthcoming if the structure of the universe is holographic as Bohm postulates, for the whole universe is enfolded in every sub-region and its entire explicate structure encoded in its every part. But in addition to the explicate order of multiplicity, there exist the implicate order of undivided wholeness where everything implicates everything (see Chapter 6).

According to Anderson, with reference to the double-slit experiment described earlier, the photon does contain information. The information is enfolded within its implicate order. Moreover, the photon is what it is and where it is by virtue of its relation to everything else. Similarly, in the case of the E.P.R. example, the momenta of each of the two "particles" are independent on the implicate level, thus a determination of one of them puts a limit on the possibility of the other, though they do not interact causally.[57]

Anderson draws a parallel between the distinction Bohm makes between the explicate and implicate order, and the distinction he makes between the personal and transpersonal consciousness. He correlates the personal consciousness to the explicate order and the undivided wholeness to transpersonal consciousness which is the experience of the all-encompassing unity.

Anderson also maintains that the brain is holographic in nature, both in the implicate and explicate orders. When the brain is no longer distracted by the flow of images and becomes quiet as in meditation, and it seems less active, there is a resonance which takes place between the brains explicate holographic structure and the implicate holographic structure. This resonance is made possible by the structural similarity between the holographic structure of the brain and that of the universe. This resonance allows for the transference of information from the implicate order to the explicate order. Since the entirety of the explicate order is encoded throughout the implicate order, the resonance provides personal consciousness with access to all knowledge (a claim made by many NDE'ers).

Anderson concludes his discourse on the holographic model, by indicating that it also provides an insight into the reasons why an expanded state of consciousness is one of the more profound experiences an individual can have. In this connection, we must consider what it is about an entity that would make us believe that it is conscious. Generally speaking, consciousness seems to be related to the complexity of an entity and the fact that it has a nervous system. We would not, for instance, consider rocks to be conscious, for they do not apparently respond intentionally or purposefully to their environment and they lack a nervous system. Anderson applies the rule "the more complex the nervous system, the higher the level of consciousness."[58] This seems to be justified because human beings appear to have a higher level of consciousness than animals lower in the phylogenetic scale. Moreover, he asserts, all be it tentatively, that human consciousness requires a holographically organized sheet of neural fibers, and that personal consciousness is localized in the cerebral cortex of the brain.[59] Holographic complexity, is assumed by Anderson, to be required for consciousness. If this is so, since the universe is holographically complex, he reasons that the universe may be conscious on the implicate level.

When persons report transpersonal experience, as is frequent in NDE cases, they often insist that the experience is ineffable and they cannot express it in words. According to Anderson's model, since the nearly infinite complexity in the implicate order cannot possibly be encoded in the explicate order, and language is an explicate phenomenon, for something to be sayable, it must be capable of being coded into the brain as explicate. This is offered as an explanation for the inability to express the experience of wholeness with everything.

Anderson has adopted both Bohm's version of "new" physics and the hologram theory of the brain, in the holographic resonance model, to account for the relation between personal and transpersonal consciousness. A weakness in the model is that complexity, *per se*, cannot be taken as an index of consciousness. Further, Bohm's model makes it clear that it is impossible to draw a sharp distinction between animate and inanimate matter – they have a common ground in the holomovement. Both the double-slit experiment and the E.P.R. paradox cited above suggest that particles may be conscious and seem to respond intentionally though they lack a nervous system. On the other hand, however, the presentation does demonstrate the usefulness of a holographic approach as a conceptual tool for investigating transpersonal or non-ordinary states of consciousness.

Chapter 11

CONCLUSION

Near-Death Experience is an authentic phenomenon in need of explanation. It is not a new phenomenon. It had occurred over many generations and in many countries. Published works, theses, and articles written on NDE, reveal a most impressive degree of consistency and universality of the core experience.

The aim of this book has been to explore the relationship between NDE as a transpersonal phenomenon and our current understanding of reality – an understanding which now requires a deep revision of our concept of the universe and our relation to it, consequent on the teachings of modern physics.

The arguments offered in this presentation could have been phrased more generally, in terms of pre-philosophic concepts or psychology, by speaking of the inner self being able to leave the body and to undertake journeys and return; and the out-of-body experience as simply the recalling and telling of the experiences of those journeys. But no attempt has been made to draw parallels between the new physics and mysticism, nor has there been any suggestion that the transpersonal experience of NDE opens a window through which we can peek into the after-life, or that the experience proves the existence of an after-life.

The holographic approach of Pribram and Bohm has been used in tandem, as a working assumption and a conceptual tool for investigating the transpersonal or non-ordinary states of consciousness of NDE. There is a tendency in Western ontology to perceive a world divided into individual and separate things: a world divided into animate and inanimate, but the distinction fades as we gain greater understanding of the nature of reality as depicted by the world of quantum mechanics.

In contradistinction to the world of separateness is the holographic world which treats the whole universe as a dynamic web of inseparable energy patterns. A world in which matter appears to be completely mutable, and all particles can be transmuted into other particles, particles which can be created from energy and can vanish into energy.

The value of the hologram in this context, as an instrument, is that it may bring to our attention in a sensibly perceptible way, a new perspective to order - implicate and explicate order. The phenomenon of NDE has certainly created a wave of wonderment and innumerable questions: does NDE grant us a fleeting access to a view of the after-life or to an extra-dimensional realm of reality? Can scientific methods be applied to find answers to these questions or do we need to conduct our investigations through a totally different system such as mysticism? Answers to these questions may not as yet have been provided, but one thing seems clear; with advancing scientific research, the Newtonian mechanistic model of the universe is inadequate in the explanation it offers of our understanding of reality, and as such, can offer no acceptable explanation of NDE. Consequently, I have sought to substitute a holographic model, which affords a scientific interpretation of the core experience. This approach is consistent with the view that paradigms in science are working models that organize existing observation, and when they are unable to account for or accommodate new knowledge they have to be replaced by more adequate ones. A world-view will last as long as it can adequately explain reality. Where problems accumulate and the world-view cannot be expanded to accommodate them, it will gradually be abandoned, sometimes even before a completely satisfactory one replaces it (see Chapter 5).

NDE is interesting because it challenges the materialistic world-view that all is physical. Moreover, according to some materialists, human beings are merely body and brain. When biological death occurs, the body disintegrates and with it the human consciousness dissipates. But modern research seems to suggest that consciousness is non-local and can violate time and space. If this is so, then NDE is believable.

The study of the brain cannot completely account for consciousness, thus, there must be something about it that is over and above the body and brain. Wilder Penfield (1978) expressed the view that "the brain has not explained the mind fully," and pointed out that one should not pretend to draw a final scientific conclusion in man's study of man, until the nature of the energy responsible for the mind-action is discovered, which he felt one day would be.[1]

The idea that consciousness is non-local, and can function independently and outside of the body, is not a new one. Much has been written, in traditional texts and reports of scholars, that Shamans can bilocate themselves, move in space, and can go far and return in an instant. The Shamanic initiation makes the trainee simply aware that the mind and consciousness are outside and above, and have always been so.[2] The idea of the separation of consciousness from the physical body is also found in Egyptian manuscripts that deal with the *ka* or double, that can separate from the physical body and travel at will (Mishlove 1993: 88).

There is now rapidly growing evidence concerning the interaction of the material and the unmanifest, comprising empirically validated data of human consciousness functioning "independent of a physical substrate – a source of mind without brain" (Wade 1966: 18). In dealing with the relation of consciousness to matter and the brain, philosophers seem to assume that it is the mind, rather than matter, that is philosophically problematic. This may be so, if we think of matter along Newtonian lines. But Newtonian conception of matter is today viewed as inadequate, if not incorrect, and the conception of quantum mechanics, as currently conceived, has replaced it. One of the philosophical consequences of this, is a changed concept of matter.

Apart from any natural scepticism and the fear of accepting, as authentic, information which may not be at present empirically verifiable, I have found no genuine grounds for dismissing NDE as hallucination or mere illusions. Whether there can be a mind-split, in which the mind splits off from the brain, must be left an open question, at this stage, as the evidence is insufficient to make a positive determination either way.

Logical positivism is no longer the predominant philosophical paradigm, as it was in the first half of the 20th century, but there remain vestiges of its principle of verification which had led us into a philosophical cul-de-sac. During the tenure of its predominance, disparaging attitudes emerged towards metaphysics, where metaphysical assertions were regarded as tantamount to philosophical nonsense, cognitively vacuous, and pronouncements about reality inherently meaningless because they were not verifiable (Aune, 1995).[3]

Today, many thinkers have come to realize that there are many things which are not now verifiable, which are not now conceivable, but may yet come to be understood. As philosophers seek "eternal truths", our enquiries may take us outside the realms of both experience and science, but philosophy should not take refuge in reduced ambitions. We can form ideas of phenomena which we do not now know how to detect. To illustrate, once the conception of a new physical particle is formed, defined in terms of a set of properties, those properties may then allow experiments to be devised which will permit their detection. Leucippus and Democritus (460 BC), the Greek philosophers, who were called the atomists, are a stout example to support this point of view. It was centuries later, after they had postulated the concept of the atom that atoms were actually detected. In fact, it was not until 1905 when Einstein published his papers on particles suspended in a liquid, that the individuality of atoms were established (Hawkins, 1988:64).

Only the most dogmatic of verificationists will deny the possibility of forming objective concepts that reach beyond our current capacity to verify. If we have departed from strict empiricism, it is because it leaves the world unexplained. We can know that something exists without knowing its nature.

The holographic paradigm, at present, offers the best available model, consistent with a changing world-view, to understand the phenomenon of NDE. It may be speculative, but then perhaps nothing short of radical speculation will give us hope of coming up with any candidates for the 'truth'. We must distinguish between the method of science and the domain of science. As such, we ought not to be reticent to speculate about possibilities outside the paradigm of science, if it forces us into relatively inflexible parameters. So ably put by William Stanley Jevons (1877: 768):

> True science will not deny the existence of things because they cannot be weighed or measured. It will rather lead us to believe that the wonders and subtleties of possible existence surpass all that our mental powers allow us clearly to perceive. We must ignore no existence whatsoever. We may variously interpret or explain its meaning and origin, but if a phenomenon does exist, it demands some kind of explanation.[4]

After all, the role of philosophy is not to propound or advocate scientifically refined and accepted hypotheses, but rather to enrich and make fecund a metaphysics which will be the mother of theories and ideas for the development of knowledge.

NOTES AND REFERENCES

Introduction

1. I have a parallel between NDE and consciousness as expressed by David Chalmers. Chalmers, David J. *The Conscious Mind.* Introduction xiii, Oxford University Press (1996)

2. *Ibid.* xiv.

3. Tarnas, Richard, *Towards a New World View - The Western World View: Past, Present and Future.* Ed. Russell E. DiCarlo. Erie, PA: Epic Publishing. (1996), p.21.

4. Wade, Jenny. *Change of Mind: A Holonomic Theory of Consciousness.* New York, State University Press, (1996), p.8

Chapter 1. NEAR-DEATH EXPERIENCE (NDE).

1. Jung, Carl G. *Memories, Dreams, Reflections*. New York: Vintage Books (1961), pp. 295-6.

2. Kubler-Ross, Elizabeth. *On Death and Dying*. New York: Collier Books, MacMillan Publishing Co. (1970), 2. See also *The Tibetan Book of the Dead*. (ed). Evans Wentz. Oxford: Oxford University Press. (1960), p.27 "The astrologer also declares what kind of evil spirit caused the death, for in popular belief - as also among the Celtic peoples of Europe - no death is natural, but it is always owing to interference by one of the enumerable death- demons."

3. *Ibid*. p.246

4. Osis, K. and E. Heraldsson. *At the Hour of Death*. (1977) New York: Hastings House Book Publishers. See "Appendices". pp. 223 et. seq. Also "Introduction". p. xii.

5. *Ibid.*, p. xv.

6. Ring, Kenneth. *Life at Death*. New York: Quill. (1980), p.32.

7. Greyson, B. and C. Flynn. Eds. "The Near-Death Experience Scale: Construction, Realibility and Validity" *Near-Death Experience: Problems, Prospects, Perspectives*. Springfield, Illinois: Charles C. Thomas. pp.45-62.

8. Noyes R. and R Kletti. "Depersonalization in the Face of Life Threatening Danger: A Description" (1976), Psychiatry 35, pp. 174-184.

9. *Op. cit.*, Ring (1980), p. 207.

10. Devereux, Jann Marie. Unpublished Thesis: *Living Life After Encountering the Light - Phenomenological Exploration of the Meaning of a Near-Death Experience*. January (1995), p. 31.

11. Ring, Kenneth. *Heading Towards Omega*. New York: Quill. (1984), p. 234.

12. *Ibid*, p. 235.

13. Sabom, Michael, B. *Recollections of Death*. New York: Harper & Row. (1982), p. 3.

14. *Ibid.* p. 2

15. Zaleski, Carol. *Other World Journeys*. Oxford: Oxford University Press. (1987), p. 108

16. *Op. cit.*, Sabom. p. 9

17. *Ibid.* p. 55

18. *Ibid.* p. 56

19. *Ibid.*, p.6

20. *Ibid.*, p.83

21. *Ibid.*, p.184

22. *Ibid.*, p.185

23. Penfield in *The Mystery of the Mind* (1978) thought that the diencephalon was the seat of the "Highest Brain Mechanism". He postulated that the anatomic brain was in reality two separate but related units. One unit he termed the "Computer Mechanism" located in the parietal lobes, the other unit the "Mind Mechanism" located in the frontal and temporal lobes, the centers of both units were separately represented in the diencephalon. These theories proposed by Sherington, Penfield and others at least established a framework in which to consider the NDE as a possible "out of body event" – a *mind-brain split* – (the "mind" and the "brain"). Could the near-death crisis event some how trigger a transient splitting of the mind from the brain in many individuals? Could the "separated self" in the NDE represent the detached mind, which according to Penfield is capable of experiencing contentment, happiness, love, compassion and awareness, while the unconscious physical body represented the remains of the "computer", a lifeless automaton? Of course, if there is a mind-brain split, it may very well be that it is the mind that retains the memory and not vice versa. Op. cit., Sabom. pp. 183-184.

24. *Ibid.*, p.186

25. *Op.cit.*, Ring (1985) p.252

26. *Ibid.*, Ring (1985) p.255

27. Professor Ring borrows the term *Homo Noeticus* from John White. John White holds the view that a new form of human life is appearing on the planet, and he states in part – Homo Noeticus is the name I give to the emerging form of humanity. Noeticus is a term meaning the study of consciousness, and that activity is a primary characteristic of members of the new breed. Because of their deepened awareness and self-understanding, they do not allow the traditionally imposed forms, controls and institutions of society to be barriers of their full development. Their changed psychology is based on expression of feelings, not suppression. The motivation is cooperative and loving, not competitive and aggressive. Their logic is multi-level/integrated/ simultaneous, not linear/sequential/either-or. Their sense of identity is all embracing – collective, not isolated individual. Their psychic abilities are used for benevolent and ethical purposes, not harmful and immoral ones. The conventional ways of society don't satisfy them. The search for new ways of living and new institutions concern them. They seek a culture whose institutions are based on love and wisdom, a culture that fulfils the perennial philosophy. See John White in *Jesus, Evolution and the Future of Humanity. Part I - Science of the Mind.* September (1981), pp. 8-17 at p.14. See also p.256.

28. See Footnote #27 above.

29. *Op.cit.*, Ring *Heading Towards Omega.* (1984), p. 252.

30. Morse, Melvin. *Closer to the Light.* (1990), p. 21.

31. See Kastelbaum R. Book Review of "Transformed by the Light." *Journal of Near-Death Studies* (1993), pp. 59-65.

32. Blackmore, Susan. *Dying to Live.* NY: Prometheus Books (1993), p. 253.

33. *Ibid.*, p. 263. It is interesting to note that recently there have been reports that Susan Blackmore has taken a "don't know" stance with respect to her former conclusions about psi and metaphysical consciousness (Skeptical Investigators Website) 1/21/2005

    She has been credited as saying in one of her recent articles that at last I've done it. I've thrown in the towel. She wrote

    > "Come to think of it, I feel slightly sad. It was just over thirty years ago that I had the dramatic out-of-body experience that convinced me of the reality of psychic phenomena. *Just a few years of careful experiments changed all that.* I found no psychic phenomena...so became a sceptic. (My emphasis)
    >
    > So why didn't I give up them? There are lots of bad reasons. Admitting you are wrong is always hard, even though it's a skill every scientist needs to learn. And starting again as a baby in a few field is a daunting prospect.
    >
    > So is losing all the status and power of being an expert. I have to confess I enjoyed my hard won knowledge.
    > ...None of it ever gets anywhere. That's good enough reason for leaving.
    >
    > But perhaps the real reason is that I am just too tired - and tired above all of working to maintain an open mind. I couldn't dismiss all those extraordinary claims out of hand. After all, they just might be true..."

34. Osis, K. and E. Heraldsson. *At The Hour of Death* (1977), p. 16.

35. Moody, Raymond. *Life After Life*. USA: Bantam (1975), pp. 19-98.

36. *Op.cit.*, Ring (1980), p. 39.

37. The Holy Bible – St. John Chapter II, Verses 14-44

38. The Russian scientist Professor Negovskii defined "clinical death" as a state during which all external signs of life (consciousness, reflexes, respiration and cardiac activity) are absent, but the organism as a whole is not yet dead; the metabolic processes of its tissues still proceed and under definite conditions it is possible to restore all its functions, i.e. the state is reversible under appropriate therapeutic intervention. If the organism in a state of clinical death is allowed to take the natural course of events, then the state of clinical death is followed by an irreversible state – biological death. During biological death, metabolic activity degradation, specific for a dead organism, sets in. Considerable experimental material gathered by several authors indicates that 5 to 6 minutes is the maximum duration of the state of clinical death which the brain cortex of an adult organism can survive with subsequent recovery of all its functions. See Gaeskaya, M. S. "Bio-chemistry of the brain during the process of dying and resuscitation" cited in Sabom, Michael, B. *Recollections of Death* (1982), p.8.

Chapter 2   SCEPTICISM AND EMPIRICISM

1. This Jamaican creole expression means that one ought to accept as credible another person's experience.

2. Santayana, George. *Skepticism and Animal Faith.* New York: Dover Publications (1923), 1923.

3. Bewaji, J.A.I. *Scepticism and Empirical Knowledge.* Unpublished PhD. Thesis. University of Ibadan, Nigeria (1990), p. 263.

4. Chisholm, R. M. *Perceiving.* Ithaca, New York: Cornell University Press (1957), Chapter 4.

5. Swinburne, Richard. *The Evolution of the Soul, The Principle of Credulity.* New York: Clarendon Press (1990), p. 12.

6. *Ibid.*, p. 13

7. Osis, K. & E. Heraldsson. *At the Hour of Death.* New York: Avon Books (1990).

8. Honorton. "Psi and Internal Attention State". B. B. Wolman (Ed.) *Handbook of Parapsychology.* New York: Van Nostrand Reinhold (1977).

9. Beloff, J. "Could there be a Physical Explanation to PSI". *Journal of the Society for Psychical Research.* (1980), p. 50 and pp. 263-272.

10. Grosso, Michael. "Towards an Explanation of Near-Death Phenomena" *The Journal of Near-Death Studies* Vol.1, No.1. July (1981) pp. 9-10.

11. Woodhouse, Mark B. "Near-Death Experience and the Mind/Body problem" *Anabiosis* – July, (1981). Vol.1, No.1 p. 57

12. Grof, Stanislav. *Books of the Dead.* London: Thames & Hudson. (1994)

13. Randall, John, Herman Jr. and Justus Buchler. *Philosophy: An Introduction.* New York/London: Barnes & Noble Books, (Harper and Row Publishers) (1971). p. 214.

14. *Ibid.*, p. 193.

15. *Ibid.*, p. 195.

16. *Ibid.*, p. 195.

17. Randall, John Herman Jr. and Buchler, Justus. *Philosophy: An Introduction.* Barnes & Noble Book, (Harper & Row Publishers). (1971). p. 195.

18. *Ibid.*, pp .192 ff.

19. Sagan, Carl. *Broca's Brain.* New York: Ballantine Books (1979), p. 335.

20. National Review Vol.38, October 14, 1988.

21. Alcock, James E. "Pseudo-Science and the Soul." *Essence* No.5 (1981), pp. 72-73.

22. However Saul 'Paul Sirag's hyperspace model of consciousness based on his version of

unified field theory creates a hierarchy of realms of consciousness which may be signposting a comprehensive theory. It certainly is an advanced model linking consciousness at a deep level with physical reality. Mishlove, Jeffrey. *The Roots of Consciousness.* New York, NY. Marlowe & Company (l993), pp. 365-368.

Chapter 3   THE DISEMBODIED SELF

1. Hume, David. *A Treatise of Human Nature.* New York: Penguin (1984), p. 81.

2. Rorty, Amélie (ed.) *The Identities of Persons.* Los Angeles, California: University of California Press, (1976). p. 11.

3. R. Descartes The Nature of Human Mind, Meditation II. The Philosophical Writings of Descartes. Translated by John Cottingham, Robert Stoothoff, Dougald Murdoch. Cambridge: Cambridge University Press. (1985).

4. Locke, John. "Of Ideas of Identity and Diversity", in *An Essay Concerning Human Understanding.* Book II, Chapter 27. Ed. John W. Yolton. London: J. M. Dent & Sons Limited (1990).

5. Hume, David. "Of Personal Identity" in a Treatise of Human Nature. Ed. Ernest C. Mossner. Penguin Books (1969), p. 299. Book I, Section vi.

6. *Ibid.,* p. 300

7. *Ibid.,* p. 301

8. *Ibid.,* p. 307

9. *Ibid.,* p. 307

10. *Ibid.,* pp. 308-9

11. *Ibid.,* Appendix p. 675

12. Kant, Emmanuel, *Critique of Pure Reason.* Trans. J. M. D. Meiklejohn. Prometheus Books. (1990.), pp. 218-9

13. *Ibid.,* p. 213

14. *Ibid.,* p. 220

15. For discussion see, Kolok, Daniel and Raymond Martin. *Self And Identity: Contemporary Philosophical Issues.* New York: MacMillan Publishing Co. (1991), p. 168.

16. *Op. cit.,* Kolok and Martin. p. 340

17. Ryle, Gilbert. *The Concept of Mind.* USA: University of Chicago Press. (1984), p.15.

18. *Ibid.* p. 340; Op. cit. Kolok and Martin. p. 340

19. Quinton, Anthony. "The Soul" in *Philosophy: An Introduction Through Literature*. Ed. Kleiman, Lowell and Stephen Lewis. New York: Paragon House. (1992), p. 212.

20. Kleiman, Lowell and Stephen Lewis. *Philosophy: An Introduction Through Literature*. New York: Paragon House, 1992. P. 204

21. *Ibid.,* p. 206.

22. *Ibid.,* p. 206.

23. *Ibid.,* p. 212

24. Strawson, P.F. *Individuals - An Essay in Descriptive Metaphysics.* (1993), London: Routledge. p.103.

25. *Ibid.,* Strawson. Dichotomizes Predicates into those kind of predicates properly applied to individuals and those which are properly applied to material bodies and which we would not dream of applying ascribing states of consciousness, these he calls M-predicates. For example – weighs 150 lbs., is in the kitchen; the other consists of all the predicates we apply to persons, which he calls P-predicates. These latter are various like 'is smiling' 'going for a walk' and so on. p.104.

26. *Ibid.,* p. 115.

27. *Ibid.,* p. 115.

28. *Ibid.,* p. 116.

29. *Ibid.,* p. 116.

30. *Ibid.,* p. 116.

31. Hart, W.D. *A Companion of Philosophy*. Ed. Samuel Guttenplan. Cambridge: Blackwell. (1994), p.266.

32. *Ibid.,* p. 266.

33. Hart, W.D. *The Engines of the Soul.* London: Cambridge University Press. (1988), pp. 50-51.

34. *Ibid.,* pp. 51-52.

35. *Ibid.,* p. 52.

36. *Ibid.,* p. 54.

37. Grice, H.P. and Robert J. Swartz, Ed. *The Causal Theory of Perception in Perceiving, Sensing and Knowing.* New York: Doubleday, (1965.), pp. 436-472.

38. *Op. cit.*, Companion of Philosophy p. 267.

39. *Op. cit.*, Engines of the Soul p. 55.

40. *Ibid.,* p. 59.

41. *Op. cit.*, Companion of Philosophy. p. 268.

42. *Ibid.,* p. 268.

Chapter 4
NEW PARADIGMS AND THE MECHANISTIC UNIVERSE

1. Kuhn, Thomas S. *The Structure of Scientific Revolution.* Second Edition (1970). Chicago: University of Chicago Press. p. 23.

2. *Ibid.,* In this context, 'normal science' means research firmly based upon one or more past scientific achievements, achievements that some particular scientific community acknowledges for a time as supplying the foundation for its further practice. P0. 10.

3. *Ibid.,* see generally pp. 24-27.

4. *Ibid.,* Where the concept of anomaly was first introduced by Kuhn, the term 'revolution' and 'extraordinary science' seemed equivalent but neither term seemed to mean more than 'non-normal science.' p. 90.

5. *Ibid.,* p. 82.

6. *Ibid.,* pp. 5- 6.

7. *Ibid.,* p. 5.

8. *Ibid.,* p. 84.

9. *Ibid.,* p. 88.

10. Grof, Stanislav. *Beyond The Brain.* (1985). Albany: State University of New York Press. p. 3. Kuhn at p.175, in his postscript, discloses that in much of his book the term 'paradigm' is used in two different senses. On one hand, it stands for the entire constellation of belief, values, techniques and so on shared by members of a given community. On the other, it denotes one sort of element in the constellation, the concrete puzzle-solutions which employed as models or examples, can replace explicit rules as a basis for the solution of the remaining puzzles of normal science.

11. *Ibid.,* p. 4.

12. *Ibid.,* p. 5.

13. *Ibid.,* pp. 22-24.

14. *Ibid.,* p. 18.

15. *Ibid.,* p. 19.

16. *Ibid.,* p. 435 Note 6.

17. *Ibid.,* To illustrate the point, Grof gives an example of a television set. He points out that the quality of the picture and sound is critically dependent on proper functioning of all the components, and malfunction or destruction of some of them will create very specific distortion. The malfunctioning component can be identified and the problem corrected by replacing or repairing the hardware in question. No one would conclude that the program must therefore be generated in the television set. His illustration seems

to suggest that the brain may be a receiver not an originator and transmitter of the product. p. 22.

18. Penfield, Wilder. *The Mystery of the Mind*. (1978), New Jersey: Princeton University Press. p. 88.

19. *Ibid.,* p. 24.

20. *Ibid.,* p. 25.

21. *Ibid.,* p. 26.

22. *Ibid.,* p. 31.

Chapter 5   THE HOLOGRAPHIC UNIVERSE

1. Koch, Winston E. *Lasers and Holography* (1981.), New York: Dover Publications. Preface, p. iii.

2. *Ibid.,* p. iii.

3. *Ibid.,* Preface p. iv.

4. *Ibid.,* Preface p. v.

5. *Ibid.,* Preface p. v.

6. Grof, Stanislav. *Beyond the Brain* (1985), Albany: State University of New York Press. p. 78.

7. *Ibid.,* p. 79.

8. *Ibid.,* p. 75. To illustrate the relationship between the whole and the part, the story is told of Fa Tsang, one of the founders of the Hwa Yen School of Buddhist thought and the Empress Wu, who was unable to penetrate the complexity of Hwa Yen literature. To give her a practical and simple demonstration of the cosmic interrelatedness, he first suspended a glowing candle from the ceiling of a room, the interior of which was entirely covered in mirrors, to demonstrate the relationship of the one to the many. Then he placed in the center of the room a small crystal and showing how everything around it was reflected in it, illustrated how, in the Ultimate Reality, the infinitely small contains the infinitely large, and the infinitely large the infinitely small, without obstruction. See also Frank, F. *The Book of Angelus Sileius* (1976). New York: The Random House.

9. *Ibid.,* p. 79.

10. Ferguson, Marilyn. "Karl Pribram's changing reality" in *The Holographic Paradigm*. Ed. Ken Wilber. (1985), Boston and London: Shambala Books. p. 18.

11. *Ibid.,* "A New Perspective on Reality " The special undated issue of the *Brain/Mind Bulletin* in the *The Holographic Paradigm,* p.5.

12. *Op.cit.,* Grof p. 80.
13. *Ibid.,* p.86.
14. Ibid., p.86
15. Pribram, Karl. H. "What the Fuss Is All About" in the *Holographic Paradigm.* p. 31
16. *Op.cit.,* Grof. p. 81.
17. *Ibid.,* p. 81.
18. *Ibid.* p. 81.
19. . *The Holographic Universe.* USA: Harper Perennial (1991) p. 1.
20. Quantum, Theory, Causality and Chance in Modern Physics. (1996), Philadelphia: University of Pennsylvania Press. Unfolding Meaning (1995), London: Routledge.
21. Bohm, David. Wholeness And The Implicate Order (1995), London. Routledge. Introduction p. x.
22. *Ibid.,* p. 150.
23. *Ibid.,* p. 11.
24. *Ibid.,* p. 53.
25. *Ibid.,* p. 59.
26. *Ibid.,* pp. 50-51.
27. *Ibid.,* p. 51.
28. *Ibid.,* p. 52.
29. *Ibid.,* p. 54.
30. *Ibid.,* p. 149.
31. *Ibid.,* p. 151.
32. *Ibid.,* p. 179.
33. *Ibid.,* p. 189.
34. *Ibid.,* p. 176.
35. Grof, Stanislav. *Beyond the Brain.* USA: State University of New York (1985), pp. 85-86.
36. Penfield, Wilder. *The Mystery of the Mind.* Princeton, New Jersey: Princeton University Press, (1978), p. 31 et Seq.
37. De Valois, Karen. K. DeValois, Russell. L. and Yund, W.W. "Responses of Straite Cortex Cells to Grafting and Checkerboard patterns". *Journal of Physiology.* Vol. 291. (1979), pp. 483-505.
38. *Op.cit.,* Talbot p. 13.

39. *Op.cit.,* Talbot. *The Holographic Universe.* p. 17. It should be noted that this astounding trait is common only to pieces of holographic film whose images are invisible to the naked eye. If one buys a piece of holographic film and can see a three-dimensional image in it without any special kind of illumination, cutting it will only produce pieces of the original image.

40. Pribram, Karl. "The Neurophysiology of Remembering". *Scientific American* 220. (Jan.1969).

41. *Op. cit.* Pribram, Karl. *Languages of the Brain.* p. 123.

42. Collier, J., Burckhardt, C. B. and Lin, L.H. *Optical Holography.* NY: Academic Press (1971).

43. *Op. cit.* Talbot, Michael. The Holographic Universe (1991), p.21.

44. Van Heerden, Pieter. "Models for the brain". Nature 227 (July 25, 1970). pp. 410-411.

45. *Op.cit.,* Talbot, Michael p. 23.

46. *Op.cit.,* Pribram, Karl. p. 169. Languages of the Brain.

47. *Op.cit.,* Talbot p. 25.

48. Pietsch, Paul. " Shufflebrain" *Harper's Magazine* 244, May, (1972). p. 66.

49. *Op.cit ,* Talbot p. 28.

50. *Ibid.,* Talbot. p. 31.

51. Pribram, Karl. "The Implicate Brain". *Quantum Implications.* Eds.B.J.Hiley, David F. Peat. Routledge & Kegan. Paul Ltd. (1991). p. 365

Chapter 6
A HOLOGRAPHIC EXPLANATION OF NDE AND OBE

1. Shields, Dean. "A Cross Cultural Study of Beliefs in Out-of-Body Experience." *Journal of the Society for Psychical Research* 49, (1978), pp. 679-741. See also Bourguigrin, Erika. "Dreams and Altered States of Consciousness in Anthropological Research" in *Psychological Anthropology* Ed. Itsu, F.L.K. Cambridge, Mass: Schenkman (1972), p. 418; Green, Celia. "Out of the Body Experiences" Oxford, England: Institute of Psychological Research (1968).

2. Tart, Charles. "A Psychophysiological Study of Out-of-Body Experiences in a Selected Subject", *Journal of the American Society for Psychical Research* 62. (1968), pp. 3-37.

3. Osis, Karl. "Out-of-Body Research" in *American Society for Psychical Research in Mind Beyond the Body.* Ed. Scott, Rogo, D. NY: Penguin (1978). pp. 162-69.

4. Talbot, Michael. *The Holographic Universe.* NY: Harper Collins (1991). p. 234.

5. *Ibid.,* p. 235.

6. Monroe, Robert. A. *Journeys Out of the Body.* NY: Anchor Press/Double Day. (1971), p. 183.

7. *Op.cit.,* Talbot, Michael. pp. 174-178 and p. 192. She has discovered that the human energy field responds to the stimuli even before the brain does. She has taken EEG readings of the brain simultaneously and discovered that when she makes a loud sound or flashes a bright light, the EMG of the energy field register the stimulus before it ever shows up on the EEG. What does it mean? Hunt says:

   I think we have an overrated brain as the active ingredient in the relationship of a human of the world. It is just a real good computer. But the aspects of the mind that have to do with creativity, imagination, spirituality and all those things, I don't see them in the brain at all, it is in the darn field.

8. Schwartz Stephen, A. *The Secret Vaults of Time,* NY: Grosset & Dunlop (1978), pp. 226-37.

9. Pollack, Jack Harrison. *Croiset, the Clairvoyant* NY: Doubleday (1964).

10. *Op.cit.,* Talbot, Michael. p. 200.

11. Scott, Rogo, D. *Psychic Break-throughs Today*, Wellingborough, Great Britain: Aquarian Press. (1987), p. 163-164.

12. Munroe, Robert. *Journeys Out of the Body* (1971), p. 184.

13. Rhine, J. B. *The Reach of the Mind.* New York: William Sloan Associates. (1947).

14. "Kinetic Effects at the Ostensible Location of an Out-of-Body Projection During Perceptual Testing". *The Journal of the American Society for Psychical Research.* Vol. 74, July 1980. p.320.

15. *Ibid.,* p.320.

16. Osis and Haraldsson. *At the Hour of Death.* New York: Hastings House Book Publishers. (1977).

17. *Op.cit.,* Osis & McCormick. P.321.

18. Tart, C. T. *Psi Scientific Studies of the Psychic Realm.* New York: Dutton. (1977).

19. Gallup, George Jr. with Proctor, William. *Adventures in Immorality.* NY: McGraw Hill (1982), p. 31.

20. Ring, Kenneth. (1980), *Life at Death.* p. 234.

21. Ferguson, M. A. *New Perspective on Reality.* Revision 1, (1978), p. 3.

22. Pribram, K. *Interview in Psychology Today.* February (1979), p. 84.

23. *Ibid.,* pp. 83-84.

24. *Op.cit.,* Ring (1980) p. 237.

25. *Op.cit.,* Talbot p. 246.

26. Myers, F.W.H. *Human Personality and* its *Survival of Bodily Death.* London: Longmans Green & Co. (1904), pp. 315-328.

27. Whiteman, J.H.M. *The Mystical Life.* London: Faber & Faber (1961).

28. *Op.cit.,* Monroe, Robert. (1971), p. 183.

29. Whitton, Joel L. and Fisher, Joe. *Life Between Life.* New York: Doubleday (1986), p. 32.

30. *Op.cit.,* Talbot p. 248.

31. *Op.cit.,* Witton & Fisher. p. 39.

32. Moody, Raymond. A. Jr. *Life After Life* New York: Bantam Books (1976), p. 68.

33. Moody, Raymond. A. Jr. *Reflections on Life After Life.* New York: Bantam Books (1978). p. 38.

34. *Op.cit.,* Talbot p. 249.

35. Ring, *Heading Towards Omega.* p. 58.

36. See: (1) *Heading Towards Omega.* New York: William Morrow (1985), p. 199; (2) Moody, Raymond, A. Fr. *Reflections on Life After Life.* pp. 9-14; (3) Moody, Raymond, A. Jr. with Paul Perry, *The Light Beyond.* New York: Bantam Books. (1988) p. 35.

37. *Op.cit.,* Monroe. p. 73.

38. *Op.cit.,* Talbot. p. 252.

39. *Op.cit.,* Talbot. p. 257.

40. Rhodes, Leon S. "Swedenborg and the Near-Death Experience" in Emanuel Swedenborg: *A Continuing Vision.* Ed. Larsen Robin. et al. New York: Swedenborg Foundation (1988), pp. 237-240.

41. Swedenborg, Emanuel. *The Universal Human and Soul-Body Interaction.* Ed and translated Dole, George F. New York: Paulist Press (1984), p. 43.

42. Dole, George. "An Image of God in a Mirror" in Emanuel Swedenborg. *A Continuing Vision.* pp. 370-381.

43. Bentov, Itzhak. *Stalking the Wild Pendulum.* New York: E. P. Dutton. (1977).

44. *Op.cit*, Ring (1980). p. 238.

45. *Ibid.,* p. 238.

46. Greenhouse, H. D. *The Astral Journey.* New York: Avon (1974). pp. 41-42

47. *Op.cit.,* Ring (1980). p. 239.

48. *Ibid.,* p. 240.

49. *Ibid.*, p. 241.

50. *Ibid.*, p. 242.

51. Jung, Carl. *Memories Dreams and Reflections.* New York: Vantage Books (1961), pp. 304-5.

52. *Op.cit.*, Ring (1980), p. 246.

53. *Ibid.*, p. 247.

54. *Ibid.*, p. 247.

55. See: (1) Eccles, J. C. *The Understanding of the Brain.* New York: McGraw Hill (1973); (2) Penfield, Wilder. *The Mystery of the Mind.* Princeton, NJ: Princeton University Press, (1976).

56. *Op.cit* , Ring. p. 248.

57. *Op.cit.*, Jung, Carl. p. 296.

Chapter 7   NON-OPHTHALMIC VISION

1. Hamlyn, W. D. "Imagination", *The Companion of Philosophy of Mind.* Ed. Daniel Guttenplan. Blackwell (1994), pp. 361-366.

2. Garrett, Don. *Companion to Metaphysics.* Ed. Jaegom Kim and Ernest Gusa. London: Blackwell (1995), p. 215.

3. "Vicky" *Vital Signs* VII No. 2. Spring (1994), The International Association of Near-Death Studies Inc. (IANDS), P. O. Box 502, East Windsor Hill. Connecticut, USA.

4. *Ibid. Vital Signs.*

5. The tunnel experience is typical of many out-of-body experiences.

6. Panoramic Life Review is another element of the core experience of many NDEers.

7. *Op. cit., Vital Signs.* p. 6.

8. Ring, Kenneth and Sharon Cooper. "Near-death and Out-of-body Experiences in the Blind: A Study of Apparent Eyeless Vision." *Journal of Near-Death Studies 16* (2). Winter (1977), New York: Human Science. p. 117.

9. *Ibid.*, p. 119.

10. *Ibid.*, p. 118.

11. Churchland, Paul M. "Knowing Qualia: A Reply to Jackson" in *The Nature of Consciousness.* Eds. Owen Flanagan, Ned Block and Güven Güzeldere. Cambridge, Mass.: MIT Press, (1997) p. 572.

12. *Op.cit., Vital Signs,* "My optic nerve was destroyed", p. 1.

13. McGinn, Colin. *Problems of Consciousness* (1974), p. 72.

14. Feigl, Herbert. *The "Mental" and the "Physical".* Minneapolis: University of Minnesota (1967), pp.66-9

15. Nemirow, Laurence. "Physicalism and the Cognitive Role of Acquaintance" p. 491 in *Mind and Cognition.* Ed. G. Lycan (1994), London: Blackwell Publishers.

16. *Ibid.,* Nemirow p.493.

17. Hart, W. D. *The Engines of the Soul. London:* Cambridge University Press. (1988).

18. *Ibid.,* p. 52.

19. *Op.cit.,* Hart. Chapter 5.

20. *Ibid.,* p. 59.

21. Hume, David. *Treatise of Human Nature* (1984), p. 223 Sec. xv.

22. Russell, Bertrand. *History of Western Philosophy,* New York: Simon and Schuster/Touchstone. (1972), Chapter 7. pp. 388-476.

23. *Op.cit.,* Hart p. 64.

24. *Ibid.,* p. 69.

25. *Ibid.,* p. 131.

26. *Ibid.,* p. 127.

27. *Ibid.,* p. 130.

28. *Ibid.,* p. 131.

29. Neumann, John, Von and Oskar Morgenstern. *The Theory of Games and Economic Behaviour,* 2nd Edition, Princeton, New Jersey: Princeton University Press. (1947), Chapter 3.

30. *Op.cit.,* Hart p. 132.

31. *Ibid.,* p. 132.

32. *Ibid.,* p. 136.

33. *Ibid.,* p. 137.

34. *Ibid.,* p. 137.

35. *Ibid.,* p. 138.

36. *Ibid.,* p. 159.

37. *Ibid.,* p. 140.

38. *Op.cit., Companion to Metaphysics.* p. 276.

39. *Op.cit.*, pp. 141-142.

40. *Op.cit.*, Ring and Cooper. p. 101 and p. 136.

41. *Ibid.*, p. 125.

42. See "Non-Ophthalmic Vision", Chapter 7, Section 7.1.

43. *Op.cit.*, Ring and Cooper p. 126.

44. Kirtley, D. D. *The Psychology of Blindness* (1975), Chicago, Ill: Nelson Hall. Ring and Cooper. p. 126.

45. *Ibid.*, Ring and Cooper. p. 126.

46. *Ibid.*, p. 129.

47. Weiskrantz, L. *Blindsight.* Oxford, England: Clarendon Press. (1986).

48. Humphrey, N. A. *History of the Mind* (1993), New York: Harper & Collins p. 90. See also Ring and Cooper. p. 130.

49. *Ibid.*, Ring and Cooper. p. 130.

50. Romains, Jules. *Eyeless Sight: A Study of Extra Retinal Vision and the Paroptic Sense.* (1924), English Translation. New York: Putnam.

51. *Op.cit.*, Ring and Cooper. p. 131.

52. *Ibid.*, p. 132.

53. *Ibid.*, p. 135.

54. *Ibid.*, p. 136

55. Cook, T. A. *The Use of Visual Concepts by Blind and Sighted Children.* Unpublished Doctoral Theses, University of Texas (1970) and N.A. Rathna. *Qualitative Analysis of the Visual Term Used by the Blind in the Spoken Language.* Indiana: Indiana State University, Bloomington, (1962).

56. *Ibid.*, p. 137.

57. *Ibid.*, p. 139.

58. *Ibid.*, p. 140.

59. *Ibid.*, p. 142.

60. *Ibid.*, p. 143.

61. Goswani. A. *Science Within Consciousness* (1994), Sausalito Ca. Institute of Noetic Sciences. p. 1.

62. Dossey. L. *Recovering the Soul* (1989), New York: Bantam. p. 98.

63. *Ibid.*, Dossey. p. 7.

64. *Op.cit.*, Ring and Cooper. p. 144.

65. *Ibid.,* p. 145.

66. *Ibid.,* p. 145.

CHAPTER 8 PROBLEMS OF CONSCIOUSNESS

1. Perry, Ralph. "Conceptions and Misconceptions of Consciousness." in *The Psychological Review XI.* Boston (1904). pp. 282 - 296.

2. Dennett, Daniel. *Consciousness Explained.* Boston: Little, Brown & Co. (1991), pp. 21-22.

3. McGinn, Colin. "Can We Solve The Mind-Body Problem?" *Mind* XC VIII.891 (1989), pp. P 349

4. Churchland, Patricia, S. "Consciousness: The Transmutation of a Concept" (1983). *Pacific Philosophical Quarterly* 64. p.80.

5. Searle, John, R. *The Rediscovery of the Mind* (1992), Cambridge, MASS: M.I.T. Press, p. 83.

6. *Ibid.,* p. 83.

7. Ladd, George, Trumbell. *Psychology: Descriptive and Explanatory.* N.Y: C.Scribner Son. (1909), p. 30.

8. Stout, George, F. *A Manual of Psychology.* N.Y: Hinds, Noble and Eldredge Publishers. (1899), p. 7.

9. James, William. *Streams of Consciousness in Nature of Consciousness.* Eds. Ned Block, Owen Flanagan and Güven Güzeldere. (1997), Cambridge, MASS: M.I.T. Press. pp. 71-72.

10. James, William. *The Principles of Psychology.* Vol.I (1950); James, William The *Principles of Psychology.* Vol.2 (1950). N.Y: Dover Publications.

11. Ibid., Vol. I. p. 185.

12. Freud, Sigmund. *New Introductory Lectures on Psychoanalysis – in complete Psychological Works of Sigmund Freud.* Vol. 20. (l964) Translated J. Stackey. London: Hogarth Press. p. 70.

13. Crick, Francis and Koch, Christof. "Towards a Neurobiological Theory of Consciousness." *Seminars in the Neurosciences.* 2. (1990) p. 263.

14. Wilkes, Katherine. "Is Consciousness Imported?" *British Journal of Philosophy of Science* 35 (1984), pp. 241--242.

15. *Op. cit., The Nature of Consciousness.* p. 5.

16. Flanagan, Owen. *Consciousness Reconsidered* (1992), Cambridge, Mass: M.I.T. Press. p.2.

17. Flanagan, Owen. "Deconstructing Dreams: The Spandrels of Sleep," *Journal of Philosophy.* 92: 1. (1995) p. 20.

18. *Op.cit., Nature of Consciousness.* p. 6.

19. *Ibid.*, Güzeldere, Güven. p. 24.

20. Miller, George. *Psychology: The Science of Mental Life.* (1962) New York: Harper & Row Publications. p. 25.

21. Gunderson, Keith. "Asymmetry and Mind-Body Perplexities." (1970). p. 127. in Rosenthal - *Materialism and the Mind Body Problem.* (1971). Englewood Cliffs: Prentice Hall. pp. 112-127.

22. *Op.cit,* Güzeldere. p. 24

23. *Ibid.*, p. 24.

24. *Ibid.*, p. 11.

25. *Ibid.*, p. 11.

26. *Ibid.*, p. 24.

27. *Ibid.*, p. 25.

28. *Ibid.*, p. 30.

29. Searle, John, R. *The Rediscovery of the Mind.* (1992). Cambridge, Mass: M.I.T. Press, p. 93.

30. *Op. cit.*, Russell, Bertrand. The Problems of Philosophy (1959)

31. *Op. cit.*, Priest, Stephen. *Theories of the Mind* (1991) p. 217

32. *Ibid.*, pp. 216-217

33. Flanagan, Owen. "Prospects for a Unified Theory of Consciousness: What Dreams are made of" (1997), in *Nature of Consciousness.* p. 97.

34. *Ibid.*, pp. 97-98.

35. See Owen Flanagan *Consciousness Rediscovered* (1992). p.1

36. *Op. cit.* Popper & Eccles *The Self and Its Brain* (1977). p.36

37. The areas of the dominant hemisphere which have linguistic and ideational performance or which have polymodal inputs are collectively called liason areas, especially Brodman, areas 39 and 40 and the prefrontal lopes.

38. *Op. cit.* Popper and Eccles. (1977). p. 371.

39. *Op. cit.* Nagel, Thomas. *The View from Nowhere.* (1986), p. 3.

40. *Op. cit.* Nagel, Thomas. *What its Like to be a Bat* (1974).

41. *The Cambridge Dictionary of Philosophy* (1995) Ed. Robert Audi. p. 606.

42. Samuel Guttenplan and Ned Block (eds.) *A Companion to the Philosophy of Mind* (1994), p. 212.

43. *Op.cit.,* Flanagan. p. 1

44. McGinn, Colin. *The Problems of Consciousness,* (1991) Chapter 2.

45. Churchland, Paul. M. "Eliminative Materialism and the Propositional Attitude" (1981). p.1. in *Nature of the Mind,* David M. Rosenthal (ed.). (1991). p. 601.

46. *Op.cit.,* Churchland (1981), p. 601.

47. *Ibid.,* p. 604.

48. *Op.cit.,* Flanagan (1992), p. 2.

49. See footnote 31 above.

50. *Op.cit.,* Flanagan (1992), p. 2.

51. *Ibid.,* p. 219.

52. *Ibid.,* p.220.

53. *Ibid.,* p. 3. Flanagan claims that the recent works by P.S. Churchland (1986), P. M. Churchland (1989), Daniel Dennett (1991) are in the same mode of constructive naturalism. That all three writers take conscious experience seriously as a phenomenon or set of phenomena which has to be explained. No one now defends the outright elimination of our common sense ways of conceiving mind. I would accept that P.S. Churchland (1986) *Neuro Philosophy;* P. M. Churchland (1989) *A Neuro Computational Perspective: The Nature of the Mind and The Structure of Science,* and Daniel Dennett (1991) *Conscience Explained,* all take conscious experience as a phenomenon or set of phenomena to be explained. The question that no one now defends the outright elimination of FP I shall leave as an open issue.

54. Churchland, P.S. *Neurophilosophy – Towards a Unified Science of the Mind-Brain.* Boston: Massachusetts Institute of Technology (1993) p. 5.

55. *Ibid.,* p. 482.

56. *Ibid.,* p. 482.

57. Chalmers, David, J. *The Conscious Mind.* New York: Oxford University Press. (1996) p.129.

58. *Ibid.,* p.154

59. *Ibid.,* p.154

60. *Ibid.,* p.155

61. *Ibid.,* p.171

62. *Ibid.,* p.120

63. *Ibid.,* p.357

64. Levine, J. "Materialism Qualia: The Explanatory Gap". *Pacific Philosophical Quarterly.* 64, (1984), pp. 351-361.

65. Fodor, J. "The Big Idea." *Times Literary Supplement.* July 3, (1992). pp. 5-7.

66. Sutherland, Stuart. *MacMillian Dictionary of Psychology.* 2nd Edition. London: MacMilliam Press. (1995), p. 95.

67. Miller, George. *Psychology of Science of Mental Life.* USA: Harper & Row Publishers (1962), p.25.

Chapter 9   THEORIES OF THE MIND

1. Descartes, R. *"Discourse on Method"* in David Rosenthal's *The Nature of the Mind.* Trans. F.E. Sutcliffe Hormondsworth. New York: Oxford University Press, (1974). p. 54.

2. Priest, Stephen. *Theories of the Mind.* (1991), N.Y: Haughton Miffin Co. p. 11.

3. Rescher, Nicholas. *Cambridge Dictionary of Philosophy,* Ed. Robert Audi.

   Cambridge: Cambridge University Press. (1995) pp. 355 ff.

4. Berkeley, George. *Principles of Human Knowledge,* with other writings. Ed. G. J. Wornock. London (1977). p. 69.

5. *Ibid.,* p. 73.

6. *Ibid.,* p. 73.

7. *Ibid.,* p. 66.

8. *Op.cit. Cambridge Dictionary of Philosophy.* p. 357.

9. Russell, Bertrand. *A History of Western Philosophy.* Chapter IX, "The Atomist". New York: Simon and Schuster (1972), pp. 33-39.

10. *Op.cit ,* Priest. p. 100.

11. Place, U.T. "Is Consciousness a Brain Process? " in the *Philosophy of Mind.* Eds. Brian Beakley and Peter Ludlow. Cambridge, Mass: MIT Press (1992) p.33.

12. *Ibid., p. 33 Philosophy of Mind.*

13. *Ibid.,* p. 34.

14. Sherrington, Sir Charles (1947) Foreward to the 1947 Edition of the *Integrative Action of the Nervous System.* Cambridge University Press. pp. XX-XXI see p. 39. *The Philosophy of Mind.* Eds. Brian Beakley and Peter Ludlow. Cambridge, Mass: MIT Press (1992).

15. *Op. cit.*, Priest, *Theories of the Mind.* p. 112.
16. *Op. cit.*, Place, U.T. *Philosophy of Mind.* p. 38.
17. *Ibid.*, Place, U.T. p. 37.
18. *Op.cit.*, Priest *Theories of the Mind.* p. 114.
19. Smart, J. J. C. *Sensation and Brain Processes, Contemporary Materialism.* London: Routledge. Eds. Paul K. Moser and J.D. Trout. (1995), p. 93.
20. *Ibid.*, p. 95.
21. *Ibid.*, p. 94.
22. Rosenthal, D.M. *The Nature of the Mind,* p. 162.
23. *Ibid.*, p. 162.
24. *Op. cit.,* Smart. *Contemporary Materialism.* p. 102.
25. Donald Davidson." Mental Events" in Readings in Philosophy of Psychology. Ed. Ned Block. p. 107.
26. *Ibid.*, p.108.
27. *Ibid.*, p.109.
28. *Ibid.*, p.109.
29. The term was coined by the scholastics in the middle ages, from the Latin verb intendo – that is, to point or aim at phenomena with intentionality, thus, to point outside of themselves to something else. The term was revived by Franz Brentano. It defines the distinction between the mental and the physical since intentionality is an irreducible feature of mental phenomena, and since no physical phenomena could exhibit it, mental phenomena could not be a species of physical phenomena. *Cambridge Dictionary of Philosophy,* p.381.
30. *Op.cit.* Davidson p.111.
31. *The Cambridge Dictionary of Philosophy.* p. 578.
32. Psychology from an Empirical Standpoint, translated by A.C. Rancuvello, D. C. Tarrel and L. L.McAlister London (1973), p. 77.
33. *Ibid.*, p. 79.
34. *Ibid.*, p. 80.
35. *Ibid.*, pp. 78-80.
36. *Ibid.*, p. 89.
37. *Ibid.*, p. 90.
38. See *The Cambridge Dictionary,* pp.347-350.
39. *Ibid.*, p. 348

40. Epoché is the Greek word meaning 'suspension of belief'.
41. Husserl, Edmund. *Logical Investigations.* Translated by J. N. Findlay, 2 Volumes, New York (1980), Chapter 2, Investigation V.
42. *Ibid.,* p. 553.
43. *Ibid.,* p. 556.
44. *Ibid.,* p. 556.
45. *Ibid.,* p. 559.
46. *Ibid.,* p. 560.
47. Sokolowski, Robert. *The Cambridge Dictionary.* p. 350.
48. *Ibid.,* p. 350.
49. *Ibid.,* p. 598
50. Spinoza. *Ethics,* London (1977). Translation: A. Boyle. p. 1.
51. *Op.cit.,* Priest p.155.
52. *Op. cit.,* Spinoza. Ethics, p. 58.
53. *Op. cit.,* Priest. p. 157.
54. *Op. cit.,* Spinoza. Ethics, pp. 45-46.
55. Strawson, P.F. Introduction to Individuals: An Essay in Descriptive Metaphysics. London: Routledge (1993), p. 10.
56. *Ibid.,* p. 89.
57. *Ibid.,* p. 89.
58. *Ibid.,* pp. 90-92
59. *Ibid.,* p. 92.
60. *Ibid.* Foot-note on p.95. In the same note he refers with approbation to Lichtenberg's dictum that instead of saying 'I think', we (or Descartes) ought to say 'there is a thought', (that is Es denkt).
61. *Ibid.,* p. 95.
62. *Ibid,* p. 96.
63. *Ibid.,* pp. 101-102.
64. *Ibid,* p. 102.
65. *Ibid.,* p. 104.
66. *Ibid.,* p. 105.
67. *Ibid.,* Strawson. p. 106.

68. *Ibid.*, Priest. p. 180.
69. *Ibid.*, Priest. p. 180.
70. Russell, Bertrand. *An Outline of Philosophy.* London (1970). p. 303.
71. *Ibid.*, p. 287.
72. *Ibid.*, p. 269.
73. *Ibid.*, p. 290.
74. *Ibid.*, p. 291.
75. A sense datum (sense data) is anything with which we are directly acquainted in perception. Sense data are not mental in themselves but anything which is a possible item of knowledge by introspection counts as mental for Russell. He calls the event, which is the act of acquaintance itself, a 'knowledge reaction' and concludes events to which a knowledge reaction of this sort occurs are 'mental'. Ibid. Russell. p. 291. See Also Stephen Priest. p. 167.
76. *Ibid.*, p. 217.
77. *Ibid.*, p. 292.
78. Chalmers, David, J. *The Conscious Mind.* p.278.
79. *Ibid.*, p. 280.
80. *Ibid.*, p. 284.
81. *Ibid.*, p. 285.
82. *Ibid.*, p. 286.
83. *Ibid.*, p. 296.
84. *Ibid.*, p. 305.
85. *Ibid.*, p. 305.
86. *Ibid.*, p. 350.
87. Op. cit. Russell p. 292.
88. "Does objective reality exist or is the universe a phantasm?" http://www.earthportals.com/hologram.html

CHAPTER 10   EVALUATION AND SUMMARY

1. Fuller, Buckminister. *Towards a New World View*. Ed. Russell DiCarlo. Erie P.A. USA: Epic Publishing (1996) p. 157.

2. *Op. cit., Towards a New World View* (1996).

3. *Op .cit.*, p.35.

4. *Ibid.*, Harmon, Willis. p. 39.

5. Ring, K. and S. Cooper, "Near Death and Out-of-Body Experiences in the Blind: A Study of Apparent Eyeless Vision." in *Journal of Near-Death Studies* 16(2) Winter (1997), p. 143.

6. *Op.cit.*, Grof, S. *Towards a New World View* (1996), pp. 104-105.

7. Einstein, A., Podolsky, B., Rosen, N. "Can Quantum Mechanical Description of Physical Reality be Considered Complete." in *Physical Review* (1935), p. 47.

8. Polkinghorne, John. "The Quantum World" in *Physics, Philosophy and Theology*. Eds. Russell, Robert John., Stoeger, William R. Coyne, George V. Vatican, Observators, Vatican State (1995), p. 338.

9. Zukav, G. *The Dancing Wu Li Masters*. New York: Bantam Books (1980), p. 48.

10. Stapp, Henry P. "Quantum Non-locality and the Description of Nature" in *Philosophical Consequences of Quantum Theory*. Eds. Cushing, Jones, T., McMullin, Ernan. Notre Dome, Indianna: University of Notre Dome Press (1989), p. 154.

11. Heisenberg, W. *Physics and Philosophy,* London: Allen and Urwin 1958.

12. *Op.cit.*, Zukav, G. p. 113.

13. Bohr, Neils. *Atomic Theory and Human Knowledge*. New York: John Wiley 1958. p. 60.

14. *Op.cit.*, Zukav. p. 111.

15. *Op.cit.*, Shimony, Abner. "Search for a World View Which Can Accommodate our Knowledge of Microphysics" in *Philosophical Consequences of Quantum Theory*. Cushjing, James. T, and Eran McMullin, Eds. Notre Dame, Indiana: University of Notre Dame. (1989), p. 25.

16. *Ibid.*, p.36

17. *Ibid.*, p. 27.

18. *Ibid.*, p. 37.

19. *Op.cit.*, Stapp, Henry P. *Philosophical Consequences of Quantum Theory*. p. 160. Einstein, in an effort to show that Quantum Theory was incomplete, along with Podolsky & Rosen (EPR), constructed an argument designed to prove this incompleteness. The EPR argument is based on two premises. The first, the LOC, which asserts that no influence of any kind can propagate faster than light. The other, QT, asserts that

the prediction for the spin correlation measurements under construction are valid. The Bell Theorem (1964) shows, in effect, that these two assumptions are mutually incompatible. The result effectively destroys the EPR argument. The conclusion that follows from the EPR-Bell argument is usually referred to as the future of 'local realism'.

20. *Op.cit.*, Zukav. p. 47

21. *Ibid.*, p. 60. In 1803, Thomas Young sought to settle the nature of light. He used an experiment that was both simple and dramatic. In front of a light source he placed a screen with two vertical slits in it. Each slit could be covered over with a piece of material. On the other side of the double-slit screen was a wall against which the light coming through the double slit could shine. When the light source was activated and one of the slit was covered up there was a spot of light. When both slits were uncovered the projection on the wall should have been the sum of light from the two slits but it wasn't. Instead, the wall was illuminated with alternating bands of light and darkness. The center band was the brightest. How could this happen? The alternating light and dark was a well-known phenomenon of wave mechanics called interference. Einstein using the photo electric effect established that light is particle-like. But how could light be both a wave and a particle? It depends on how the observer views them.

22. Walker, Evan, H. "The Nature of Consciousness." in *Mathematical Biosciences*. (1970). pp. 175-176. He says, "Consciousness may be associated with all Quantum mechanical processes... since everything that occurs is ultimately the result of one or more quantum mechanical events, the universe is 'inhabited' by an almost unlimited number of rather discrete conscious, usually no-thinking entities that are responsible for the detail working of the universe".

23. Jung, C. G. *Synchronicity*. Trans. R.F.C. Hull. Bollingen Series, Princeton University Press (1973), See also p. 23 Peat, David E. *Synchronicity*. New York: Bantam Books (1988).

24. Capra, Fritjof. The Tao of Physics. The Milesian's (6th Cent.B.C.) were called 'holozoists' or 'those who think matter is alive', by later Greeks, because they saw no distinction between animate and inanimate, between spirit and matter. So far as I can ascertain they had no word for matter, for to them, all forms of existence are manifestations of the 'physis' which was endowed with life and spirituality. 'Physis' was the essential nature, or real constitution of things which they sought to discover; simply put, the essential nature of all things (1991), p. 20.

25. *Op.cit.*, Zukav. p. 80.

26. *Ibid.*, p. 80.

27. Freeman, David, H. *Discover*, June (1994), pp. 90-94.

28. Op.cit., Grof, S. *Towards a New World View.* p. 104.

29. *Ibid.*, p. 104.

30. *Ibid.*, p. 105.

31. *Ibid.*, p. 105.

32. *Op.cit.*, Dychtwald, Ken. The Holographic Paradigm. pp. 105-106.

33. Bohm, David. *Wholeness and the Implicate Order.* New York & London: Routledge. (1980), Chapter 6.

34. Op.cit., Capra, Fritjof. *The Tao of Physics.* Boston: Shambhala (1991). p. 320.

35. Ring, Kenneth. *Life at Death.* New York: Quill (1980). pp. 234-7.

36. Braude, Stephen. E. "The Holographic Analysis of Near-Death Experiences: of The Perpetuation Some Deep Mistakes." In Essence, Volume 5, Number 1. (1981). pp. 53-63.

37. *Ibid.*, p. 53.

38. *Ibid.*, p. 54.

39. *Op.cit.*, Pribram K. H. What the fuss is all about - The Holographic Paradigm. p. 32.

40. Chew, G. F. "Bootstrap: A Scientific Idea." Science. Vol. 161, May 23, (1968). pp. 762-5.

41. Capra, Fritjof. *The Holographic Paradigm.* Ed. Ken Wilber. Shambhala. (1985). p. 115.

42. Ring, K. *Life at Death.* (1980), p. 234.

43. *Op.cit., The Holographic Paradigm.* p. 115.

44. *Op.cit.*, Braude, S. E. pp. 54-5.

45. *Op.cit.*, Pribram. K. H. *The Holographic Paradigm.* p. 33.

46. *Op.cit.*, Braude, S. E. p. 55.

47. Fourier, Jean, B.J. An Eighteen Century Frenchman, had invented a type of calculus, a mathematical way of converting pattern, no matter how complex, into a language of simple waves and how they could be converted back into the original pattern. This enabled Gabor, who first formulated the hologram, to convert a picture of an object into the blur of interference patterns on a piece of holographic film and back into an image of the original object.

48. Talbot, Michael. *The Holographic Universe,* Harper - Perennial (1992), p. 27.

49. DeValois, Karen. DeValois, Russell. L. and Yund, W. W. Responses of Straite Cortex Cells to Grafting and Checkerboard Patterns. *Journal of Physiology*, Vol. 291. (1979). pp. 483-505 The Holographic nature of the brain is further evidenced by the fact that the visual system is sensitive to spatial frequency patterns (that is coarseness and fineness of texture) in the environment (Campbell 1974). See Campbell, F. W. "The Transmission of Spatial Information Through the Visual System," in F. O. Schmitt and F. G. Worden, Eds. The Neurosciences: Third Study Programme. Cambridge, Mass: MIT Press. (l974). Also Op.cit., Michael Talbot. p. 27.

50. *Op.cit.*, Braude. p. 56.

51. *Ibid.*, Braude. p. 56.

52. *Ibid.*, Braude. p. 57

53. Anderson, Robert M. Jr. "A Holographic Model of Transpersonal Consciousness." in *The Journal of Transpersonal Psychology.* Vol. 9, Number 2, (1977), p. 119.

54. *Ibid.*, p. 120.

55. *Ibid.*, p. 122.

56. *Op. cit.*, Anderson, R. p. 123

57. *Ibid.*, p. 123. See also Bohm (1995) Wholeness and Implicate Order. p. 133

58. *Ibid.*, p. 126

59. *Ibid.*, p. 126

Chapter 11   CONCLUSION

1. Penfield, Wilder. *The Mystery of the Mind.* New Jersey: Princeton University Press. (1978). p. 88 and p. 114

2. Mishlove, Jeffrey. *The Roots of Consciousness.* New York: Marlow & Company. (1993). p. 87

3. Jevons, William, Stanley. *The Principles of Science.* (1877). London and New York: MacMillan & Co. p. 768.

BIBLIOGRAPHY

Abel, Reuben. *Man is the Measure*. New York: Free Press (1976).

Aune, Bruce. *Metaphysics - The Elements*. USA: Minnesota Press (1995).

Adler, Mortimer, J. *Ten Philosophical Mistakes*. New York: MacMillan Publishing Company, (1987).

Almeder, Robert. *Death and Personal Survival*. Maryland: Rowman and Littlefield Publishers Inc. (1992).

Allen, Reginald, E. Ed. *Greek Philosophy*. New York: MacMillan Publishing Company (1966).

Arendt, Hannah *The Life of the Mind*. New York: Harcourt Brace and Company (1977).

Armstrong, D.M. *A Materialist Theory of the Mind*. London: Routeledge (1968).

Audi, Robert. ed. *The Cambridge Dictionary of Philosophy*. London: Cambridge University Press (1995).

Bailey, Alice A. *The Soul and its Mechanism*. Lucis Publishing Company (1987).

Beck, Lewis, White. *Introduction: Prolegmena to any Future Metaphysics*. Immanuel Kant. New York: MacMillan Publishing Company (1989).

Bentov, Itzhak. *Stalking the Wild Pendulum*. New York: E. P. Dutton (1977).

Berkeley, George. *Principle of Human Knowledge, with other writings*. ed. by G. J. Warnock. London (1977).

Bewaji, J.A.I. *Scepticism and Empirical Knowledge*. Unpublished PhD Thesis. University of Ibadan, (1990).

Bhakywedanta, A.C. and Swami Prabharpada. *The Science of Self Realization*. Los Angeles, California. International Society for Krishna Consciousness.

Blackmore, Susan. *Dying to Live*. New York: Prometheus Books (1993).

Block, Ned, Owen Flanagan and Güiven Güzeldere, Eds. *The Nature of Consciousness - Philosophical Debates*. Cambridge, Mass. A Bradford Book. The MIT Press, (1997).

Block, Ned. *Readings in Philosophy of Psychology*. Vol. 1. USA. Harvard University Press (1980).

Bohm, David. *Wholeness and the Implicate Order*. New York: Routledge (1995).

Bohm, David. *Causality and Chance in Modern Physics*. London: Routledge and Paul Kegan (1957).

Bohm, David. *Unfolding Meaning*. London: Routledge (1995).

Bohr, Neils. *Atomic Theory and Human Knowledge*. New York: John Wiley (1958).

Bradley, F. H. *Writings on Logic and Metaphysics*. James W. Walford and Guy Stock, Eds. Oxford: Clarendon Press (1994).

Brentano, Franz. *Psychology from an Empirical Standpoint*. Trans. A.C. Rancurello, D.B. Terrell and N. L. McAlister. London (1973).

Brinkley, Dannion and Paul Perry. *Saved by the Light*. New York: Villard Books (1994).

Broughton, Richard, S. *Parapsychology: The Controversial Science*. Toronto and USA. Ballantine Books, Random House (1991).

Boyd, Richard, Philip Gosper & J. D. Trout, Eds. *The Philosophy of Science*. A Bradford Book. Cambridge, Mass. MIT Press (1991).

Capra, Fritjof. *The Tao of Physics*. USA. Bamtam, Shambhala (1991).

Chalmers, David, J. *The Conscious Mind*. New York: Oxford University Press (1996).

Chisholm, R M. *Perceiving*. Ithaca, New York: Cornell University Press (1957).

Churchland, Patricia, S. *Neurophilosophy: Towards a Unified Science of the Mind/ Brain*. Massachusetts Institute of Technology (1993).

Churchland, Paul, M. *Scientific Realism and the Plasticity of the Mind*. New York: Cambridge University Press (1979).

Churchland, Paul, M. *The Engine of Reason: The Seat of the Soul- A Philosophical Journey into the Brain*. USA. MIT Press (1994).

Churchland, Paul, M. *Matter and Consciousness*. USA. MIT Press. Revised Edition (1990).

Churchland, Paul, M. A. *Neurocomputation Perspective: The Nature of Mind and the Structure of Science*. Cambridge: MIT Press (1989).

Collier, J., C.B. Burckhardt and L.H. Lin. *Optical Holography*. N.Y. Academic Press (1971).

Cook, T. A. *The use of visual concepts by blind and sighted children*. Unpublished Doctoral Theses. University of Texas (1970) and N. A. Tathna, Qualitative analysis of the visual term used by the blind in their spoken language. Indiana State University (1962).

Copleston, Frederick, S. J. "A History of Philosophy". Vol.II - *Modern Philosophy*. New York: Doubleday (1994).

Cushing, James, T. and Ernon McMullin. Eds. *Philosophical Consequences of Quantum Theory.* Nortre Dame, Indiana: University of Notre Dame Press (1989).

Dennett, Daniel. *Consciousness Explained.* Boston: Little, Brown & Company (1991).

Descartes, Rene. "Of the Nature of Human Mind - Meditation II." In David Rosenthal's *The Nature of the Mind.* New York: Oxford University Press (1991).

Descartes, Rene. "Discourse on Method" in David Rosenthal's *The Nature of the Mind.* New York: Oxford University Press, (1991).

Devereux, Jann, Marie. *Living After Encountering the Light: A Phenomenological Exploration of the Meaning of NDE.* Unpublished Doctoral Thesis, Jan. (1995). Presented to the Union Institute.

DiCarlo, Russell, E. ed. *Towards a New World View.* Epic Publishing (1996).

Dodds, E. R. *The Greeks and the Irrational.* USA: University of California Press (1966).

Doore, Gary. PhD. ed. *What Survives.* Los Angeles, California: Jeremy P. Tarcher Inc. (1990).

Dole, George. "An Image of God in a Mirror." Swedenborg Emanuel. *A Continuing Vision.* Ed. Larsen, Robin et al. New York: Swedenbord Foundation (1988).

Dossey. L. *Recovering the Soul.* New York: Bantam (1989).

Durrant, Will. *The Story of Philosophy.* NY: Washington Signaro Publication (1961).

Eadie, Betty, J. and Curtis Taylor. *Embraced by the Light.* USA: Gold Leaf Press (1992).

Eccles, John, C. *Evolution of the Brain: Creation of the Self.* London: Routledge (1989).

Eccles, John, C. *The Human Psyche.* London: Routledge (1989).

Eccles, John. C. *The Understanding of the Brain.* New York: McGraw Hill (1973).

Ferguson, Marilyn. "Karl Pribram's changing reality" in *The Holographic Paradigm.* Ed. Ken Wilber. (1985), Boston and London: Shambala Books.

Flanagan, Owen. *Consciousness Reconsidered.* USA: MIT Press (1972).

Flanagan, Owen. Prospects for a Unified Theory of Consciousness, What Dreams are made of in *Nature of Consciousness.* Cambridge Mass. MIT Press (1997).

Flew, Anthony, ed. *Body, Mind and Death.* New York: MacMillan (1964).

Foster, John. *The Immaterial Self.* London and New York: Routledge (1996).

Frank, F. *The Book of Angelus Sileius.* New York: Random House (1976).

Freud, Sigmund. *New Introductory Lectures on Psychoanalysis.* In Complete Psychological Works of Sigmond Freud. Vol. I. Translated by J. Stackley London: HoGarth Press (1964).

Frost, S. E. Jr. *Basic Teachings of Great Philosophers: A Survey of Their Ideas.* USA: Anchor Books, Doubleday. Revised Edition (1989).

Gallup, George Jr. with William Proctor. *Adventures in Immorality*. New York: McGraw Hill, (1982).

Globus, Gordon, G., Glover Maxwell, F. W. Savodnik. Eds. *Consciousness and the Brain*. New York and London: Plenum Press (1977).

Goswami, A. *Science Within Consciousness*. Ca. Sausalito Ca. Institute of Noetic Sciences, (1994).

Graham, George. Philosophy of the Mind. UK: Blackwell Publishers (1993).

Greenhouse, H. D. *The Astral Journey*. New York: Avon (1974).

Greyson, B. and Charles Flynn. Eds. "The Near Death Experience Scale: Construction, Realibility, and Validity". *In The Near Death Experience: Problem, Prospects, Perspectives*. Springfield, Ill. Publisher: Charles C. Thomas (1984).

Grice, H.P. *The Causal Theory of Perception in Perceiving*, Sensing and Knowing Ed. Robert J. Swartz. New York: Doubleday, (1965).

Grof, Stanislav. *Beyond the Brain*. USA: State University of New York (1985).

Grof. Stanislav and Christian Grof. *Beyond Death*. London: Thames and Hudson Limited (1990).

Grof, Stanislav. *Books of the Dead*. London: Thames and Hudson Limited (1994).

Grossman, Reinhardt. *The Existence of the World – An Introduction to Ontology*. London: Routeledge (1994).

Guttenplan, Samuel. Ed. *Companion to the Philosophy of Mind*. London: Blackwell Publishers (1994).

Hady, Joan. *A Psychology With a Soul: Psychosynthesis in Evolutionary Context*. London: Penguin (1989).

Hart, W.D. *The Engines of the Soul*. London: Cambridge University Press (1988).

Hawkins, Stephen. *A Brief History of Time*. New York: Bantam Books (1988).

Heisenberg, W. *Physics and Philosophy*. London: Allen and Urwin (1958).

Hady, Joan. *A Psychology With a Soul – Psychosynthesis in Evolutionary Context*. London: Penguin. (1989).

Hamlyn, D. W. *Metaphysics*. London: Cambridge University Press (1994).

Hamlyn, D. W. *The Companion to Philosophy of Mind*. Ed. Daniel Guttenplan. London: Blackwell (1994).

Hudson, Yeager. *The Philosophy of Religion*. California: Mayfield Publishing Company (1991).

Hume, David. *A Treatise of Human Nature*. New York: Penguin (1984).

James, William. *The Principles of Psychology*. Vol. I. NY: Dover (1950).

James, William. *Pragmatism*. USA: Prometheus Books (1991).

Jevons, N. Stanley. *The Principles of Science*. London and NY: Macmillan (1877).

Jung, Carl, G. *Synchronicity*. Trans. R. F. C. Hull Bollingen Series. USA: Princeton: University Press (1973).

Jung, Carl, G. *Memories, Dreams, Reflections*. New York: Vintage Books (1961).

Jung, Carl, G. *Archetypes and The Collective Unconscious*. Trans. R. F. C. Hull. Bollingen Series XX. Princeton University Press (1990).

Kant, Immanuel. *Critique of Pure Reason*. Trans. by J. M. D. Merklejohn Prometheus Books (1990).

Kim. Jaegwon. *Philosophy of Mind*. Boulder, Colorado: Westview Press (1996).

Kirtley, D.D. *The Psychology of Blindness*. Chicago, Ill: Nelson Hall (1975).

Kleiman, Lowell, and Stephen Lewis, Eds. *Philosophy: An Introduction Through Literature*. New York: Paragon House (1992).

Kock, Winston E. *Lasers and Holographs*. New York: Dover (1981).

Kolak, Daniel, and Raymond Martin. *Self and Identity: Contemporary Philosophical Issues*. New York: Macmillan Publishing Co. (1991).

Kripke, Saul S. *Naming and Necessity*. Cambridge, Mass. Cambridge University Press (1980.)

Kübler-Ross, Elizabeth. *On Death and Dying*. NY: Collier, Macmillan (1969).

Kuhn, Thomas S. *The Structure of Scientific Revolutions*. USA: University of Chicago Press. 2nd Edition Enlarged (1970).

Ladd, George. Trumbell. *Psychology: Descriptive and Explanatory*. New York: C. Scribner & Son (1909).

LaMettie, Julien, Offray. *Man a Machine and Man a Plant*. Indiana, USA: Hackett Publishing Company, (1994).

Lashley, K. S. *Brain Mechanism and Intelligence*. Chicago: Chicago University Press, (1929).

Locke, John. *An Essay Concerning Human Understanding*. London; J. M Dent & Sons Ltd. (1990).

Lockwood, Michael. *Mind, Brain and the Quantum: The Compound I*. UK: Blackwell Publishers, (1989).

Lovejoy, Arthur, R. *The Great Chain of Being*. USA: Howard University Press (1964).

Lyons, William. *Modern Philosophy of Mind*. London: J. M. Dent - Orion Publishing Group (1995).

Martinich, A.P. *Philosophical Writings*. USA: Blackwell Publishers (1997).

Miller, George. *Psychology of Science of Mental Life*. USA: Harper & Row Publishers (1962).

Miller, David. ed. *Popper Selections*. New Jersey: Princeton University Press (1985).

Mishlove, Jeffrey. *The Roots of Consciousness*. NY: Marlow & Company (1993).

Moody, Raymond, A. Jr. *Reflections on Life After Life*. Foreword by Elizabeth Kübler-Ross. USA. A Bantam Book. Mockingbird Books (1976).

Moody, Raymond, A. with Paul Perry. *Reunions*. New York: Villard Books (1993).

Moore, G. E. *Some Main Problems of Philosophy*. London: George Allen & Urwin& Urwin (1953).

Moore, Thomas. *Care of the Soul*. NY: Harper Collins Publishers Inc. (1992).

Monroe, Robert, A. *Journeys Out of the Body*. New York: Anchor Press (1971).

Morse, Melvin, with Paul Perry. *Closer to the Light*. New York: Ballentine Books (1990).

Morse, Melvin, with Paul Perry. *Transformed by the Light*. New York: Ivy Books (1992).

Moser, Paul and J.D. Trout, Eds. *Contemporary Materialism*. London: Routeledge (1995).

Myers, F. W. H. *Human Personality and its Survival of Bodily Death*. London: Longmans, Green & Co. (1904).

McGinn, Colin. *The Problems of Consciousness*. UK: Blackwell Publishers (1991).

Nagel, Thomas. *A View From Nowhere*. New York: Oxford University Press (1986).

Nagel, Thomas. *What Does it all Mean?* New York: Oxford University Press (1987).

Neumann, John Von and Oskar Morgenstern. *The Theory of Games and Economic Behaviour*. 2nd Edition. New Jersey: Princeton University (1947).

Ornstein, Robert. *The Evolution of Consciousness*. New York: Touchstone (1991).

Osis, Karlis, and Erlender Heraldsson. *At the Hour of Death*. New York: Hastings House Book Publishers (1977).

Peat, David, F. *Syncronicity*. New York: Bantam Books (1988).

Penfield, Wilder. *The Mystery of the Mind*. New Jersey: Princeton University Press (1978).

Ponty, Merlean, M. *The Structure of Behaviour*. Boston: Beacon Press (1967).

Popper, Karl, R. and John C. Eccles. *The Self and Its Brain*. London: Routeledge (1993).

Pollack, Jack, Harrison. *Croiset the Clairvoyant*. New York: Doubleday (1964).

Pribram, Karl. *Languages of the Brain*. NJ, Englewood Cliffs: Prentice Hall (1971).

Priest, Stephen. *Theories of the Mind*. London: Penguin Books (1991).

Quinton, Anthony. *Philosophy of Religion*. William L. Rowe and William J. Wainwright, Eds. Orlando, Florida: Harcourt, Brace Jovanovich (1973).

Randall, J. H. Jr. and J. Buchler. *Philosophy: An Introduction*. New York: Quill (1980).

Randles, Jenny and Peter Hough. *The After Life*. NY: The Berkley Publishing Group (1993).

Rescher, Nicholas. *Cambridge Dictionary of Philosophy*. Robert Audi ed. UK: Cambridge University Press (11995)

Restak, Richard, M. *The Mind*. Bantam Books (1985).

Rhodes, Leon, S. *Swedenborg and the Near-Death Experience in Emanuel Swedenborg: A Continuing Vision*. ed. Larsen Robin et al. New York: Swedenborg Foundation (1988).

Rhine, J. B. *The Reach of the Mind*. London: Faber and Faber (1947).

Ring, Kenneth. *Life at Death*. New York: Quill (1982).

_____ *Heading Towards Omega*. New York: Quill (1984).

Ring, Kenneth & Valarino Evelyn Elasasser. *Lessons from the Light*. New York: Plenum Press (1998).

Rinpoche, Sogyal. *The Tibetian Book of Living and Dying*. San Francisco: Harper (1993).

Rorty, Amélie, Oksenberg. *The Identities of Persons*. Los Angeles, California: University of California Press (1976).

Ross, Sir David. *Plato's Theory of Ideas*. UK: Oxford, Clarendon Press (1963).

Rosenthal, David, M. *The Nature of the Mind*. NY: Oxford University Press (1991).

Rowan, John. *Supersonalities - The People Inside us*. London: Routledge (1990).

Rowe, William L. and William J. Wainwright. *Philosophy of Religion - Selected Readings*. Florida: Harcourt Brace Jovanovich, (1989).

Russell, Bertrand. *Human Knowledge*. London: Routledge (1992).

___. *The Problems of Philosophy*. New York: Oxford University Press (1959).

___. *Our Knowledge of the External Worlds*. New York: Routledge (1993).

___. *A History of Western Philosophy*. Chapter IX The Atomist. Eds. Brian Berkeley and Peter Ludlow. Simon Schuster (1972).

___. *An Outline of Philosophy*. London, (1970).

Russell, J. Robert, William R. Stoeger, S.J. and George V. Coyne, S. J. Physics, Philosophy and Theology. Vatican Observatory, Vatican City State (1995).

Ryle, Gilbert. *The Concept of Mind*. USA: University of Chicago Press 1984.

Sabom, Michael, B. PhD. *Recollections of Death*. NY: Harper and Row (1982).

Sagan, Carl. *Broca's Brain*. New York: Ballantine (1993).

Santayana, George. *Scepticism and Animal Faith*. NY: Dover Publications (1923).

Schilpp, Paul, Arthur. *The Philosophy of G. E. Moore*. 1942: A Reply to My Critics. USA: Open Court. The Library of Living Philosophers Vo. IV (1968)

Schwartz, Stephen, A. *The Secret Vaults of Time*. New York: Grosset & Dunlop.

Scott, Rogo, D. *Psychic Breakthroughs Today*. Wellingborough, Great Britain: Acquarian Press (1987).

Searle, John, R. *The Rediscovery of the Mind*. Cambridge, Mass: MIT Press (1992).

Sherrington, Sir Charles. *Integration Action of the Nervous System*. Cambridge University Press (1947).

Sherbok, Dan Cohn and Christopher Lewis. Eds. *Beyond Death*. London: Macmillan Press Ltd. (1995).

Spinoza, Baruch. *Ethics*. Translation: A. Boyle. London (1977).

Stairs, Allen. *Quantum Mechanics, Mind and Self*. NY: Macmillan (1991).

Stout, George, F. *A Manual of Psychology*. New York: Hinds, Noble, and Eldredge Publishers (1899).

Strawson, P. F. *Individual*. London: Routledge (1993).

Swedenborg, Emanuel. *The Universal Human and Soul-Body Interaction*. Edited and Translated by George F. Dole. New York: Paulist Press (1984).

Swinbourne, Richard. *The Evolution of the Soul*. London: Clarendon Press (1986).

Talbot, Michael. *The Holographic Universe*. New York: Harper Collins (1991).

Tarnas, Richard. *Towards a New World View - The Western World View: Past, Present and Future*. Ed. Russell E. DiCarlo. Erie, PA: Epic Publishing (1996), p.21.

Thurston, Bonnie, Colleen. *Consciousness and the Evolution of Conceptual Frameworks*. Unpublished Doctoral Thesis. British Colombia, Canada: University of British Colombia (1981).

Van Inwagen, Peter. *Metaphysics*. San Francisco/Colorado, Westvent Press (1993).

Wade, Jenny. *Changes of Mind - A Holonomic Theory of Consciousness*. USA. State University Press (1996).

Ward, Keith. *Defending the Soul*. Oxford, London: Oneworld (1992).

Weiskrantz, L. *Blindsight*. Oxford: Clarendon Press (1986).

Wentz, Evans. Ed. *The Tibetan Book of the Dead*. New York: OUP (1960).

Werner, Jaeger. *Aristotle*. New York: Oxford University Press (1962).

Whiteman, J. H.M. *The Mystical Life*. London: Faber and Faber (1961).

Whitton. Joel, L. and Joe Fisher. *"Life Between Life."* New York: Doubleday (1986).

Wiggins, Wilvin. *Recent Philosophy*. Jamaica: University of the West Indies (1983).

Wilber, Ken. Ed. *The Holographic Paradigm and other Paradoxes*. Boston: Shambhala (1985).

Wilber, Ken. Ed. *Quantum Questions*. Boston: Shambhala (1985).

Williams, Bernard. *Problems of the Soul*. NY: Cambridge University Press (1991).

Zaleski, Carol. *Otherworld Journeys*. New York: Oxford University Press (1987).

Zukav, Gary. *The Seat of the Soul*. New York: Simon & Schuster (1989).

Zukav, Gary. *The Dancing Wu Li Masters*. New York: Bantam Books (1980).

ARTICLES

Alcock, James.E. "Pseudo Science and the Soul." *Essence.* No.5, (1981).

Anderson, Robert. M. Jr. "A Holographic Model of Transpersonal Consciousness." *Journal of Transpersonal Psychology.* Vol.9 No.2, (1997).

Beloff, J. "Could There be a Physical Explanation of Psi." *Journal of the Society of Psychical Research* (1980).

Bourguigrin, Erika. "Dreams and Altered States of Consciousness." *Anthropological Research in Psychological Anthropology.* ed. Itsu, F. L. K. Cambridge, Mass: Schenkman, (1972).

Braude, Stephen, E. "The Holographic Analysis of Near- Death Experiences: The Perpetuation of Some Deep Mistakes." *Essence* 5, Number I, (1981).

Capra, Fritjof. "Holonomy and Bootstrap." *The Holographic Paradigm.* ed. Ken Wilber. Boston: Shambhala. (1982).

Chew, G. F. "Bootstrap A Scientific Idea." *Science* Vol.161, May 23, 1968.

Churchland, Paul, M. "Knowing Qualia - A reply to Jackson" in *The Nature of Consciousness.* Eds. Owen Flanagan and Güven Güzeldere. (1997).

Churchland, Paul, M. "Eliminative Materialism and the Propositional Attitude." *Journal of Philosophy.* LXXVIII, 2. February, 1981.

Churchland, Patricia, S. "Consciousness: The Transmutation of a Concept." *Pacific Philosophical Quarterly* 64.(1983).

Crick, Francis and Christof Koch. "Towards a Neurobiological Theory of Consciousness." *Seminars in the Neurosciences* 2, (1990).

Descartes, Rene. "Meditations on First Philosophy" *Nature of the Mind.* Ed. David Rosenthal. New York: Oxford University Press, (1991).

DeValois, Karen. K., Russell L. DeValois and W. W. Yund. "Responses to Straite Cortex Cells to Grafting Checkboard Patterns." *Journal of Physiology* Vol.291, (1979).

Dychtwald, Ken. "Reflections on the Holographic Paradigm." *The Holographic Paradigm.* Ed. Ken Wilber. London: Shambhala, (1982).

Einstein, A. B. Podolsky and N. Rosen. "Can Quantum Mechanical Description of Physical Reality be Considered Complete?" *Physical Review* (1935).

Feigl, H. "The 'Mental' and the 'Physical'." *Minnesota Studies in Philosophy of Science* 2: 370-492, (1958).

Ferguson, Marilyn. ed. Ken Wilber. *The Holographic Paradigm* Boston and London: Shambhala Books, (1985).

Ferguson, M.A. "Karl Pribram's Changing Reality." *A New Perspective on Reality*. Revision. I, (1978).

Flanagan, Owen. "Deconstructing Dreams: The Spandrels of Sleep" *Journal of Philosophy* 92.1, (1995). - "A Unified Theory of Consciousness, or, What Dreams are Made of" in *Nature of Consciousness*. Eds. Ned Block and Güiven Güzeldere. p. 97.

Fodor, J. "The Big Idea." in *Times Literary Supplement*. July 3, 1992.

Freedman, David, H. "Quantum Consciousness." *Discover the World of Science*. Vol.15. No.6. June, 1994.

Gaeskaya, M.S. "Bio-Chemistry of the brain during the process of dying and resuscitation" New York Consultants Bureau,(1964).

Giles, James. "Bodily Theory and Theory of the Body" *Philosophy* Vol.66 No.257. July, 1991.

Green, Celia. "Out of Body Experiences." England, Oxford. Institute of Psychological Research (1968).

Grosso, Michael. "Towards an Explanation of Near Death Phenomena." *Anabiosis: The Journal for Near-Death Studies* Vol.I No.1. July, 1981.

Gunderson, Keith. "Asymmetry and Mind-Body Perplexities" 1970, Rosenthal *Materialism and the Mind-Body Problem*. Englewood Cliffs, Prentice Hall.(1971).

Hart, W.D. "Dualism" in *A Companion to the Philosophy of Mind*. Ed. Samuel Gutenplan. pp.265-269. (1994).

Hempel, Carl, G. "Logical Analysis of Psychology" from *Readings in Philosophy of Psychology*. Ed. Ned Block. Vol 1. 1980. Intentionality, Mind and Language. Ed Ausonio. Marras, (1972).

Honorton "Psi and Internal Attention States." B. B. Wolman, ed. Handbook of *Parapsychology*. New York: Van Nostrand Reinhold, (1977)

James, William. "Streams of Consciousness." *Nature of Consciousness*. Eds. Ned Block, Owen Flanagan and Güzeldere. USA: MIT Press, Cambridge Press, (1997).

Kastelbaum, R. "Transformed by the Light." *Journal of Near Death Studies*, (1993).

Levine, J. "Materialism Qualia: The Explanatory Gap" *Pacific Philosophical Quarterly* 64. (1983).

Lewis, David. "Mad Pain and Martian Pain." *Readings in Philosophy*. Ed. Ned Block. Vol 1.

McGinn, Colin. "Can We Solve the Mind Body Problem?" *Mind* XC VIII: 891, (1989).

Moody, Raymond. "Life After Life: Implication of Near-Death Experience." *Towards a New Worldview*. Ed. Russell E. DiCarlo. Epic Publishing (1996).

Morse, M. "Near-Death Experience and Death Related Vision in Children." *Current Problems in Pediatrics* 24(2) 1994 pp.45-92

Nagel, Thomas. "What its Like to be a Bat." *Readings in Philosophy of Psychology*. New York: Oxford University Press, (1974).

Nemirow, Laurence. "Physicalism and the Cognitive Role of Acquaintance." *Mind and Cognition*. ed. G. Lycan. USA: Blackwell Publishers, (1994).

Noyes, R. R. Kletti. "Depersonalization in the Face of Life Threatening Danger: A Description." *Psychiatry* 35, (1976).

Osis, Karl. "Out of Body Research at the American Society." *Mind Beyond the Body* Ed. Rogo D. Scott. New York: Penguin, (1978).

Perry, Ralph. "Conceptions and Misconception of Consciousness." *The Psychological Review* XI. Boston, (1904).

Pietsche, Paul. "Shufflebrain" *Harper's Magazine* 244, May, 1972.

Place, U. T. "Is Consciousness a Brain Process?" *British Journal of Philosophy* Printed in *Philosophy of Mind* 1992. Eds. Brian Berkeley and Peter Ludlow. Cambridge, Mass: MIT Press.(1956).

Polkinghorne, John. "The Quantum World." *Physics, Philosophy and Theology*. Eds. Russell, Robert, John Stoeger, William, R. Stoeger and George V. Coyne. Vatican State: Vatican Observator, (1995).

Pribram, Karl. "The Neurophysiology of Remembering." *Scientific American* 220, January, 1969.

Pribram, Karl. "What the Fuss is All About." *The Holographic Paradigm*. (1985).

Pribram, Karl. "Interview" in *Psychology Today*. February, 1979.

Pribram, Karl. "The Implicate Brain." *Quantum Implications*. Eds. Hiley. B. J., and David F. Peat. Rutledge & Kegan Paul, (1991).

Putnam, Hilary. "Nature of Mental States." *Readings in Philosophy of Psychology* Vol .I. ed. Ned Block USA: Harvard University Press, (1980).

Putnam, Hilary. Ed. "Language and Reality." *Philosophical Papers*. Vol.2 (1980). Cambridge.

Quinton, Anthony. "The Soul." *The Journal of Philosophy*. LIX 15. July 19, 1962.

Ring, Kenneth. "Near-Death and Out-of-Body Experiences in the Blind: A Study of Apparent Eyeless Vision." *Journal of Near-Death Studies* 16 (2) Winter (1997).

Romains, J. "Eyeless Sight: A Study of Extra Retinal Vision and the Paroptic Sense." New York, NY. (1924).

Serdaly, W. "A Pediatric Near Death Experience Terminal Variants." (1989 - 1990), *Omega* 20 pp55-62

Sherrington, Sir Charles. Foreword to Edition of the "Integrative Action of the Nervous System." *Cited by Place in Philosophy of Mind* pp. XX-CCI. 1947. Cambridge University Press.

Shields, Dean. "A Cross Cultural Study of Beliefs in Out of Body Experience." *Journal of the Society for Psychical Research* 49. (1978).

Shimony, Abner. "Search for a World-view which can accommodate microphysics." *Philosophical Consequences of Quantum Theory.* Eds. Cushing, James T. and Eran McMullin. University of Notre Dame Press. (1989).

Smart, J. J. "Sensation and Brain Processes." *Contemporary Materialism.* Eds. Moser, Paul, K. and J. D. Trout. London: Rutledge. (1995).

Stapp, Henry, P. "Quantum Non-locality and the Description of Nature." *Philosophical Consequences of Quantum Theory.* Eds. Cushing, James, T. and Eran McMullian. University of Notre Dame Press, (1989).

Tart, Charles. "A Psychophysiological Study of Out-of-Body Experiences in a Selected Subject." *Journal of the American Society of Psychical Research* 62. (1968).

Van Heerden, Pieter. "Models for the Brain." *Nature* 227. (July, 1970).

Vicky : "Vital signs" *The International Association of Near-Death Studies Inc. (IANDS).* XIII No.2 Spring (1994). Connecticut, USA.

Walker, Evan, H. "The Nature of Consciousness." *Mathematical Biosciences,* (1970).

White, John. "Jesus Evolution and the Future of Humanity." *Part I Science of the Mind,* September, 1981.

Wilkes, Katherine. "Is Consciousness Imported?" *British Journal of Philosophy of Science* 35. (1984).

Woodhouse, Mark, B. "Near-Death Experience and the Mind-Body Problem." *Anabiosis,* Vol. I No.1, July 1981.

APPENDIX I

COMMENTS ON NON-OPHTHALMIC VISION

Dr. Hugh Vaughn, Eye Surgeon
Kingston, Jamaica
March 31, 1999.

Vision is a complex process in which an organism is consciously aware of its environment by the detection of light in its environment. The awareness of one's environment is a function of being conscious. The awareness is present provided that a person is conscious, and this awareness is what defines being conscious. The awareness is present regardless of the sensory input. Vision is differentiated from other senses by the fact that it uses light from the environment to provide the awareness of the environment. It is the use of light to provide this awareness that makes the sense of vision. Hearing is peculiar in that it uses sound to provide the awareness of the environment. Temperature awareness is provided by the skin, and so all the senses provide inputs into the awareness of the environment which is conscious-ness. The physical apparatus to receive and interpret light information consists of the sense organs, i.e. the eye and the rest of the visual pathway, the optic nerves, the optic chiasm, optic tract, the lateral geniculate bodies, the optic radiation and the visual cortex, as well as the visual association areas. Malfunction of any of these can lead to blindness, which is the lack of visual information inputting into one's consciousness. The consciousness will be there despite the lack of visual input. So non-ophthalmic awareness of the environment is real, whether it should be called vision is a moot point. The fact that one may interpret the awareness of the environment is a kind of map generated by vision is not necessarily a characteristic of vision. This map may be present in one's consciousness and all sensory inputs fill in information on this map. This may be envisaged like a video monitor, which may display vision as in the case of a television or an ultrasound image in the case of an ultrasound, or magnetic resonance in the case of magnetic resonance imaging, or X-ray appearances in the case of Cat scanning. So there may be in one's consciousness a device similar to a video terminal which can display sound, temperature, light, and all the sensory inputs, and display them in a position appropriate to the position assigned to the object of their origin. In this way we could see the form of an object based on its image, and hear sounds coming from it accurately placing the origin of the sound or any other information peculiar to that object. If this is so then a consciousness of the environment will be there and it will be imaged in a particular way, that way being determined by the structure of our consciousness (the video terminal screen), and not the modality of the sensory input. Hence we could see things which we never saw physically. This would explain why persons who have never had sight could "see" things.

The model of our environment need not necessarily have been formed by our own experiences as the information can be passed on from parent to offspring in the genetic material. An example of this is information and behaviour, which we often ascribe to instinct in animals. For example, an insect or a lizard may never have seen its parent yet it knows where there is a source of food and a source of shelter in its environment. The migration of the Monarch Butterfly is a classic example of this. The butterfly originates in a part of Mexico and migrates to USA and Canada reproducing as it goes along with the return to Mexico completed in some five or so generations to complete the cycle. This is genetic programming or sometimes called "hard wiring", a well known concept in biology. Hence the fact that persons may see images even though they have never had sight is not particularly remarkable or farfetched. It may be and probably is the way nature works normally.

Hugh Vaughn

Index

A

agnosticism 120, 121

Alchemy 51

Anabiosis 2

Aquinas, Thomas (St.) 23

At The Hour of Death 5, 14

Autoscopic hallucination 25, 26

Autoscopic NDE 9, 26

Ayer, A.J. 26, 71

B

Bacteria 174

Bats 120

Behaviourism 37, 141

Bentov, Itzhak 84

Berekeley, George 135-6

Bewaji, John Ayotunde 17

Big bang 51

Blackmore, Susan 13, 14

Blindsight 101, 102

Braude, Stephen 177, 178, 179, 180, 181

Brentano, Franz 144, 146, 147-151

C

Camera Obscura 54

Cartesianism 144, 159

cerebral cortex 183
Chalmers, David 127, 128, 129, 162, 163, 189
Churchland, Patricia 111, 126
Churchland, Paul 124

D

Da Vinci, Leonardo 83
Davidson, Donald 143-146
Delirium 25
Dementia 25
Demerol 25
Democritus 23, 137, 188
Dennett, Daniel 110
Descartes, René 23, 29, 32, 33-5, 41, 44, 49, 50, 51, 132, 153, 154, 157
DeValois, Karen
DeValois, Russell
DiCarlo, Russell E. 169
Double/ Dual Aspect theory 109, 128-9, 152-153, 165
Dreams 2, 3, 6, 12, 41, 81, 83, 101, 118, 136, 175
Dualism 22-3, 40, 43-4, 50, 127-9, 132-4, 142, 144, 152, 153, 155, 172
Dying Brain Hypothesis 13

E

Einstein, Albert 59, 170, 188
Eliminative Materialism 123-4
Emotion 147
Emperor's New Mind 174
Empiricism 17, 18, 19, 21, 23, 25, 27, 135, 136, 188,
Engram 57, 65, 66
Epistemology 93, 96, 114, 172
Esse est percipi 136
explanatory gap 130
Extra-sensory perception (ESP) 74, 75, 101
Extrasomatic hyphothesis 74, 76

F

feelings 6, 11, 68, 115, 116, 118-9, 130, 148, 156
Feigl, Herbert 93-4, 142
Flanagan, Owen 112, 117, 121, 124-6
Floyd, Keith 164
Folk Psychology (FP) 123, 124
Freud, Sigmund 112

G

Gravity 50, 110
Greyson, Bruce 6, 7
Grof, Stanislav 48, 49, 50, 52, 53, 175
God 13, 151, 85, 135, 151, 154, 155, 158
Güzeldere, Gürven 114
Gunderson, Keith 113

H

Hart, W.D. 40-1, 43-4, 95-100
Heading Towards Omega 11, 12, 77
Hobbes, Thomas 135
Holograms 44, 56, 64-5, 67
Holographic theory 7, 44, 64, 78, 79, 87, 109, 176, 177
Holomovement 59, 60-1, 63-4, 164, 176, 177, 179, 184
Hume, David 29-30, 31-3, 40, 42-3, 90, 95, 135
Husserl, Edmund 146, 149, 150-2
Huxley, Aldous 71
Hylozoism 174

I

Idealism 134-5, 137, 153, 174
Imagination 3, 38, 40, 89-90, 147, 150
interference holography 68
Integrationist intuition 114
Intentionality 144, 148-9, 150-152
Intrasomatic hypothesis 74

J

James, William 111, 112
Janus 122
Jesus 20
Jevons, William Stanley 188
Jung, Carl 3, 86, 88

K

Kreutziger, Sarah 8
Kübler-Ross, Elizabeth 3, 4
Kuhn, Thomas 46-48

L

Ladd, George Trumbell 111
Languages of the Brain 59, 65
Lashley, Karl 57, 66 Brain Mechanism and Intelligence 57
Lawrence, D.H. 71
Leucippus 23
Life after Life 5, 8-9, 20
Life at Death 5, 77
Locke, John 29, 36, 135
Logical positivism 187

M

McGinn, Colin 93, 110, 121-123
Memory 25-6, 28-9, 31, 36-7, 56-7, 60-1, 65-9, 73,125-6, 152, 161, 174, 178, 180-1
Metaphysics 96, 155, 159, 164, 171-2, 187
Miller, George 113, 131
Mind-body dualism 23, 129, 155
mind-body problem 38, 44, 110, 117, 122, 165, 172-3
mind-brain identity theory 137-9, 140-1
Monroe, Robert 72-4, 80, 82
Monism 128-9, 134, 141, 143-5, 153-4, 159-161
Moody, Raymond 5, 6, 8, 10, 12, 15, 20, 81, 85

Morphine 25
Morse, Melvin 12, 13

N

Nagel, Thomas 120-1
Naturalism 23, 112, 120-1, 123-6
Nemirow, Laurence 94
New Mysterianism 112, 121
Newton, Isaac (Sir) 49, 50-1, 97
non-naturalism 117, 118
Non-mental Naturalism (See New Mysterianism)
non-ophthalmic vision 89, 92, 102

O

objectivity 3, 51, 88, 109, 120, 170
occult 42, 95, 123
On Death and Dying 3, 5
Oxygen 25, 26, 90

P

Penfield, Wilder 12, 52, 65, 87, 186
Perry, Ralph 110
phenomenological fallacy 140
phenomenology 125, 128, 146, 149, 152, 163
Photons 173, 174, 182
physics 24, 27, 40, 48, 59, 70, 78, 83, 104, 129, 135, 140, 142, 159, 160-4, 170-3, 175, 178, 184-
Pietsch, Paul 69, 180
Place, U.T. 138, 140-1
Plato 2, 23, 29, 35, 132
Pribram, Karl 56, 57, 59, 64-70, 74, 78-9, 84, 176, 178-181, 185
Priest, Stephen 116, 117, 140
Psychokinesis (PK) 74, 75
Psychology 5, 11, 27, 52, 64-5, 77, 100, 112-3, 123, 125-6, 150, 159, 162, 185
Psychosis 24, 52

235

Q

Quantum Physics 24, 59, 70, 135, 170
Quantum Theory 63, 64, 170
Quinton, Anthony 35-8

R

Reality 7, 21, 23-4, 26, 49, 52-3, 56, 58-64, 70, 72, 74, 77-9, 84, 86-8, 95, 101, 104, 121-2, 125, 131, 135, 145, 146, 149, 150, 151, 155, 159, 164, 165, 168-1, 174-9, 181, 185-7
Reductionism 7
Religion 5, 52
Republic, The 2
Rescher, Nicholas 134
Ring, Kenneth 5, 6, 7, 11, 12, 27, 77, 78, 79, 81, 85-87, 92, 100-5, 177, 179, 181
Romains, Jules 102
Russell, Bertrand
Ryle, Gilbert 34, 142, 194

S

Sabom, Michael 7-11, 27
Scepticism 17, 18, 47, 124, 187
Schizophrenia 25, 26
Schlick, Moritz 157
Scientific American 66
Searle, John 111, 115
segregationalist intuition 114
sensations 35, 39, 99, 110, 115, 130, 136, 137, 138, 141-2, 150, 152, 161, 164
Sherrington, Charles (Sir) 139
Shimony, Abner 172
Smart, J.J.C. 141-143
Soul 3, 11, 12, 18, 22, 23, 29, 30, 35-8, 95, 160, 164
Soul-phase 36
Spinoza, Baruch 95, 153-5, 159
Spirit 2, 4, 23, 29, 83
Stapp, Henry 171, 174
Stoke, George 55

Subjectivity 109, 115, 120, 121 124

Supernatural 118, 122

Swedenborg, Emmanuel 83, 84

T

The Engines of the Soul 95

Thorazine 25

Transcendental self 32-34

V

Van Helmholtz, Herman 70

Van Heerden, Pieter 68

Van Newmann, John 67

Vishnu 20

W

Walker, E.H. 173

Weiskrantz, Lawrence 101

Whitton, Joel 80

Wilkes, Katherine 112

Willis, Harmon 169

About the Author

Dr. Oswald G. Harding, Q.C.

Dr. Oswald G. Harding is an English Trained Barrister of the Inner Temple and the London School of Economics, who had obtained an Honours Degree in Anthropology from McGill University where he began post graduate work.

He became a public figure in his native Jamaica after being appointed Attorney General and Minister of Justice, as well as President of the Senate. He taught law at the Norman Manley Law School for Five (5) years and is now an Honorary Tutor.

Dr. Harding has published several articles in The West Indian Law Journal and other journals. He is now a Senior Research Fellow in Philosophy and Law in the Graduate School at the University of the West Indies and lectures in philosophy.

www.ingramcontent.com/pod-product-compliance
Lightning Source LLC
Chambersburg PA
CBHW020353170426
43200CB00005B/146